P9-CIV-121

Advance Praise for
BRAINWASHED

"Ben Shapiro's courage and insight should provide inspiration not only for other young conservatives on campus, but also for their parents. His book is a welcome sign that all is not lost for this new generation."

—MICHAEL MEDVED,
nationally syndicated radio host and
author of *Hollywood vs. America*

"Don't tell me a book this brilliant was written by a college kid barely out of his teens. It's got to have been written by a gutsy old sage who somehow got himself embedded into UCLA and whose piercing observations have the power to save the oncoming generation from tyrants with tenure."

—BARRY FARBER,
nationally syndicated radio host

"With wit and verve, Ben Shapiro—America's youngest national columnist—provides a firsthand account of how liberal pieties masquerade as the only truth in today's corrupted universities. With luck, his critique will help others begin to the take those steps needed to fix the campus and return it to its esteemed place in our national life."

—DANIEL PIPES,
founder of Campus Watch and
columnist for the *New York Sun*

"Been there. Done that (Tulane, A&S, '91). Ben gets it exactly right about the modern collegiate brainwash. Thankfully, beer and Mardi Gras saved me from full indoctrination. But Shapiro's unassailable book, most assuredly, is the healthier blueprint to avoiding Marx and Engel's witting accomplices."

—ANDREW BREITBART,
co-author of *Hollywood, Interrupted: Insanity Chic in Babylon—
The Case Against Celebrity*

"A brilliant new voice for a new generation of activists: Don't miss Ben Shapiro's new book!"

—HUGH HEWITT,
nationally syndicated radio host and
author of *In, But Not Of*

"This book reveals how deeply entrenched a noxious culture of hatred for America and Western values has become among those who teach our nation's young men and women. Shapiro delivers a sobering wake-up call for all Americans, detailing the pressing need to—as the Left might put it—take back our colleges and universities."

—ROBERT SPENCER,
director of Jihad Watch and
author of *Onward Muslim Soldiers* and *Islam Unveiled*

"In *Brainwashed*, Ben Shapiro rips the liberal university system to shreds. With an arch wit and insider's perspective, Shapiro exposes how liberal group-think has spread bacteria-like through our education system and is threatening to squash genuine debate in our schools."

—ARMSTRONG WILLIAMS
nationally syndicated columnist

"Shapiro has a razor-sharp pen. His pointed criticism is directed at the overwhelming percentage of college professors who believe Islam is good and Christianity is bad, who don't accept that capitalism beat socialism because capitalism is ending centuries of destitution, and who worship skin-color diversity but who blithely create strict campus rules against diversity of speech."

—JILL STEWART
"Capitol Punishment" syndicated columnist,
radio and television political commentator

BRAINWASHED

HOW UNIVERSITIES
INDOCTRINATE
AMERICA'S YOUTH

BEN SHAPIRO

WND BOOKS
A Division of Thomas Nelson Publishers
Since 1798

www.thomasnelson.com

Copyright © 2004 by Ben Shapiro

All rights reserved. No portion of this book may be reproduced, stored in a retrieval system, or transmitted in any form or by any means—electronic, mechanical, photocopy, recording, scanning, or other—except for brief quotations in critical reviews or articles, without the prior written permission of the publisher.

Published in Nashville, Tennessee, by WND Books.

Library of Congress Cataloging-in-Publication Data

Shapiro, Ben.
    Brainwashed : how universities indoctrinate America's youth / Ben Shapiro.
    p. cm.
    ISBN 0-7852-6148-6
    1. Education, Higher—Political aspects—United States. 2. Education, Higher—Social aspects—United States. 3. College teachers—United States—Attitudes. 4. College students—United States—Attitudes. I. Title: How universities indoctrinate America's youth. II. Title.
    LC89.S484 2004
    378.73—dc22

                                                                    2004001945

Printed in the United States of America

04 05 06 07 08 BVG 5 4 3 2 1

To my parents,

who taught me the difference between right and wrong
and gave me the strength to confront falsehood.

CONTENTS

CONTENTS

PUBLISHER'S NOTE

These are strange times on America's university campuses. While professors use their position to indoctrinate their students, the classical liberal view of higher learning has given way to the modern liberal view of lower living.

Reporting on this decline has posed a bit of a problem for WND Books because to paint the full picture has required author Ben Shapiro to quote some fairly crude material and deal with offensive subject matter. Publishing material of this sort is not something we as a publisher do; it's against our corporate policy. But in this instance we have done so for one simple and vital reason: To know what students are really getting themselves into requires they know what's really going on.

We do not publish this material to appeal to prurient interests but to more fully advise and inform students, parents, and those concerned about the university system and what they can expect from it.

DAVID DUNHAM
Publisher, WND Books

FOREWORD

BY DAVID LIMBAUGH

I can't tell you how many times I've heard people—including myself—muse how interesting it would be if they could relive their lives as teenagers or college students with the knowledge, savvy, and experience they have acquired through their additional years. Of course it's idle fantasy, but as I've come to know Ben Shapiro over the past few years, I've been reminded of that very thought.

I've met my share of precocious young adults who were talented in their own way but never one with the intellectual maturity and insight of Ben. To borrow the cliché, he has wisdom well beyond his years. Which is what makes his book, examining the university culture, unique.

It seems that most of these types of books are written either by professors or those outside the system. By contrast, this book is an insider's look at academic indoctrination from one currently being victimized by it. But Ben's perspective is not limited to that of a university student with blinders to everything but his studies. He is also an astute political analyst and cultural critic, already writing a nationally syndicated column. So with *Brainwashed* we get a sophisticated and firsthand critique of the university as an institution of ideological propaganda for the leftwing, secular worldview. And the book delivers—confirming our worst fears about modern academia.

It covers, topic by topic, all the major issues on college campuses and all the major aspects of college life, convincingly documenting the overt liberal bias among professors and shattering the conventional wisdom that their bias is irrelevant to their teaching. The bias has deep historical roots in this country and is growing in intensity. It covers the gamut, from accusing Republicans of stealing the presidential election in 2000, passing tax cuts for the rich, robbing seniors of their Social Security benefits, and poisoning our air and water, to praising the failed system of Marxism and denouncing capitalism. The outrage doesn't end there. Shapiro also documents the shocking professorial promotion of sexual deviancy and even their inexcusable justifications of terrorism.

Shapiro goes beyond merely exposing the bias. Using hard data and reasoned argument, he also debunks the myths and distortions propagated by a professoriate incapable of objective analysis because of its ideological enslavement. An example is its blind advocacy of minimum wage laws to help the poor even though most economists oppose them because they lead to job cutbacks.

As Shapiro demonstrates, most professors—and not just those in the political and social science departments—don't even aspire to present a balanced perspective. In many cases, part of their mission is to influence the students' outlook. And they are succeeding. He cites surveys and exit-polling data showing that while slightly more college freshmen identify themselves as liberal than conservative, that gap widens substantially as they become upper-classmen.

The brainwashing of students transcends the classrooms, to the student media (using tuition funds), and student groups—which themselves often become instruments of leftwing professorial indoctrination. While the Left glorifies diversity of race and ethnicity, it actively opposes diversity of thought, considering only leftist ideas acceptable for dissemination. The very ideal of education to create an atmosphere of open inquiry is tacitly mocked in favor of the monolithic liberal agenda.

But academic integrity is not the only victim of doctrinaire leftwing academic bias. Truth itself is a casualty as the result of a disturbing trend in academia to fully embrace postmodern moral relativism. How can ideas flowing from traditional values receive a proper airing when the prevailing dogma emphatically rejects moral absolutes? How can students be expected to further their grasp on reality when the university atmosphere teaches that truth is a social construct largely defined by power? Yet, as Shapiro shows, "the assault on absolute morality is the basis for every brainwashing scheme of the Left."

We should all shudder when we realize that the university establishment is training our youth to believe "there is no such thing as a neutral or objective claim" and that there is no such thing as evil, except, perhaps, for political conservatives and "big corporations." When a prominent Princeton University professor is not ridiculed and shunned but celebrated for arguing that it is moral to murder disabled newborn human beings, we ought to understand that something is seriously wrong with our campus culture. And these warped perspectives can't help but have a stunningly damaging impact on the future of this nation, as today's students are tomorrow's leaders.

Despite the bleak picture Shapiro paints, he does not close on a pessimistic note. In his three-step action plan, he offers a number of practical solutions as part of a multi-pronged strategy to deal with this multifaceted problem. *Brainwashed* is a sober and engaging treatment of a serious problem that should concern every parent, student, and lover of liberty in America today.

INTRODUCTION

INDOCTRINATING THE YOUTH

*"It is imperative that our classrooms be free of indoctrination.
Indoctrination is not education."*
—ROBERT M. BEHRDAHL
Chancellor, University of California, Berkeley[1]

If only our educators believed this. For years, the university system has brainwashed its students to believe fervently in the tenets of liberalism. The universities accept into their waiting clutches young, open-minded students ready to learn. They turn out mainstream liberals, spouting the Democratic party line—and that's just the "moderate" students. Students often graduate believing in the mythic power of Marxism and hating the "racist American system."

From race to the environment, from religion to sex, from the War on Terror to the Arab-Israeli conflict, universities push a never-ending line of liberal claptrap. The higher education system indoctrinates America's youth.

The vast majority of the professoriate is leftist. This is an uncontested fact. A poll conducted of Ivy League professors and administrators at liberal arts and social science faculties showed that 84 percent voted for Al Gore in 2000, as opposed to 9 percent for George W. Bush. Fifty-seven percent identified themselves as Democrats while only 3 percent identified themselves as Republicans.[2]

Leftists argue that professorial bias is irrelevant to their teaching. They say that even if a professor is liberal, he or she will undoubtedly offer a balanced view. This is blatantly false. As they do in the mainstream media, liberals dominate the "higher education" scene. And just as in the media, the liberal tilt is extremely real and extremely influential.

Professors generally feel no need to keep their personal biases out of the classroom. American Association of University Professors General Secretary Mary Burgan explains that to separate bias from teaching would be "impossible . . . It is the job of the faculty to decide which critical, relevant and commanding [viewpoints] to concentrate on in the classroom." University of California at San Diego Professor Linda Brodkey argues that to teach both sides of the story is unnecessary—rather, students must only be assured that "there is always free debate." UCSD provost David Jordan is more blunt: "Why should I teach a point of view I don't agree with?"[3]

College students are attacked with bias from the moment they step on campus until the time they leave it. The effect is devastating.

The typical college student has just left the cocoon of the lower educational system. A Fall 2001 survey of entering college freshmen revealed that "29.9 percent of students entering four-year colleges and universities characterize their political views as 'liberal' or 'far left'" while "20.7 percent . . . consider themselves 'conservative' or 'far right.'"[4] This leaves a ten-percentage-point differential between right and left.

By the time students become upper-classmen, a ten-point political gap often becomes a fifty-point canyon. In an informal exit poll conducted by the *UCLA Daily Bruin* during the 2000 presidential election, Gore garnered 71 percent of the UCLA student vote, with Bush receiving a mere 20 percent. Ralph Nader came in a close third, at 9 percent.[5]

Just wait until these students graduate. By that time, they will be walking, talking leftists babbling nonsensically about "tax cuts for the rich" and "exploitation of African-Americans, Latinos, Muslims, women, children, and lab animals."

BELLY OF THE BEAST

I know all of this not because of polling data (which confirms my stated observations) or talk radio (which is often far more reliable and accurate than network news), but from personal experience: I have been a student at the University of California at Los Angeles since age sixteen. I am a political science major and have taken dozens of courses throughout my UCLA career. I have seen firsthand the leftist brainwashing occurring on campus on a daily basis.

The mechanisms of indoctrination are not limited to professors lecturing to a captive audience. Student media play a large role in shaping the views of the student body at UCLA and other campuses around the country. Student groups use tuition money to spew propaganda: propaganda that invariably touts a leftist view of the world. I wrote an opinion column for the *UCLA Daily Bruin* for nearly two years; they fired me for revealing the newspaper's systematic bias in favor of the Islamic community.

The student media and student groups are often used by professors for brainwashing students. For example, at UCLA, professors write to the *Daily Bruin*, seek interviews with other student media, or speak at events sponsored and organized by student groups. Professors pose as experts on a wide variety of topics unrelated to their area of expertise.

Indoctrination is not limited to UCLA. The same bias exists in universities around the country. Comparing notes with friends around the country or merely following the news shows a concerted pattern of leftism throughout the "higher education" system.

I do not suggest that all professors are to the left of Stalin. Some of the most complimentary letters I have received regarding either my *Daily Bruin* column or my syndicated column are from professors. On the other hand, it would be intellectually dishonest to claim, as liberals often do, that because exceptions exist to a rule, the rule is no longer relevant. The vast majority of professors identifies with leftist politics and rarely misses an opportunity to plant those rancid seeds in the minds of their students.

BATTLING THE BEAST

The burgeoning problem of brainwashing by the universities must be combated. The diversity touted by the university system reaches only as far as skin color or country of origin. The spectrum of ideas extends only from the left to the far left. Assistant Professor Heather K. Gerken of Harvard puts it thus: "When the faculty is as liberal as it is, we end up breaking down into liberals and progressives."⁶ Students aren't likely to get a well-rounded view of the world.

This problem cannot be underestimated. American men and women go to universities to be educated and exit knowing only one side of the story. Those who protest against the totalitarian rule of leftist thought are patronized or frightened into submission.

As a columnist for the *Daily Bruin*, I once received a laudatory e-mail from a UCLA administrator. I replied to the e-mail and asked the author if I could forward his letter to my editor for possible publication in the *Bruin*. The author replied, "As a father of three and a career staff member, I'm afraid I could not handle the potential damage my express thoughts would do to my career as an administrator here. . . . Sadly, for those of us who earn our living here as staff, it's professional suicide to engage in free expression."⁷

This book will delve into the world of the university. It will rip the cover off of a system that for too long has claimed diplomatic immunity while simultaneously feeding students a steady diet of leftism. It will reveal, in full detail, one of the greatest problems facing America: the brainwashing of its youth.

1

NO MORAL ABSOLUTES

"There is no such thing as a neutral or objective claim,"[1] said Professor Joshua Muldavin of UCLA. It was early in the quarter, and the professor was explaining to our class that there is no such thing as capital-T Truth. There is no right and wrong, no good and evil, he taught. We must always remember that we are subjective beings, and as such, all of our values are subjective.

It's a load of bunk. Of course evil exists. Anyone who believes there is an excuse for rape is evil. Anyone who believes in killing disabled children is evil. Anyone who flies planes into buildings with the intent of killing civilians is evil.

But not according to the professors.

When Professor Orlando Patterson of Harvard University was interviewed on *NewsHour with Jim Lehrer* regarding President Bill Clinton's perjury, he said, "I think it's important to emphasize the fact that there are *no absolutes in our moral precepts*. Kant may have believed that, and some fascists do. . . . [P]erjury is not an absolute. You don't have absolute rules here."[2] Wow. Perjury is okay because there are no absolutes. And if you don't agree, you're a "fascist."

Professor Stanley Fish of the University of Illinois at Chicago wrote in a submission to the *New York Times*: "relativism will not and should not end, because it is simply another name for serious thought."[3] In the same article, Fish pushes Americans to "understand" the September 11 terrorists, and to condemn "false universals." How sophisticated—and pathetic.

This is typical of professors. A National Association of Scholars/Zogby poll conducted from April 9 to April 16, 2002, revealed the overwhelming use of this professorial dogma. The poll calculated the opinions of 401 randomly selected college seniors. When asked which statement about ethics their professors most often voiced, 73 percent picked: "what is right and wrong depends on differences in individual values and cultural diversity." Only 25 percent of the students selected the option reading: "there are clear and uniform standards of right and wrong by which everyone should be judged."[4]

All this classroom propaganda has a major effect on the students. John Leo, a nationally syndicated columnist, reported that "Several years ago, a college professor in upstate New York reported that 10 percent to 20 percent of his students could not bring themselves to criticize the Nazi extermination of Europe's Jews."[5] You heard that correctly: *Students would not condemn the Nazis for the Holocaust.* This is what American students are being taught at "institutions of higher learning."

THE LEFT'S MORAL BLINDNESS

After trashing moral absolutes, professors are free to advocate anything—even murder.

Professor Peter Singer of Princeton University advocates the killing of disabled newborns. Reports the *New York Times*, "To Singer, a newborn has no greater right to life than any other being of comparable rationality and capacity for emotion, including pigs, cows and dogs."[6] This is evil. Equating newborn humans with animals is absolutely sickening. But that is what Singer is teaching in his course at Princeton.

Moral relativism is a widespread disease. A book by Paul Ehrlich, a professor of population studies and biology at Stanford, was assigned in my Life Science 15 course, Spring 2002. In the book, Ehrlich compares the Holocaust to the dropping of the A-bomb on Japan.[7] To compare the slaughter of six million innocents with a military action that saved hundreds of thousands of American and Japanese lives is reprehensible. Of course, this type of moral relativism is nothing new for Ehrlich, who is most famous for his laughably erroneous 1968 tome, *The Population Bomb*. In that book, Ehrlich claims that "The battle to feed all of humanity is over. In the 1970's the world will undergo famines—hundreds of millions of people are going to starve to death." His solution? "The birth rate must be brought into balance with the death rate . . . We can no longer afford merely to treat the symptoms of the cancer of population growth; the cancer itself must be cut out."[8]

Without any set of stable morals, professors argue in favor of thugs and criminals. One professor played the "song" "Cop Killer" by that illustrious artist, Ice-T. To quote from the song: "I got my twelve gauge sawed off / I got my headlights turned off / I'm 'bout to bust some shots off / I'm 'bout to dust some cops off! / Cop killer, it's better you than me / Cop killer, f— police brutality / Cop killer, I know your family's grieving (F— 'em) / Cop killer, but tonight we get even (ha, ha, ha, ha, yeah!)."[8] The Parents Music Resource Center (PMRC) protested this charming little ditty, even making statements on the floor of the United States Senate. The ACLU responded in defense of Ice-T, whose music "provides an outlet for anger and encourages listeners to think about the issue of police misconduct and the antagonism it creates."[9]

The professor followed up the "song" by asking the class: "What do you think? Is the government censoring musicians by acknowledging the legitimacy of groups like the PMRC?"[10] How is that for a leading question?

Besides defending gangsta rap, professors will also defend convicted and admitted murderers and murderesses—as long as those killers are leftists.

Mumia Abu-Jamal is the convicted murderer of New York police officer Daniel Faulkner. After Faulkner made a routine traffic stop on Abu-Jamal's brother, Billy Cook, Abu-Jamal stumbled upon the scene, pulled out a gun, and shot Faulkner three times, then stood over him and shot him in the head for good measure. Abu-Jamal is guiltier than sin but has become an international *cause célèbre* because of his political position: far left. He used to be a member of the Black Panthers and was a radical radio host.[11]

Naturally, professors rush to defend him. Mary Brent Wehrli, a self-described radical and professor of social work at UCLA, says, "His case is a blight on the democratic process we all believe in. Information which would have changed the outcome of the trial was not admitted and the judge appears to be racist and not open-minded—not unbiased."[12]

Another campus celebrity is Sara Jane Olson (a.k.a. Kathleen Soliah), a former member of the Symbionese Liberation Army, a domestic terrorist organization. She pled guilty on November 1, 2001, to the attempted murder of two Los Angeles police officers in 1974. As part of the SLA, she planted bombs under the cars of the two police officers.[13]

Predictably, professors also support Olson. Wehrli was listed on the Web site of the Sara Olson Defense Fund Committee as an endorser and honorary member of the committee. She says, "I support Sara Jane Olson. Olson has been denied the right to a fair trial." Erwin Chemerinsky, professor of law at USC, agrees with Wehrli. His name was above hers on the list of endorsers and honorary members of the committee. Other professors on the list included Peter Rachleff, a history professor at Macalaster College in St. Paul, Minnesota, and William Ayers ("Distinguished Professor of Education").[14]

"Distinguished Professor of Education" William Ayers is a professor of education at the University of Illinois in Chicago. In the 1960s and 70s, he was a member of the radical Weather Underground group (also known as the Weathermen). His wife, Bernadine Dohrn, now a member of the law school faculty and director of the Northwestern Children and Family Justice Center, was also a member. The Weather Underground was responsible for numerous antiwar bombings, including an attempted bombing of the Pentagon and a bombing at an army base. Ayers is unrepentant for his actions; he wrote a book, *Fugitive Days*, describing his experiences with the Weathermen. Ayers says, "I have no regrets . . . you have to act in an imperfect world and we did and would again."[15]

Northwestern and the University of Illinois are backing these unabashed terrorists. Northwestern law school dean David Van Zandt says of Dohrn, "Her career here at the law school is an example of a person's ability to channel one's energy and passion into making a difference in our legal system."[16] It's nice to know that one's energy and passion for terrorism can be converted toward teaching students, isn't it?

DEBASING MORALITY

The assault on absolute morality is the basis for every brainwashing scheme of the Left. It even bestows upon them the leeway to defend murderers and thugs.

Higher learning, indeed.

2

PARTISAN POLITICS

Liberal Democrats dominate the university scene. This shouldn't come as much of a surprise, but the extent of the Democratic domination is mind-boggling. The percentage of Democrats teaching in the university system closely parallels the percentage of communists in the Cuban government.

To review: 84 percent of professors voted for Al Gore for president in the 2000 election; only 9 percent voted for George W. Bush. While 57 percent of professors are self-identified Democrats, only 3 percent identify themselves as Republicans.[1] A whopping 79 percent of professors said that George W. Bush's politics were "too conservative."[2] Of the seventy-eight political science professors at Colorado's state universities, forty-five are registered Democrats, and just nine are registered Republicans.[3] At Williams College, there are only four registered Republican professors on campus out of two hundred professors. At Brown University, registered Democrats outnumber Republicans 54-3; at Berkeley, 59-7; at Stanford 151-17; at the University of California at San Diego, 99-6.[4]

Stanford's History Department has twenty-two Democrats but only two Republicans. Cornell's has twenty-nine Democrats and zero Republicans. Dartmouth's has ten Democrats and no Republicans. At the University of Colorado at Boulder, the English, History, and Philosophy Departments have a combined sixty-eight Democrats, and not a single Republican. At that same university, 184 of the 190 social science and humanities professors identified themselves as Democrats.[5]

At my own beloved UCLA the numbers are just as frightening. There are thirty-one English professors with registered party affiliation. Twenty-nine of them are affiliated with the Democratic party, the Green party, or another leftist political party. Out of thirteen journalism professors with registered affiliation, twelve are affiliated with leftist parties. Fifty-three out of fifty-six history professors are affiliated with leftist parties. Sixteen out of seventeen political science professors are affiliated with leftist parties. Thirty-one of thirty-three women's studies professors are affiliated with leftist parties.[6]

The few professors who *are* conservative are unable to "come out of the closet" for fear that they will be targeted by their colleagues and the university administration. Professor Robert Maranto of Villanova University explains: "While colleges strive for ethnic diversity, they actively oppose ideological diversity. Surveys find that only about 10 percent of social science and humanities faculty vote Republican." Maranto cites the case of a sociologist who quit academia after turning conservative: "When I decided to become a registered Republican, it was a sensation," the sociologist relates. "It was as if I became a child molester. You don't want to be in a department where everyone hates your guts."[7]

INDOCTRINATION

Professors spouting the party line have a definite effect on the student population. An informal exit poll at UCLA revealed that 71 percent of students voted for Al Gore in the 2000 election with another nine percent voting for Ralph Nader.[8] At Tufts, 51 percent of the students identify themselves as liberals, 14 percent identify as moderate, 16 percent "did not know," and only 10 percent identify as conservative or right-of-center.[9] In more conservative states, the majority of college students might identify themselves as Republicans, as at the University of Tennessee.[10] Even at these universities, however, the percentage of conservatives is extremely low compared to the general population in the surrounding areas.

I took a political science class during the winter of 2001, just following the 2000 presidential elections. The title of the course was "Introduction to World Politics," and there were about 300 students enrolled.

Early on in the quarter, the professor asked for a quick show of hands:

Who voted for Al Gore, and who voted for George W. Bush? About 250 hands went up for Al Gore, and about 15 went up for George W. Bush (I raised my hand even though at the time I had just turned seventeen; I figured Bush needed all the help he could get in *that* classroom). The professor then asked: "Who thought the election process was fair?" About 15 students, including me, raised their hands. The professor finally asked: "If Al Gore had won, who here would have thought the election was fair?" This time, almost every one raised a hand. It was typical of a Democratic constituency: the system only works if we win.

The Democrats running the universities don't separate politics and teaching. At all. In fact, the Democratic party platform provides a great description of the material professors shove down the throats of their captive audiences.

"PRESIDENT-SELECT" GEORGE W. BUSH

Immediately following the 2000 presidential election, professors started depicting George W. Bush as an illegitimate, "selected" president. They spewed all the usual rhetoric about Bush's alleged stupidity and illiteracy. The legacy of democracy had been shattered by Bush's highway robbery.

English Professor Robert Watson of UCLA submitted an article to the *Daily Bruin* the week before George W. Bush's inauguration. It was a brutal, cynical, and altogether outrageous piece. "We can't stop him from taking office," Watson wrote. "We also can't let him pretend he deserves it."

Watson invented charges, accusing the Bush campaign of "mob intimidation" and "stalling legal tactics." He played the race card; Bush only gained his "mythical official edge," Watson said, because he "systematically deprived" racial minorities and the poor of "equal voting rights." He ripped the "conservative Republican majority on the US Supreme Court" for overriding state law.

Bush spokespeople were men of "intellectual dishonesty, ethical indifference and spiritual ugliness," and Attorney General John Ashcroft had a "lifelong record of opposition to African Americans and racial justice." Awash in melodrama and metaphor, Watson stated, "Let's meet on Jan. 20, while George W. Bush takes his oath to serve the Constitution he's undermining. Maybe, for symbolic value, we can each hold a candle, and burn a piece of paper marked 'Ballot' and 'Democracy' on one side and 'Truth' and 'Equality' on the other."[11]

Watson wasn't finished with his one-man protest. He held a meeting of roughly thirty people the night of Bush's inauguration. "Something truly outrageous and destructive had happened, and the Bush handlers were cynically counting on everybody wanting to forget about it. I thought it was important for people who were willing to resist to know they weren't alone, to improve each other's understanding by discussion and to figure out what can be done to limit the damage," said the English professor-cum political expert. Watson then dragged out his sobbing wife who managed to sniffle: "I don't believe in God. The Constitution and the Declaration of Independence are narratives to me of how the world should work, and what happened in the last election destroyed that."[12] She's God-less. She's Constitution-less. She's world-less. She's brainless.

Political science Professor Matthew Baum of UCLA said that the 2000 election "stretched legitimacy."[13] Thomas Cronin, president of Whitman College, and Michael A. Genovese, political science professor at Loyola Marymount, said that Bush faced "compelling questions about whether he possesses enough '*gravitas*' to be president."[14] September 11 answered those questions pretty definitively.

Princeton professor Richard Falk called the Supreme Court decision "dubious to the point of scandalous, seemingly inconsistent with the conservative view of federalism, and suspiciously linked to the promotion of a partisan political outcome."[15] Fellow Princeton professor Stanley Katz concurred: "What the Supreme Court decided, in the end, was that we should be governed by John Ashcroft, Donald Rumsfeld and Richard Cheney. It should remind the Democrats how much is at stake in presidential politics—and that partisan politics are the name of the game."[16] Professor Gwendolyn Mink of UC Santa Cruz declared: "The Supreme Court not only stole the 2000 election from the people, it deranged our constitutional order." To hear these professors talk, you would think that the Supreme Court is full of neo-fascists who burn American flags for fun.

Bush is illegitimate and lacks *gravitas*. John Ashcroft is a bigot. The

Supreme Court is partisan and politically motivated. Thank goodness the professors are here to save America from such rotten people.

"TAX CUTS FOR THE RICH"

A favorite shtick of the professors is the tried-and-true anti-Republican "tax cuts for the rich" argument. According to professors, the rich don't deserve their money. Rather, the poor deserve the money of the rich. Therefore, the government should take the money of the rich and give it to the poor through high taxes. If an administration either fails to take enough money from the rich or gives back money to the rich, that administration is evil and hates the poor. Hence, tax cuts only benefit the rich.

The "tax cuts for the rich" argument is completely specious. To start, most of those who are categorized as "rich" by the Left are hardly rolling in dough. My family would probably be classified as rich based on my parents' combined income, but my parents pay private school tuition for three children and have a mortgage and living expenses. I have yet to see a tux-clad servant named Alfred around my house. Still, according to some, my mother, a hard-working television executive, and my father, an author and composer, should pay nearly 50 percent of their money to the government. Why? To support socialist programs that discourage hard work and favor reliance on the government.

There's no denying that tax cuts return money to rich people, but that is because rich people pay the vast majority of taxes. Tax cuts provide money to the upper class, but that upper class doesn't just tuck it into a mattress and sit on it. They use it to start businesses; they invest in the stock market; they provide jobs and income for the lower classes.

Not according to professors, of course.

Less than 10 percent of professors support Bush's tax plan, and only 3 percent of tenured faculty support it.[17]

UCLA history professor Mary Corey finds any "request for permanent lower taxes rather bothersome."[18] Rather bothersome? A toothache is rather bothersome. Tax cuts are requirements for a healthy economy.

UCLA Professor Lynn Vavreck labels as confused those who "want to help the poor, but also want lower taxes."[19] Last time I checked, lowering taxes not only does not hurt the poor, it helps them greatly. Simply put, if people have more money to spend, they will invariably create new industries, new markets, etc. This provides more jobs for the unemployed, and provides new capital for entrepreneurs. When Ronald Reagan pursued tax-cutting during his administration, median family income, median household income, and average household income all rose;[20] from 1982 to 1989, the unemployment rate declined by 4.3 percent.[21] And Vavreck says tax-cutting is bad for the poor?

Professor Joel Blau of the State University of New York at Stoneybrook stated, "Instead of 'compassionate conservatism' and calls to leave no American behind, we are faced with a proposal that *caters to the wealthiest segment of the population.*"[22] One question: If the wealthiest segment of the population has no money, who gives the poor their jobs? The government? There's a name for that economic philosophy—communism.

Professor Ellen Frank of Emmanuel College agreed with Blau: "If these tax cuts pass, Congress will have succeeded in . . . using surplus Social Security and Medicare revenues to finance tax cuts for the very wealthy."[23] Horse manure. The Bush tax cuts cut taxes across the board, not just for the wealthy. And again, why is there such a backlash against the rich keeping more of their own money?

David E. Kaun, a professor of economics at UC Santa Cruz said that the Bush tax plan would "serve not to stimulate the economy and increase investment as advertised, but rather would further aggravate the *unfairness* that is rife across the nation."[24] If Kaun is so concerned about "unfairness," why doesn't he care that the people who work the hardest are those who are taxed the most? Why doesn't he care that the current tax structure penalizes those who work their way to the top? Kaun isn't concerned about fairness. He's jealous of those who earn their money in the real world rather than the ivory towers of academia.

MIT Professor of Economics and Dean Emeritus Lester Thurow fears that "If Bush and the Republicans come in and have a huge tax cut as Reagan did in 1980, we'll be right back into the deficit hole."[25] Aha. Three questions. First, didn't Reagan take over from Jimmy Carter, who had run the economy straight into the ground? Second, didn't the American economy experience the largest peace-time economic growth rate in history under Reagan? And third, why isn't cutting government spending a viable alternative to maintaining high taxes?

In a submission to the *Daily Bruin*, UCLA Professor Robert Watson again puts in his two cents: "It's wonderful how many reverse Robin Hoods leap out of the woods to protect the rich and powerful from criticism."[26] Sensing any class envy here?

After UCLA economics professor Theodore Andersen confronted Watson's economic illiteracy in a letter to the *Daily Bruin*, Watson fired back. (Note: Professor Watson occasionally does teach classes, when he can fit his teaching around writing submissions to the student newspaper.) Watson expressed his anger at right-wing politicians "who justify . . . limiting social services in order to provide tax-breaks for the already wealthy."[27] The professor has it backwards. Social services are not limited to provide for tax breaks; tax dollars fund the social services in the first place. To act as though money for social services magically appears and that tax cuts steal that magical money and hand it to the rich is absolutely false.

But, then again, since when have leftists cared about truth?

"MEDIA BIAS? WHAT MEDIA BIAS?"

The university view of the media says that the *New York Times* is entirely objective, not wildly biased. Ditto for the *Los Angeles Times*. So too for CNN. In fact, the only non-objective news sources are Fox News, the *Wall Street Journal*, and the *Drudge Report*. There is no liberal bias in the media.

Geoffrey Nunberg, a professor who has taught at UCLA, said that "If there is a bias here, in fact, the data suggest that it goes the other way—that the media consider liberals to be farther from the mainstream than conservatives are."[28] Has this guy ever picked up a newspaper or turned on the network news? If he thinks that the media is conservative, he must be bonkers.

Professor David Domke of Washington University admits that there is "some evidence that the media leans to the left, but the amount of that lean is small."[29] Hell will freeze over before the amount of bias at the *New York Times* is small. The liberal media hates Republicans, the military, and Israel. Take, for example, the following teaser on ABCNews.com for Ted Koppel's *Nightline*: "Tonight: Reaction to Israel's deadly attack on Gaza City." When that link was clicked, the headline that popped up read: "Cycle of Violence."[30] From original headline, it would seem that Israel, unprovoked, launched an attack on Gaza City, killing civilians for the fun of it. In reality, Israel was targeting the chief terrorist of Hamas, Saleh Shehadeh, a man responsible for several major attacks on Israeli civilians.

Professor Steven Spiegel of UCLA characterized *Harper's Magazine* and the *New Republic* as "centrist."[31] The editor of the *New Republic* is Martin Peretz, a notorious liberal and the longtime mentor of Albert Gore. *Harper's Magazine* is a leftist rag; knee-jerk liar Stanley Fish appears frequently in *Harper's* as did the equally outrageous Edward Said until his death last year. If these are centrist publications, then Pat Buchanan is a Ralph Nader backer.

When they're not properly labeling media outlets, professors show their leftist colors (various shades of red) by simply ignoring media not biased to the left. Professor Lynn Vavreck of UCLA characterizes the following media sources as "hard news": The evening news reports of ABC, CBS, and NBC, CNN, MSNBC, Fox News, *New York Times, Los Angeles Times, Time, Newsweek, U.S. News and World Report.*[32] Notice anything missing? Only the *Wall Street Journal,* the largest daily newspaper in the United States.

An in-class assignment for a political science course at UCLA asked students to study the amount of "negative news" reported about a given candidate for political office. The professor wanted students to draw the conclusion that the level of media criticism was equal across party lines, and that Republican candidates only garnered more criticism since they were elected to the executive office more times—in short, that no media bias existed. Only one problem: *This assignment had nothing to do with media bias.* The question of media bias is not whether the media covers more scandals concerning Republicans than Democrats. It is a question of whether the media covers the same story differently depending on whether the subject is right-wing or left-wing.

To cut them some slack, professors are usually on the far left of the Democratic party, so I suppose the *New York Times* must seem moderate by comparison.

THE QUEST FOR "SOCIAL JUSTICE"

For Democrats, the goal of society should be to ensure "social justice"—a nice-sounding abstraction that boils down to ham-fisted government intervention.

"Just being responsive to the market won't ensure that social justice is preserved," said Professor Scott Bowman, guest lecturing to one of my political science classes. "Law isn't only the key to the marketplace, it's the key to social justice."[33] Professors believe that the free market forgets the little guy. They believe that the market only acts in the interest of the big corporation and seeks to exploit the ordinary Joe trying to earn a living. So, they say, government must step in to protect Joe with social programs. As an assigned political science textbook reads, "state jurisdiction over public goods that fall within its borders offers real advantages."[34]

Welfare is a big favorite of the professors. And not the watered-down version of welfare embodied in the 1996 Welfare Reform Act. They like the big, expensive, useless form of welfare that keeps teen pregnancy high, work ethic low, and the upper class paying massive taxes.

Professor Sheldon Danziger of the University of Michigan ripped into the 1996 Welfare Reform Act: "The harsh realities of the labor market mean that restricting assistance for welfare mothers will increase economic hardship. The likelihood that the new welfare law will cause harm will increase over time."[35]

Likewise, Professor Sheila Kamerman of Columbia University predicted that Welfare Reform would be a gigantic flop. "There is a fantasy that these changes are going to significantly reduce out-of-wedlock childbirth and teenage pregnancy. But very little attention is being paid to the consequences for children."[36]

Kamerman knows the trick: When you have no grounds for a real argument, weep for the children—a tactic (perhaps learned from leftist comrades in Congress) that gets good play in the press most every time it's tried. Said

Professor Peter Edelman of Georgetown University, "The new law doesn't promote work effectively and doesn't protect children. The old system involved at least a framework that was right."[37]

But, of course, Danziger, Kamerman, Edelman, and their ilk are wrong. The old framework *hurt* children. The Welfare Reform Act caused poverty, child poverty, illegitimate childbirth, and black child poverty to decline drastically.[38]

Another favorite social policy of the Left is Social Security. With Boomers ripening at such a fast rate, the program will soon be overtaxed, but don't even think about privatizing any part of it! Money is best left in the hands of government. The citizens of the United States are too stupid to save for the future.

Professor Patricia E. Dilley of the University of Florida nearly went apoplectic in her attempt to demonize privatization. "A call to totally privatize the program would effectively end Social Security as we know it, and could endanger retirement benefits for countless Americans," she said. When reminded that Social Security is in serious trouble, Dilley remarked, "whether society as a whole shares the cost of paying for their retirement through Social Security, or whether each individual has to save for his or her own retirement, the same amount of goods and services will have to be devoted to the elderly, either way. *It's just a matter of how the burden is distributed.*"[39]

Say what? She's seriously advocating a no-change policy, saying that even if the worst happens, the taxpayers will pay for it. Remembering that the nation's "rich" pay the biggest share of taxes, this is nothing more than class envy in action.

Professor Alicia Munnell of Boston College, a former Clinton staffer, denied any problems with Social Security: "The system is not broken . . . they want to restructure it and cut Social Security benefits and replace it with individual accounts. I think that's a bad idea."[40] This is a fundamental mischaracterization of Social Security privatization. Conservatives do not want to cut benefits to the already-retired. They merely want to give people the option of placing their benefits in safe stocks and bonds, instead of handing them over to the government. That's a bad idea?

Associate Professor Brad Roth of Wayne State University insulted any plan including privatization as "an ideological effort on the part of Republicans to undermine the role of government in serving people's needs."[41] Excuse me, but it is not the job of the government to "serve people's needs." The government has only one basic role: to protect lives and property from harm and fraud. Mandating that citizens pay money into a government retirement fund shouldn't be a part of the game plan.

Minimum wage laws are also popular with the professors. If we're going to subscribe to the free market on a global scale, they say, we must make sure the little person isn't stepped upon. We must assure him a "living wage." In reality, minimum wage laws create unemployment by forcing companies to cut back costs. The little guy is the one most hurt by the minimum wage.

But professors don't see it that way.

According to Boston University Professor Kevin Lang, there would be "little or no" job losses if minimum wages were raised.[42] Professor Robert Pollin of the University of Massachusetts at Amherst concurs: "The impact on businesses and governments is very small. If there were any evidence otherwise, it would have shut down the living-wage movement a long time ago."[43] That's not exactly true. Most economists oppose minimum wage laws, but that never prevents the laws from being written. The living wage movement lives on, not because of any merit, but because it's a popular political move to back anything that "helps the poor."

Professor Alan Krueger of Princeton declared, "There's no indication that the last increases have had an adverse impact on employment."[44] Krueger and Professor David Card of UC Berkeley co-authored a study on minimum wage that concluded that any minimum wage would have little or no effect on employment.[45] How is it possible that a minimum wage would not cause a decline in employment or curtail a rise in employment? The answer is, it's not possible. As Larry Elder relates in his book, *The Ten Things You Can't Say in America,*

> When other researchers tried to duplicate the results [of the Krueger-Card study], they could not. Turns out that those working for Card and Krueger simply picked up the telephone and asked employers whether they intended to increase, decrease, or keep employment flat.

Researchers seeking to duplicate the results of Card and Krueger went one step further. They requested *payroll cards* in order to verify employment. When researchers requested payroll cards, the non-effect of hiking minimum wage completely disappeared. In fact, both Pennsylvania and New Jersey suffered a decrease in employment following their minimum wage hike.[46]

The Democratic tendency of the professors isn't confined to laws already on the books. For example, many professors support nationalization of the health care industry, in accordance with the Hillary-care plan.

A "debate" at Oral Roberts University pitted Professor George Gillen and Professor William Walker (pro-nationalization) against Professor Timothy Brooker (anti-nationalization). Gillen stated that the reason for rising prescription drug prices is the fact that the pharmaceutical industry is an oligopoly – only a few companies control the entire field. His solution? Nationalize the health care system. Brooker, Gillen's supposed opponent, explained that the free-market system drives innovation in the pharmaceutical industry. Still, in the end, Brooker conceded, and he and Gillen agreed that nationalization was required to some extent.[47] So much for defending your principles. I'm sure the students felt very enlightened after hearing "both sides of the story."

Ray Moseley, an associate professor of medical ethics at the University of Florida College of Medicine, claimed that "Americans are becoming aware that those in countries with nationalized health programs are receiving better medical care than in the United States . . . Other countries are spending half as much and getting better results."[48] That's interesting. Last time I checked, heads of state came to America for health care, not Cuba. And socialized medicine is having its problems in Canada. Canada lags behind America in its medical technology and its ability to cope with an overcrowded system.

The answer to every "social justice" question is more taxes and regulation, say the professors. People are poor and have illegitimate children to support? Tax the rich and give money to the poor. People are unemployed? Tax the rich and pay the unemployed. A small percentage of the elderly can't plan for the future? Make everyone pay into Social Security. A small percentage of people aren't getting proper health care? Nationalize the whole system.

If we listened to the professors, we'd be living like the Cubans already.

STUPID REPUBLICAN TRICKS

Being good little Democrats, professors think that Republicans are the scourge of the Earth. The dastardly Republican party is stupid, bumbling, and destructive to America. It's a good thing the brilliant Democrats are here to prevent Republicans from killing all the poor people and setting up an aristocracy with David Duke as king.

Conservatives are just plain stupid. A UC Berkeley study by Jack Glaser and Frank Sulloway, John Jost of Stanford University, and Arie Kruglanski of the University of Maryland at College Park, detailed the conservative mindset. According to the researchers, the basis of political conservatism is tolerance for inequality and resistance to change; some psychological factors associated with conservatism are dogmatism and intolerance of ambiguity, fear and aggression, uncertainty avoidance, need for cognitive closure, and terror management. In short, conservatives are mentally defective.

The authors stated that conservatives across the board share the afore-mentioned qualities and lump Ronald Reagan and Rush Limbaugh together with Hitler and Mussolini. Not only that—they attempt to cate-gorize Stalin, Khrushchev, and Castro as "conservative."

Just because conservatives are less "integratively complex," Professor Glaser mouths, "it doesn't mean they're simple-minded."[49] How reassuring.

One of my teaching assistants addressed "conservative stupidity" while tangentially discussing the nature of taxi drivers. "I've met some genius taxi drivers, and I've met some people who listen to Rush Limbaugh all day." He paused, then continued: "and they're clearly on crack because even *they* don't even understand what Rush is saying."[50] The implication: only an idiot would listen to Rush Limbaugh. There sure are a lot of idiots out there—twenty million, in fact. I'm one of them.

Conservatives are portrayed as members of a conspiratorial power structure. Lane Community College Ethnic Studies Professor Mark Harris believes we should "look at all cultural perspectives to sustain hope and energy in the face of a conservative power structure."[51] But while right-wingers are busy being nefarious and diabolical, liberals are uniformly deeply concerned and brilliant. Professor Robert Watson of the UCLA English Department describes radical-leftism as "the determination to ask hard questions about the things a society has been most comfortable assuming."[52] University of Oregon Survival Center co-director Randy Newnham agrees: "'I would describe more students as being radical because many of the students that I work with are anti-capitalism, pro-labor equality, pro-liberation and think critically about world events.'"[53]

HOW THE REPUBLICANS RUINED AMERICA

The first week of lecture in my "National Institutions: Congress" course, Professor Barbara Sinclair dragged out the liberal playbook. Republicans were "extreme," she told the class, while Democrats were "more diverse." House Majority Leader Tom DeLay was "extremely conservative," while House Minority Leader Nancy Pelosi was "answerable to her constituents," and "couldn't be *that* liberal."[54] This kind of propaganda flows from professorial podiums every day. So it should be no surprise when professors claim that Republicans are ruining our country. After all, they're the "extremists," while Democrats are more tolerant and "diverse."

UCLA Professor Kenneth Schultz says, "Republicans have not historically been the party of human rights."[55] Oh. So all that stuff about Lincoln and the slaves was a big lie?

Professor Lynn Vavreck of UCLA taught my "Introduction to American Politics" class during Winter 2002. She had a field day with George H.W. Bush's 1988 "Revolving Door Ad." The ad, run by the Bush campaign against Michael Dukakis, highlighted Dukakis's softness on crime. Vavreck first told the class that the ad revived memories of the independently-produced "Wille Horton Ad," which revolved around Willie Horton, a violent felon given furlough under Dukakis's Massachusetts administration. With furlough in hand, Horton went on to rape a woman in Maryland and stab her boyfriend. After connecting the two ads, Vavreck detailed all of the inaccuracies in the "Revolving Door Ad" with verve and vigor. About half an hour later, she showed her "favorite" campaign ad, a Michael Dukakis ad depicting a sweaty, fat Republican talking about politics.[56] For some strange reason, she did not critique the ad or discuss *its* inaccuracies.

An assigned text in that political science class states: "From 1929 until 1933, the Republican party presided over the worst depression in American history."[57] Funny how that works. According to the text, the Great Depression only lasted for four years. In reality, the Great Depression lasted another eight years after that, for two Democratic administrations under FDR. And as historian Jim Powell has argued, Roosevelt's economic policies actually made matters worse, prolonging and deepening the Depression.[58]

Professors hate the very notion of missile defense as proposed by those war-mongering Republicans. Some 74 percent strongly oppose a national missile defense system, as opposed to 70 percent of the general public who favor it.[59] Albert Carnesale, the chancellor of UCLA, says that "a missile defense shield is not the answer to the threat of weapons of mass destruction."[60] More than thirty professors and members of the Union of Concerned Scientists urged the Bush administration to forego national missile defense at least for the present.[61]

Don't even ask about school vouchers. Despite their stunning success wherever they have been tried, professors would rather hang themselves with their shoelaces than condone vouchers. About 67 percent of professors oppose the use of school vouchers.[62] Professor Paul Peterson of Harvard University wrote a book lauding school vouchers, and immediately came under attack from his fellow intellectuals. Professor Henry M. Levin of Stanford University claimed that Peterson was biased: "There's no question that he's a passionate advocate for vouchers . . . And that certainly dominates his perspective on these evaluations."[63] Bruce Fuller, a researcher from UC Berkeley insulted Peterson's research technique: "Even when he has limited data, he's always squeezing out whatever data he can to arrive at a predetermined answer."[64] This is typical. If you don't follow the party line, you get slammed.

Professors never forget the dastardly antics of the rotten Republicans and the manic media during the Clinton impeachment debacle. They remember "Kenneth Starr's *sprawling* $40 million, five-year investigation of Bill and Hillary Clinton"[65] and "the news media's *obsessive* coverage of the scandal."[66]

After all, professors were some of the biggest backers of Clinton during his scandals. Four hundred professors signed an ad urging the GOP-controlled Congress not to impeach Clinton, while at the same time insisting that they were "non-partisan."[67] Professor Sean Wilentz of Princeton testified on behalf of President Clinton: "If you believe [Clinton's crimes] do rise to that level [of impeachment], you will vote for impeachment and take your risk at going down in history with the zealots and the fanatics."[68]

And then there are the extremists. Professors Bill Mullen and Kevin Borgeson of Stonehill College likened prominent conservative David Horowitz, a Jew, to radical Holocaust denier Bradley Smith. Attorney General John Ashcroft, a devout Christian who as Missouri governor asked his weekly prayer meetings to be non-denominational so as not to offend those of other faiths, was slurred as a member of a phantom "racist right."[69]

On a wide variety of issues, the professors hew to the party line, and that means the Right can do no right. It's no coincidence, and it's an educational travesty.

OUT, DAMNED CONSERVATIVES!

Republicans are not welcome on campus. Conservatives are not even allowed to speak at college graduations. The Center for the Study of Popular Culture researched the political views of graduation speakers over a ten-year period, covering thirty-two colleges, including all Ivy League schools. Speakers with liberal ideas outnumbered speakers with conservative ideas by a margin of 226-15. Twenty-two of the thirty-two schools surveyed did not invite a single conservative to speak; during the same period, they invited 173 liberals.[70]

When UCLA invited First Lady Laura Bush to speak at the Graduate School of Education and Information Studies commencement, all hell broke loose. Even though it was clear from the first that Bush would not accept, students protested the invitation with all the strength in their leftist bodies. "We will not stand by and allow her presence to go uncontested," vowed Estela Zarate, a doctoral student in education.[71]

Meanwhile, leftists are welcomed with open arms. Al Franken, vitriolic liberal, had an academic fellowship at Harvard University during 2003. He was given fourteen assistants to help him research his book, *Lies and the Lying Liars Who Tell Them: A Fair and Balanced Look at the Right.* This great work of scholarship includes chapters entitled "Ann Coulter: Nutcase," and "I Bitch-Slap Bernie Goldberg."[72]

And that's not all. Franken used official Harvard University letterhead to play pranks on prominent conservatives. Franken sent a letter to Attorney General John Ashcroft asking Ashcroft to share his experience with abstinence for "a book about abstinence programs in our public schools entitled, 'Savin' It!'" He told Ashcroft that the story would be used to show that the Bush Administration is "setting the right example for America's youth." He informed Ashcroft that he had "received wonderful testimonies from HHS Secretary Tommy Thompson, William J. Bennett, White House Press Secretary Ari Fleischer, Senator Rick Santorum, and National Security Advisor Condoleezza Rice." The entire letter was bogus. In fact, Franken wanted material for his book. As columnist Michelle Malkin puts it, "Ridiculing chaste young people and their abstinent role models as oddballs and prudes may score Franken a few points at Hollywood and Harvard cocktail parties."[73]

DONKEY U.

Tax cuts are evil. Welfare reform is evil. Social Security privatization is evil. Lack of a "living wage" is evil. Private ownership of health care is evil. Missile defense is evil. School vouchers are evil. The entire history of the Republican party is evil. Well, then, what are all the poor students to do?

Vote Democrat.

3

WORKERS OF THE WORLD, UNITE!

There are the Democrats, and then there are the Reds.

If the twentieth century taught us one lesson, it is that socialism fails wherever it is tried. It failed in the Soviet Union. It failed in China. It failed in Tanzania, North Korea, and Cuba. And it hasn't exactly made Sweden, France, or Finland world powers. The last century is hard evidence that without a capitalist economy, a country will find itself in dire straits.

Professors still haven't learned that lesson.

Classes on Marxism exist at major universities across the country, including Brown University, Columbia University, Cornell University, Dartmouth College, Harvard University, Princeton University, University of Pennsylvania, Yale University, Bucknell University, Carnegie-Mellon University, Duke University, Emory University, New York University, Stanford University, Syracuse University, University of Chicago, Amherst College, Carleton College, Oberlin College, Reed College, Vassar College, Wellesley College, University of Arizona, University of Colorado, University of Florida, University of Iowa, University of Kentucky, University of Massachusetts, University of Michigan, University of Minnesota, University of Missouri, University of North Carolina (Chapel Hill), Pennsylvania State University, Rutgers University, University of Texas, University of Virginia, University of Washington, University of Wisconsin, and virtually the entire University of California system.[1]

Amherst College offers "Taking Marx Seriously." The University of

California at Santa Barbara offers "Black Marxism." Rutgers University offers "Marxist Literary Theory." University of California at Riverside offers a Marxist Studies minor.[2]

Professor Richard Sklar of UCLA described socialism as a "great idea"[3] and communist dictator Mao Tse-Tung as a "great leader."[4] Implementation of socialism has resulted in more deaths than all the international wars of the twentieth century combined. Is socialism really a "great idea"? Mao caused the deaths of millions of his own people. Does that constitute great leadership?

Professor Dirk Struik, mathematician at MIT, stated that "From my student days on, I found the study of Marx' way of thinking has been helpful."[5] Professor Cornel West's biographical sketch, quoted on numerous Web sites, describes his philosophy as one that "seeks to revive the best of liberalism, populism and democratic socialism."[6] Professor A. Belden Fields of the University of Illinois leads the socialist group on campus in monthly discussions.[7]

When Tony Kushner, poisonously socialist playwright, spoke at Cornell University, he wittily remarked, "Capitalism sucks, we all know it."[8] Kushner, according to the *Cornell Chronicle*, "discussed the evils of capitalism and individualism" and "as an alternative, he offered socialism, which he said embodies beneficial cooperation rather than competition."[9] Great alternative. At least, that's what the professors thought.

Ron Wilson, a professor of theater and film, lauded Kushner: "Kushner's combination of whimsy with intellectualism made for an interesting evening." According to the article, Professor Joyce Morgenroth, associate professor of dance, "said she liked the way Kushner weaved together many different themes but kept touching ground. 'He kept bringing the audience back to earth.'"[10]

I recall sitting in my Geography 5 class early during my freshman year at UCLA. Professor Joshua Muldavin taught the course. Along with learning that Western nations destroy the earth's peoples and ecosystems, we also learned about his virulent anti-capitalism; the only question was whether he was a full-fledged communist. He answered that, and fast. Relating the story of a student who had asked about his communist leanings, the professor addressed the class, "So he asked me if I was a communist. I said, 'If being a communist means that I care about all people, that I want to reduce inequality and help the poor, then yes, I'm a communist.'" I sat there, stunned. The rest of the class laughed and applauded.

The far left of the university faculty are as red as overripe tomatoes. And they're bombarding students every day.

CAPITALISM: THE FLAWED SYSTEM

The Leon Trotsky wing of the university hates capitalism with a vengeance. According to this faction, capitalism does nothing good; it only broadens the gap between rich and poor and results in the exploitation of people for the sake of money. Any economic growth is not due to a free-market economy, but to some other factor.

Professor Sklar told our class that "intellectuals aren't as anti-capitalist as they were twenty-five or thirty years ago."[11] I wasn't around that long ago, but if professors now are *less* anti-capitalist than they were then, I can't imagine how bad it was then.

An assigned article for UCLA's Geography 5 course in Winter 2001 stated, "'market-oriented' systems of production and distribution do not have a good track record in feeding people, nor in tackling the underlying structures of poverty which consign over one quarter of the world's population to hunger."[12] That's a surprise. Last time I checked, non-"market-oriented" systems had starved twenty million people in the USSR, thirty million people in China, and millions more throughout the world. Guess I must have missed the part in America's history where its market-oriented system killed millions of citizens.

The course syllabus for UCLA class Geography 4, entitled "Globalization: Regional Development and the World Economy," reads, "At the end of the course students should be able to understand the basic features of the world economy, how it developed historically and *how these processes create inequality and poverty.*"[13] It is implicitly assumed that capitalism causes inequality and poverty. Excuse me? Every country that takes part in the world market has experienced economic growth. If the gap between rich countries and poor countries widens, that does not mean that the poor aren't also getting richer; it's a question of comparison. Let's say, for example, that I make $100,000 per year as an executive, and you make $30,000 per year as a teacher. At Christmas, I get a raise of $5,000, and you get a raise of $1,000. Our income gap just widened by $4,000, but you are still making more money than you used to. Inequality by itself does not imply creation of poverty.

Professor Robert M. Solow of MIT, a Nobel laureate, echoed complaints about capitalism causing "inequality": "laissez-faire capitalism tends to generate *vast inequalities of income and even vaster inequalities of wealth*."[14] Fellow MIT Professor Kenneth Arrow, another Nobel laureate, agreed: "capitalism itself doesn't work very well when it's not regulated and when there aren't checks and balances on it."[15]

Professor Thomas Sugrue of the University of Pennsylvania in Philadelphia sees capitalism as the cause of black underdevelopment. Capitalism causes inequality, he says. (Haven't we heard this before?) And not only does capitalism cause inequality, "African Americans have disproportionately borne the income of that inequality."[16] Wrong. Sorry, professor, you don't win the free car. Want to try for a washing machine? Robert Higgs of the Independent Institute and Robert Margo of Vanderbilt University calculated that over the last century "the average black income has increased much faster than average white income."[17]

The most pro-capitalism philosopher in recent history, Ayn Rand, is lambasted by professors. Professor John Russon of Penn State said, "There's nothing particularly original or interesting in her ideas and she certainly doesn't make it onto the list of philosophers to study."[18] Associate Professor Michael F. Szalay of UC Irvine concurs: "her stuff, philosophically and politically, is kind of crackpot stuff . . . Objectivism is not taken seriously by philosophers anywhere."[19] As a religious person, I do not agree with much of Ayn Rand's profoundly negative view of religion. Still, to minimize her contribution to philosophy is ridiculous. Her espousal of capitalism is incredibly important, today more than ever before. With taxes rising and government intervening in all sectors of life, her libertarian philosophy is required at least to balance the debate.

Avowed Marxist and tenured professor at the University of Texas, David Michael Smith, called capitalism "a system based on exploitation and oppression and domination and racism and war—and lots of other things."[20] Right. And socialism is a system based on pretty butterflies and flowers and tolerance of all living creatures.

"PROFIT" IS A DIRTY WORD

Professors make "profit" into a curse word. If something is bad, it must be because people are doing it purely for profit. Providing a service is only worthy if it is done altruistically. Professors ignore the fact that man is a reward-driven being and that profit is the surest incentive for hard work.

Perhaps the best example is professors' hatred for the tobacco industry. Professors rip tobacco companies because they operate based on profit motive. Professor Fletcher Baldwin of the University of Florida is happy that "My state is stripping the profit of the tobacco industry in the United States."[21] Will that be such a great thing when thousands of people lose their jobs?

"Tobacco terrorists hate our freedom . . . They hate our freedom from nicotine addiction and premature death," says Professor John Creed of the University of Alaska. "Big Tobacco makes big profits from this completely preventable epidemic that kills 400,000 Americans annually."[22] Oh, come on. Tobacco terrorists? Are they flying planes loaded with cigarettes into buildings? All tobacco companies do is provide a product to an eager market. Is that such a crime?

It is according to David Kessler, dean of Yale Medical School: "It is too easy to be swayed by the argument that tobacco is a legal product and should be treated like any other. A product that kills people—when used as intended—is different. No one should be allowed to make a profit from that."[23] Wait . . . aren't people voluntarily buying tobacco products? I haven't seen any Philip Morris employees breaking into people's houses and forcing innocent people to smoke cigarettes at gunpoint.

Let's not forget Burger King and McDonalds, those horrible proponents of heart disease. Professors hate them as well, for similar reasons.

Marion Nestle, a professor at New York University and author of *Food Politics: How the Food Industry Manipulates What We Eat to the Detriment of Our Health*, sees Americans as stupid baboons forced into being fat by advertisements. "It's not fair," Nestle whines. "People are confronted with food in every possible way to eat more. The function of the food industry is to get people to eat more, not less."[24] Naw, really? You mean food companies, like, want us to eat their food so they can make money? How awful!

People like junk food? That's just too bad for them. "I want to get to the point where people are in the hallway and see a vending machine and say, 'That's bad, that shouldn't be there,' in the same way as if they saw a cigarette vending machine," says Tom Farley of Tulane University.[25] Winning that battle "will not be easy," says a determined Tony Robbins of Tufts University. "People need to be creative about [defeating junk food], but tobacco was no minor opponent, either."[26]

This is all the fault of profit. If there were no profits to be made, no one would eat fast food and everyone would look like Cindy Crawford and Matt Damon. And no one would smoke, and the air would be clean, and no one would die of lung cancer.

Yeah, right. Besides, whatever happened to the right to choose?

GREEDY CAPITALIST PIGS

The commie wing of the university system doesn't just hate capitalism; it hates capitalists. And nothing signifies capitalists better than rich white guys.

There's something inherently wrong with being rich. It means you stole from others. It means you're racist. It means you can afford to bend the law, to bias politics, to kill peasants.

Oy.

Professor Paul Ehrlich of Stanford sneers: "Wealth . . . keeps poor people and nations relatively powerless to seek equality."[27] Yeah, things would be better if we were all poor. Then we could run around beating each other with sticks to "seek equality."

UCLA Professor Robert Watson explains that professors are more noble than everyone else and therefore despise money: "people who are willing to give up the extreme wealth that some careers offer, preferring instead the opportunity to teach young people and to retain intellectual independence, tend also to be people who will question the self-worship and money-worship of American culture."[28] Thank goodness we have professors who are so pure and altruistic!

Professor Muldavin, the self-described communist, quoted Plato in class one day, saying: "Ignorant wealth is more evil than poverty."[29] He didn't cite a source for the quotation, but the point he was making was clear: If you're rich and not a leftist, you're evil.

Muldavin also assigned a propaganda piece called *LA's Lethal Air.* The author states, "For the well-to-do, however, one person's misfortune is another person's gain."[30] Funny, that's not what I think when I see a poor person's dog get hit by a car. Or when I hear that someone has lost his job. One of the greatest things about the capitalist system is that we all prosper together or we fail together. A recession doesn't just hit the poor, and neither does an economic wave. The better the poor guy does, the better it is for everyone's pocketbook.

EVIL CORPORATIONS

If the well-off are symbols of capitalism, then corporations are the well-off to the nth degree. Professors *hate* corporations. Corporations rape the environment. Corporations exploit poor workers. Corporations are tyrannical, exceeding their moral bounds for the evil of evils, profit.

To Professor Muldavin, corporations are exploiters of the Third World: "Loss of control is a historical and social process. In the Third World, the loss is by local communities and increase is by *large and distant entities.*"[31] Spooky stuff.

Professor Robert Watson weighed in on corporations, as he does on most topics, in a submission to the *UCLA Daily Bruin.* "You don't need universities to assure Americans that . . . big corporations are kind-hearted and good for everyone—they hire publicists, they own the media outlets, they buy the legislators," he said. "American universities have thrived, like the society as a whole, because we have a system for resisting the natural tendency of the authorities to want to dictate belief."[32] Like most of his other views, Watson's anti-corporate tendencies stem from his rebellion against authority. And he passes the same garbage on to the "thousand UCLA students who have worked with [him]."[33]

Watson's counterpart, University of Texas Professor Dana Cloud, wrote a submission to the *Daily Texan*, which she called "Pledge for the workers." Her revised "Pledge of Allegiance" reads: "I pledge allegiance to all the ordinary people around the world, / to the laid off Enron workers and the WorldCom workers / the maquiladora workers / and the sweatshop workers from New York to Indonesia, / who labor not under God but under the heel of multinational corporations."[34] From this letter, you'd think multinational corporations rape cows, eat children, and drop nuclear waste into preschools. What a load of garbage.

UCLA Professor Marilyn Raphael sees corporations as disgusting polluters. "If people get away with polluting," she says, "you know industry gets away with it."[35] This is flawed logic. People get away with polluting because the government does not have the resources to oversee every single individual. Corporations, on the other hand, have government employees on top of them every moment of every day.

A text by the Labor/Community Watchdog in Los Angeles, assigned by Professor Muldavin, agrees with Raphael. According to that text, corporate executives must "assume the lion's share of the responsibility for the environmental dangers to public health and the threat to the planet's long-term viability."[36] Corporations spend their time "Defiling Politics, Culture, and the Air,"[37] and they "*determine our choices* through advertising, market share, pricing, and other forms of power in the marketplace."[38] Did you get that? Corporations are brainwashing customers with advertising. They're taking control of our brains. Cue music from *The Matrix*.

Another assigned text in Professor Muldavin's course says, "Today's claim by corporations of an unfettered right to allocate wealth we all helped to create may be closer to the concept of the divine right of kings than it is to the principles of democracy."[39] This is psycho. The divine right of kings would allow corporations to chain workers to their chairs and pay them nothing, motivating them with a whip. In reality, corporations usually pay well. And as for the right to allocate wealth, if you make it, you take it. Corporations can divvy it up however they see fit.

When I took his Geography 4 class at UCLA, Professor Jurgen Essletzbichler explained industrial capitalism. His class notes had computer graphics in them to make the learning more visually accessible. The cartoons he posted for industrial capitalism were 1) a fat-cat industrialist riding in a carriage alongside a skeleton symbolizing death[40] and 2) a fat-cat industrialist representing England, with arms coming out of the head grabbing less industrialized countries.[41] Wonderful. I love the smell of indoctrination in the morning.

Essletzbichler also posted a graphic that was supposed to represent trickle-down economics. The graphic showed a fat cat industrialist standing atop a globe, urinating upon the lower half of the globe. Not exactly an objective depiction of the mechanics of an economic theory.

Apparently at a loss for words, Essletzbichler showed the movie *Roger and Me* during lecture time.[42] *Roger and Me* is a documentary about layoffs by General Motors at its plant in Flint, Michigan. The protagonist, Michael Moore (author of *Stupid White Men* and *Dude, Where's My Country?*), chases around GM chairman Roger B. Smith. As Amazon.com reviewer Sean Axmaker puts it, "Moore ambushes his corporate subjects."[43] According to the professor, however, this wasn't an ambush—it was an accurate depiction of real life events. It showed the "downside of globalization."[44]

Professors also push the notion that corporations are all corrupt. Professor Eugene White of Rutgers University stated that the recent spate of corporate corruption scandals is "all very typical."[45] Professor Jeffrey Garten, dean of the School of Management at Yale, concurs: "I think it is fair to say that there was *nobody* in the business community who is not implicated in this in some way."[46] As the *Washington Post* reported, Harvard Business Professor Jay Lorsch originally believed that corporate corruption was relatively rare; but "[n]ow he's not so sure."[47]

All of this is having an impact on the students. A poll of college seniors revealed that a plurality, 28 percent, chose business as a profession in which "an 'anything goes' attitude [is] most likely to lead to success." This ranked above journalism, law, teaching, science/medicine, and civil service, among others.[48] When students were asked whether the only difference between Enron and other businesses was that "Enron got caught," 56 percent agreed, and only 41 percent disagreed.[49] Meanwhile, only 10 percent of the general public felt that corporate corruption occurred at most companies.[50] This contrast is frightening. If college students think business is evil, it's easy to see what they think of capitalism.

THE BIG LABOR/UNIVERSITY ALLIANCE

There's some dirty business going on between the professors and the labor unions. Labor unions are notoriously anti-capitalist. Leninists thought of a Marxist Revolution as a revolution of the workers against the "aristocracy." Labor unions were needed decades ago, when collective bargaining power was a must; now, labor unions are merely a nuisance, allying with the Democratic party to thwart the workings of the market. Professors are buddy-buddy with Big Labor, and they encourage students to become just as buddy-buddy.

A 1996 report in the *New York Times* detailed this burgeoning friend-ship. According to the article, professors nationwide are advising students to become union organizers. Professors are also giving pro bono courses to union officials. As the *Times* writes, "today's intellectuals promise that their support for labor will prove far more substantial than mere talk at teach-ins." In short, professors are supporting labor by brainwashing their students. Following are some details of this incestuous relationship:

> Cornell University professors held a conference with the AFL-CIO on how to do more organizing. . . . in early October, several dozen aca-demic luminaries will join union leaders at Columbia University for a 1960's style teach-in intended to give the academic world's imprimatur to labor's new leadership and to explore how intellectuals can do more to advance the goals of organized labor.
>
> Similar teach-ins will be held at a dozen other schools, including the University of Wisconsin, the University of Florida, Eastern Illinois University, Wayne State University in Detroit and the University of Texas at El Paso . . .
>
> . . . Acknowledging that their new-found friendship with labor is not altogether altruistic, officials with the association say they hope the AFL-CIO will back their fights to preserve tenure, win raises and reverse cuts in education spending.[51]

At UCLA, professors counseled the AFL-CIO on how to institute its Union Summer program. Over one thousand students worked for unions and helped set up unions at small factories all over Los Angeles.[52]

Scary isn't it? It's even scarier when you look up just what the AFL-CIO, the other half of the university/Big Labor alliance, is promoting. Their Web site carries their mission statement which says: "We will fight for an agenda for working families at all levels of government. We will empower state federations. We will build a *broad progressive coalition that speaks out for social and economic justice.*"[53] As discussed earlier, progressive always means extremely liberal/communist, and "social and economic justice" always means governmental redistribution of income.

In practice, this means that the AFL-CIO overwhelmingly pushes Democratic candidates. They contributed $712,284 to Democratic federal candidates during the 2002 election cycle. Other labor unions contribute even more. The Laborers Union and Teamsters Union gave a combined $2,211,121 to Democratic federal candidates during the 2002 election cycle.[54]

Union activism is a central cause supported by the professors. And so it becomes a central cause for the student body as well.

THE CHINA SYNDROME

Take China, Cuba, or any other socialist/communist country. If you ask a professor what he thinks of them, you'll probably get a thumbs-up. China has a good economic system, recently weakened by its slow transition to capitalism. Cuba has a great health care system. Pick any socialist country out of a hat, and you can guarantee professors will believe it to be superior to the United States.

I call this admiration for communism/socialism the China Syndrome.

The prototype for this disorder is Professor Muldavin of UCLA. According to Muldavin, China is a "model of development."[55] He lauds the Maoist development model, which he says "was founded on a strategy of self-reliance . . . its successes in such areas as education, health and social welfare, and the development of both rural and urban infrastructure are widely acknowledged."[56] He scorns China's slow growth toward capitalism:

"There are a number of structural environmental and social problems in the reforms that will not be solved, indeed *are actually exacerbated, by continued transition to a market-oriented economy.*"[57] (Translation: Moving toward a capitalist system doesn't help China or its citizens—capitalism hurts them.)

Muldavin continues: "One of the most disturbing things to have transpired is the dismantling of China's social welfare system . . . I saw overnight, within two or three years, the complete collapse of these systems. Nothing— no state agencies, no 'private sector initiative'—is stepping in to take up the slack."[58] Therefore, obviously, the only solution is a totalitarian communist regime. And their social welfare system wasn't working too well in the first place—this is the country with a one-child policy, remember?

When confronted by a student with the fact that Mao's Great Leap Forward led to the deaths of thirty million Chinese citizens in the largest man-made famine in world history, Muldavin answered, "I certainly did not mean to whitewash this famine. . . . [The famine] does not discount in any way other aspects of collective economy that may be beneficial, nor that there may be negative aspects to privatization."[59]Oh. So killing thirty million people doesn't discount a development strategy. By that token, Stalin's plan, which killed only twenty million Russians, must be considered a brilliant development strategy.

If they like China, they *love* Cuba.

"In Cuba, there seems to be an even-handedness about how resources, admittedly limited, are allocated, and there is universal health care free of charge with an extensive nationwide delivery system," says Professor Steven Schendel of Stanford University. "Yes, there are shortages of materials, but there is a lot of compassion."[60] And of course, we all know how much compassion helps when you're dying of cancer. Sorry, Mrs. Esquivel, we don't have the means to do chemotherapy and you're going to die because of it, but we *feel* bad for you.

Professor Sharon Frey of Saint Louis University believes that "From a sense of community, global perspective and compassion they are way ahead of us."[61] Isn't this the country that relies on sugar production to fuel its pathetic way of life?

Professor Mario Coyula of Harvard, a visiting lecturer from Cuba, is proud that Cuba didn't fall after the fall of the Berlin Wall. He's also proud of Cuba's lack of a class system: "People set up tables in the street for play-ing dominoes. There is always a corner grocery where people hang out. It is an atmosphere in which the social classes are leveled."[62] Now there's something to tell the world about. People playing dominoes. Over here, we spend our time creating a massive economy upon which the entire world relies. Over there, they play dominoes.

"NO MORE PROPERTY RIGHTS!"

This is the crux of the matter. To solve all of the "shortcomings" of capital-ism, professors advocate a new definition of property. Property rights must be abolished, they say, to make the system more equitable for everyone. This is communism. It was Karl Marx who said, "the theory of the communists may be summed up in the single sentence: abolition of private property."[63] *This* is what professors want.

"Working against hunger requires a fundamental rethinking of the meaning of ownership," reads an assigned text in a UCLA geography course.[64] When people are hungry, damn private ownership. That's the strategy.

Professor Laurence Tribe of Harvard Law School feels that the Constitution impedes progress. According to Tribe, the Constitution has a "built-in bias against redistribution of wealth." Such a bias benefits "entrenched wealth." As Thomas Sowell says, "When the rule of law is seen as a bias . . . the principles of the American Constitution [have been] qui-etly repealed."[65]

Abolishing private property means the unlimited right to redistribute wealth. "If the cause of poverty is the grossly unequal distribution of the world's wealth, then to end poverty, and with it the population crisis, we must redistribute that wealth, among nations and within them," says far-left Professor Barry Commoner.[66] And what gives Professor Commoner the right to take someone's property and hand it over to someone else? Only if there were no property rights would such a thing be acceptable.

In pragmatic terms, these Marxists are looking for a plan which would "involve a massive redistribution of wealth through taxation of higher-income people, primarily those making $100,000 or more, and even more significantly, far higher corporate taxes," according to Paul Ehrlich in an assigned text in UCLA's Geography 5 course.[67] Also, according to Ehrlich, "Wasteful consumption in rich countries must be reduced to allow for needed growth in poor countries. . . . Our sociopolitical systems also must undergo dramatic revision in the direction of increasing equity at all levels."[68] In a world designed by the intellectuals, the "rich" would slave their lives away and then have their money robbed from them and given to the poor.

The Democratic Socialists of America, the largest socialist organization in the US, is riddled with university faculty. Honorary chairs include Professor Bogdan Denitch of City University of New York and Professor Cornel West of Princeton University. Professor Frances Fox Piven of City University of New York is a vice president of the organization, as is Professor Rosemary Ruetheur of the Graduate Theological Union.[69] The DSA statement of purpose says: "We are socialists because we reject an international economic order sustained by private profit."[70]

RED ALERT

Not all professors are communists. In fact, the vast majority of them are not. But there is a concerted movement within universities to revive the "glory" that was once socialism. They do it by minimizing the value of capitalism which they say is unfair to the lower classes. They do it by making "profit" a dirty word. They do it by demonizing the rich as leeches sucking blood from the hard-working poor. They do it by depicting corporations as rapists of the environment and the Third World. They do it by allying with Big Labor. They do it by glorifying communist dictatorships like China and Cuba. They do it by preaching a re-evaluation of the very definition of private property.

Marxism is dying globally. But it's alive and kicking at America's universities.

4

"NOT JUST FOR THE RICH AND WHITE!"

On March 14, 2001, I stood alone atop Ackerman Student Union and looked down at Westwood Plaza. Three stories below me, a throng of more than one thousand in strength yelled and chanted. Most of the crowd were black, but some students were Hispanic. Even some Asians stood with the protesters. Together, this conglomeration of races barraged the campus with sound. Many wore red shirts reading: ACCESS DENIED. Many had been bused in from high schools around the Los Angeles area. Exhorted to new heights of fanaticism by a few lone figures carrying bullhorns, they screamed the same batch of tired civil-rights slogans over and over. It was race-baiting at its finest.

"EDUCATION IS A RIGHT! NOT JUST FOR THE RICH AND WHITE!" they chanted, ignoring that the majority of those in the UC system are not white, and that there are more Asian Americans than whites on UC campuses.[1]

"THIS IS WHAT DIVERSITY LOOKS LIKE!" they proclaimed, forgetting that no whites were in the crowd.

"UC REGENTS: WE SEE UC RACISTS!" they shouted, slurring a board that contains more liberals than it does conservatives.

And, to the regents, "YOU WORK FOR US!" not for the people of California.

These militant affirmative action protesters were attempting to change the stated policy of the University of California admissions system, a policy that was set forth in two acts called SP-1 and SP-2. These provided that 50 to 75 percent of all freshmen applicants would be admitted based on grades and SAT scores alone, not on race. And it was this policy that had all the race-baiters in a tizzy.

So the protesters weren't too happy when they looked up and to the left and saw me holding a large poster board sign that read:

MERIT BEFORE DIVERSITY
SAVE SP-1 AND SP-2

At first, only a few of the screamers saw me. These laughed derisively and tapped their friends. Soon, about a third of the thousand were looking up and either yelling at me, staring, or flipping me the bird.

Later, the crowd began marching through campus shouting their stupidity. I knew that they would have to take a certain route through the campus; I cut them off at the pass. I held my sign where every one of them would have to see it. The rally organizers, sensing possible trouble, were forced to station rally organizers around me in order to prevent the protesters from jumping me.

The bottom line of this story is that this kind of violent, emotional, race-based liberalism doesn't arise in a vacuum. It comes from somewhere. And in the case of the colleges, it's coming straight from the faculty.

"US/THEM" AND "THE OTHER"

Professors often play a semantic game. They define "racism" as the division between "Us" and "Them," and the maltreatment of "the Other." The only way for peace to bloom between people of different cultures and ideologies, they say, is for each person to consider all of humanity "Us." Using the word "Them" objectifies other people, and separates you from them. It all sounds so deep. Too bad it's baloney.

"The imposition of social inequalities between 'Us' and 'Them' is now recognized as racism,"[2] says an assigned text for an UCLA biology course. (Translation: If anyone or anything creates inequality between two groups, that's racist.) This is half-witted. Sometimes it is life itself that imposes social inequalities; is life then racist? If society imposes "social inequalities" between law-abiding citizens ("Us") and violent criminals ("Them"), are we racist?

Griffith Chaussee, lecturer of Hindi-Urdu at the University of Virginia, criticized "the us/them mentality" many people have when it comes to different cultures: "The modern nation-state concept has become hegemonic, propagating binary thinking."[3] (Translation: States promote "we're great, everyone else stinks" type thinking.) So what? Binary thinking is good. It keeps America safe. As long as we don't get too buddy-buddy with "the Other," "the Other" has a tough time getting close enough to bomb our buildings. The more clear the distinctions drawn between the good and the bad, the better and safer life will be.

Chaim Seidler-Feller is a sociology professor at UCLA, as well as the head of UCLA Hillel. At a Holocaust memorial he compared Nazi treatment of Jews to Jewish treatment of Palestinians, and urged students to "Think about the others, the other, the other . . . The Holocaust happened because people did not think of 'the other.'"[4] Actually, no. The Holocaust happened because the Nazis were evil maniacs intent on killing Jews and because much of Europe let them get away with it. Nazis thought about "the others" and then they murdered them. "The Other" is a foolish, vague abstraction that means nothing when push comes to shove.

This scorn for any Us/Them dichotomy is a favorite semantic game of the Left in general. I once spoke at a public high school about the Arab/Israeli conflict. "As long as they [the Arabs] continue to attack us [Americans and Israelis]," I said, "I believe that we should racially profile Arabs." One of the students angrily blurted: "Why do you separate 'Us' and 'Them'? Isn't that racist?" "No," I replied, "that's proper grammar." Unfortunately, the Left has so corrupted ordinary use of the English language that it is almost impossible to avoid some linguistic snake pit.

The "Us/Them" and "the Other" garbage is an excuse for accommodationist philosophy, which believes that in any conflict of ideology, surrender is the best option. A group is behaving badly? Well, we can't call them "Them," or "the Other," so they must be some of "Us"; we must be responsible for their behavior. It's all our fault. We must change *our* behavior. If you are unwilling to accept blame, you're a racist. It's a nice Catch-22. If someone does something wrong, it's your fault. Or be called a racist for driving a wedge between "Us" and "Them."

WINNERS WRITE HISTORY

History professors across the country believe that teaching world history is too often taught from a "Eurocentric" viewpoint. European history is given more time in the classroom than African history; American history is given more time in the classroom than American Indian history.

Instead of merely accepting the fact that European and American history have had more of an impact on today's world than American Indian or African history, professors attempt to rectify this imbalance. They teach history from the "African point of view," or the "Native American point of view."

Thus, in colleges across the country, history is taught from a "multicultural perspective." As Dinesh D'Souza described in his book, *Illiberal Education,* "Most American universities have diluted or displaced their 'core curriculum' in the great works of Western civilization to make room for new course requirements stressing non-Western cultures, Afro-American studies, and Women's Studies. . . . professors who are viewed as champions of minority interests . . . are permitted overtly ideological scholarship, and are immune from criticism even when they make excessive or outlandish claims with racial connotations."[5]

At Carnegie-Mellon University, the History Department offers "Gender Roles and Social Change," a course studying "women's and men's roles, behaviors, and beliefs in a variety of societies." Stanford University offers students History 36N: "Gay Autobiography"—"gender, identity, and solidarity as represented in nine autobiographies."

New York University students get the chance to enroll in "Race, Gender and Sexuality in US History." The course description states that "throughout US history, the social, economic, moral, and political arguments advanced to sustain the subordination of people of color, women, and gays and lesbians have frequently revolved around the sphere of sexuality."

At Oberlin College, the History Department gives students the incredible opportunity to take "Unbearable Whiteness: The Social Construction of a Racial Category." "Throughout the history of the US," the course description avers, "people deemed to be 'white' have accrued social, legal, and economic privileges at the expense of others deemed non-white."[6] This sounds like a history class about pre-civil rights America. It isn't. Texts include *Racial Formation in the United States: From the 1960s to the 1990s*, *How Jews Became White Folks and What That Says About Race in America*, and *The Possessive Investment in Whiteness: How White People Profit From Identity Politics.*[7] This class revolves around *continuing* white oppression of minorities.

Edward Said describes Western views of the Middle East as "ethnocentric" and inherently racist in *Orientalism*. He writes that the only "unbiased" observers of the Middle East and Orient are Arabs.[8]

Professor John Esposito echoes Said's gibberish in his book *The Islamic Threat*. He describes Americans as "ethnocentric," especially with respect to the American style of democracy. He also calls for an end to the study of any linkage between Islam and terrorism because it reinforces stereotypes.[9] Universities should whitewash Islam, rather than showing it for what it is— because people might "stereotype" Muslims. When feelings clash with facts, facts just have to be changed.

As it turns out, "multicultural history" does little for college students in the way of teaching useful information. A 2001 study showed that of the seniors at the top fifty-five colleges in the country, "only 23 percent could identify James Madison as the Father of the Constitution." Only "40 percent could identify the correct fifty-year time period in which the Civil War was fought."[10]

But at least the seniors aren't Eurocentric.

THOSE POOR, VICTIMIZED MINORITIES

All minorities are poor. All minorities are undereducated. All minorities are unfit because they have been subjugated and victimized. If you don't believe me, just ask the professors.

According to one assigned reading, minorities are "the most vulnerable members of the working class,"[11] they "suffer because of their class position in society and because of their race," and their "burdens of class and race continue."[12] This stuff is reminiscent of the old joke about the *New York Times:* The day before the world ends, the *Times* runs the headline: "World to End: Women and Minorities Hit Hardest."

On campus, the same civil rights struggle that began long ago continues today. An assigned book for a political science course entitled "Introduction to American Politics"states: "African Americans have been engaged in a two-hundred-year struggle for civil rights."[13] Uh-huh. So we're supposed to believe that no gains have been made in the civil rights struggle? That the civil rights of African Americans haven't been guaranteed by the government of the United States? Heck, the civil rights people have done such a good job that anyone who even *criticizes* minority communities can expect a mailbox full of letters calling him racist.

The same text later states, "African Americans, along with numerous other minority groups . . . share a history of discrimination first-hand. Whites tend to think that legal equality has now been achieved and that any special effort to overcome the effects of past discrimination is unfair to whites."[14] (Translation: While minorities have well-informed views of the world because they have seen discrimination "first-hand," whites think that no discrimination exists.) Okay, wait a second here. First off, to assume that the white community is monolithic is as racist as to say that all black people support Jesse Jackson. Second, this statement implies that if you are white, you have never experienced discrimination. In short, it is promoting a lie.

Blaming the problems in some minority communities on the white majority, UC Irvine professor Diego Vigil said that "young, second generation immigrants. . . . are marginalized on many levels and thus drawn to street life."[15] Most of the people in America are the descendants of immigrants to America, yet somehow they have been able to rise to the top. Why is it that only *this* generation of immigrants is being oppressed and "marginalized"?

Professor Noel Ignatiev of Harvard University identifies himself as an "abolitionist" seeking to abolish "whiteness." "White people must commit suicide as whites in order to . . . change from the miserable, petulant, subordinated creatures they are now into freely associated, fully developed human subjects," Ignatiev told a crowd at the University of California-

Berkeley. "By attacking whiteness, the abolitionists seek to undermine the main pillar of capitalist rule in this country." Ignatiev also attacked the police force, which he feels is a tool of the racist state: "The cops look at a person and then decide on the basis of color whether that person is loyal to the system they are sworn to serve and protect. They don't stop to think if the black person whose head they are whipping is an enemy; they assume it."[16] According to Ignatiev, "every group within white America has at one time or another advanced its particular and narrowly defined interests at the expense of black people as a race." For those who know Ignatiev's record, this should come as no surprise. Ignatiev is the founder of the magazine *Race Traitor*. The first issue of the magazine bore the slogan "Treason to whiteness is loyalty to humanity."[17]

In 1993, Nation of Islam spokesperson Khalid Abdul Muhammad spoke at Kean College in New Jersey. In his babbling, hate-filled diatribe, Muhammad portrayed the black community as a victim of "the Jewish conspiracy." "You see everybody always talk about Hitler exterminating six million Jews. That's right. But don't nobody ever ask what did they do to Hitler?" He then turned to South Africa, where as reparations for apartheid he advocated giving the white man "twenty-four hours to get out of town, by sundown. That's all. If he won't get out of town by sundown, we kill everything white that ain't right in South Africa. We kill the women, we kill the children, we kill the babies. We kill the blind, we kill the crippled, we kill 'em all. We kill the faggot, we kill the lesbian, we kill them all."[18]

According to Professor Vernellia R. Randall of the University of Dayton School of Law, "because of institutional racism, minorities have less education and fewer educational opportunities."[19] It's actually rather pathetic. Because professors are running out of real racists in positions of power to criticize, they blame everything on some institutional racism. And the great thing for them is, it's impossible for anyone to debunk *institutional* racism. How can race-baiters lose?

Professor Wallace Sherwood of Northeastern University parrots the "if you're white, you're a racist" line: "There are a lot of white people who genuinely don't believe that black people are as intelligent as they are. . . . In discussions, they tune out. Comments don't register in their minds unless they come from a white person."[20] Professor Sherwood is black, so I can't comment on his statement—I already tuned out.

RODNEY KING AND THE LOS ANGELES "UPRISING"

No event better illustrates the racial issue on campus than the professorial reaction to the events surrounding Rodney King. Professors sympathize fully with him, they condemn the police, and they use these events to promote their own causes. Here is moral relativism at its finest.

Jorja Prover, a professor of social welfare at UCLA, was teaching at USC when the Rodney King trial took place. During a lecture on violence in Los Angeles, a student rushed into her classroom to announce that the officers on trial in the beating had been acquitted. "I was basically fighting back the tears," Prover said.[21] Terrific. She "fights back the tears" when cops are acquitted for beating a large, drugged-up and resistant thug, because of the feeling that the black community was once again being oppressed. Does Professor Prover cry for the police officers murdered by such thugs every year?

The reaction of a law professor at the University of Georgia was this: "What happened to Rodney King was no fluke; it was not an isolated incident involving rogue cops. Beatings and other forms of police brutality, though carefully and cleverly concealed from the public, have always been, and continue to be, standard police behavior throughout this nation."[22] The police must be pretty clever to find ways to beat up all black criminals without anyone seeing. Perhaps they have magical invisibility shields.

Sympathy for Rodney King is at least a bit justified; one could argue the police overreacted to King. What is not justified is embracing the so-called "Los Angeles Uprising" as a legitimate protest to racism. (Professors, like many on the Left, call the Los Angeles Riot an "uprising" in an attempt to legitimize it.) Professor Jody Armour of USC stated that "racial discrimination, especially against young African American and Latino men, continues to corrupt the criminal justice system and could prompt a similar uprising in the future. 'We are still living in a tinder box,' he said."[23] When in doubt, blame all horrific behavior from any minority group on the problem of racism.

Professor Edward Chang of the University of California at Riverside predicted: "We are not confronting the cause of the problem [that led to the riot], so there will be another riot." What were the causes of the 1992 riot and what will be the causes of future riots? "Poverty and a growing gap between the 'haves' and 'have nots,' pervasive racial discrimination and segregation, lack of employment and educational opportunities for minorities and widespread police abuse."[24] In short: racism causes everything bad. Not single motherhood, or high crime rates, or lack of work ethic. Minorities are being kept down by the oppressive hand of the white man.

Professor Kyeyoung Park of UCLA is more opportunistic than her blustery colleagues, using the "uprising" as an excuse to tout "diversity requirements"—classes designed to "enhance multicultural sensitivity." These useless courses which students would never take voluntarily serve only to keep superfluous professors employed. But Park really believes these requirements help with explosive racial tensions: "We don't provide the mechanisms for people to learn about other groups," she explained, as if diversity class kumbaya would stop looters from burning down L.A.[25]

"Rodney King was about police abuse, O.J. was about police incompetence . . . That's a pretty grim picture for the LAPD," stated Laurie Levenson, a Loyola University Law School professor.[26] It's creative the way Professor Levenson equates the Rodney King incident with the O.J. trial— creative and disgusting. Rodney King was about the police using excessive force in subduing a criminal; O.J was about a brutal murderer slaughtering his ex-wife and her friend.

Only at university is a riot an "uprising," a police officer a thug, and a criminal a hero.

"YOU CAIN'T TELL ME I DON'T BE SPEAKIN' GOOD ENGLISH!"

Those with a leftist mindset assault the English language. I don't mean that they redefine words for their own purposes, although that is also a serious problem. I mean that university professors assault the actual grammar of English. They do this in order to equate improper use of English and proper use, thereby allowing those who speak improper English to advance in the system. They pretend that speaking English incorrectly is still okay; they push for bilingual education to preserve the "diversity of language."

I took a linguistics course at UCLA during Spring 2001, entitled "Introduction to the Study of Language." The first activity assigned to the class was a pre-test. A portion of the pre-test was a series of true/false statements. One read, "We should say 'It's I' rather than 'It's me.'"[27] Being the diligent student of English that I am, I naturally responded true. Wrong. The answer was false: We can say "It's me" just as well as "It's I." I was stunned. Grammar clearly requires that we say "It's I," and yet here the students were being told it is just as correct to say "It's me." Incredible.

Professors equate bastardized forms of English, mainly Ebonics, with grammatical English. In fact, it was Professor Robert Williams of Washington University who created the term "Ebonics" in 1973. Williams believes that "Teachers must recognize Ebonics as a language and not devalue it. . . .When children are criticized on the way they talk, their self esteem is hurt."[28] If teachers actually taught with the goal of boosting self-esteem, most adults would still be illiterate.

Says Professor Ernie Smith, formerly of Cal State Fullerton: "If Ebonics is not a language, then neither is English."[29] Professor Mikelle Omari of the University of Arizona concurs: "It is now time to work together to remove the social stigma associated with Ebonics."[30] Black English: Separate, but equal.

Dr. Ronald Bailey of Northeastern University went even further, claiming that Ebonics is "the African American version of the Boston Tea Party"—he believes that black youths who speak Ebonics do so to resist the white oppressors.[31] Professor Geneva Gay of the University of Washington feels similarly, explaining that "Taking [Ebonics] away would destroy African-American culture." According to Gay, the only reason that anyone would oppose Ebonics is racism.[32]

Bilingual education, states Professor Richard Ruiz of the University of Arizona, allows people to maintain "a sense of their ethnic identity, who they are, and of their community, while at the same time, pledging an allegiance to the United States." Professor Ruiz opposes any ballot proposition aimed at preventing bilingual education. Such measures "[tie] the hands of the people who are trying their best to teach children through bilingual education."[33]

A guest lecturer, Professor Pamela Munro, came to speak to my linguistics class. During the course of the lecture, she casually said, "What can be done to save our vanishing linguistic heritage? Discourage discrimination against bilinguals or people who speak minority languages."[34] (Translation: Force companies and businesses to hire people who speak "minority languages.") How about, instead, *teaching people English*? What a concept.

SLAVERY REPARATIONS

Professors are tickled pink when it comes to slavery reparations. Some 40 percent of professors would love to see reparations become a reality, as opposed to a mere 11 percent of the general public.[35] Since big government is the solution to every problem, the solution for the troubled black community must come in the form of cash garnered from tax dollars.

First, they rev up the pity machine to justify slavery reparations. An assigned history text reads: "Because slaves made up the overwhelming majority of the labor force that made the plantation colonies so profitable, it is fair to say that Africans built the South."[36] To emphasize this point, the text stresses: "Although African Americans received *nothing in return*, their labor helped build the greatest accumulation of capital that Europe had ever seen."[37] You can see where this is going. If the slaves received "nothing in return," the obvious solution is to give their descendants something—except, of course, both the oppressors and oppressed are long dead and the descendants of the former owe nothing to the descendants of the latter.

But professors continue to use this history of "subordination" to justify demands for slavery reparations—even when those reparations will be paid by people who had nothing to do with slavery and will be paid to blacks who are not affected by slavery.

Chris Ogletree, a Harvard Law professor, said there is a "blistering racial divide" in the United States because insufficient discussion of racial issues has taken place, one that could only be solved by slavery reparations. "We are not just taking action against the government, but also institutions and individuals who directly profited from slavery."[38] Just to let Mr. Ogletree know, everyone who directly profited from slavery is dead.

Professor Richard Lobban of Rhode Island College agrees. He said to a crowd of students at Brown University that "we need to have a sense of national apology." He continued, saying that slavery went on for longer and killed more people than the Holocaust, and its victims are just as deserving of compensation.[39] Lies. There is no way that slavery in the United States caused more than thirteen million deaths, the number of people murdered in the Holocaust (counting Jews, other "non-Aryans," and Christians).

And don't dare to challenge the leftist view of slavery reparations. Just ask David Horowitz. Horowitz attempted to run an ad entitled "Ten Reasons Why Reparations for Slavery is a Bad Idea and Racist Too." It was originally accepted by the UC Berkeley *Daily Californian*. The next morning, papers were stolen and burned by students to prevent the ad from having any impact. Later, the editor of the *Californian* ran an apology for the ad.

Professor Lewis Gordon of Brown University characterized the ad as "both hate speech and a solicitation for financial support to develop anti-black ad space" and believed that it would "embolden white supremacists and anti-black racists."[40] Horowitz is hardly a white supremacist—he's Jewish. And rather than combating the actual ideas Horowitz espoused, Gordon chose to slander the ad as "hate speech."

Professor Ernest Allen Jr. of the University of Massachusetts also slandered the ad as "a racist polemic against African Americans and Africans that is neither responsible nor informed."[41] When you can't combat the argument, call it racist—works every time. Professor Allen, as well as Women's Studies Professor Arlene Avakian, also picketed a Horowitz speech at the University of Massachusetts.[42] Don't these people have to prepare for classes?

When Horowitz spoke at Arizona State University in Spring 2001, he was counterbalanced by no less than three professors from the university, as well as a "moderator"—another professor. Professor James Weinstein (Law) emphasized the importance of free speech just as Horowitz did, saying "If it guaranteed Horowitz the right to make obnoxious and patently wrong assertions, it also gave [the opposing professors] the right to protest vigorously against his views." Professor Joseph Graves (Biology) accused Horowitz of being "blatantly racist." Professor T.J. Davis (History and Law) essayed that

Horowitz and his arguments "flew in the face of three decades of authoritative scholarship on the subject of slavery." According to the *moderator*, Dr. Michael Mitchell (Political Science and African American Studies), Horowitz was "contentious and closed to any truly civil dialogue."[43] Of course, being stuck on stage with four professors to fight off would *never* make anyone testy. It's fair and balanced—just like CNN.

"IT'S NOT YOUR FAULT"

Failing to gain admission into a school is never a minority's fault. It's all the fault of some institutional racism or biased testing procedure. Just ask Paul Ehrlich. "[I]s Pedro loaded with smart genes but deprived of an opportunity to develop his potential and held back by a meaningless score on a biased test?" he asks rhetorically.[44] Of course, yes. Never let it enter your mind that Pedro isn't the sharpest knife in the drawer. Even though there are plenty of dumb Jacks and Jills, to acknowledge such a thought about Pedro would be racist.

Calling the SAT a biased test is the latest excuse for allowing less qualified students to get into schools on more than just merit. Richard Atkinson, the former UC president, advocated omitting the SAT I from the UC admissions process as part of "a series of steps aimed to increase the accessibility of the university to students from different backgrounds."[45] Said Atkinson, "This proposal is about fairness in educational decision making."[46] Atkinson claims that the test is biased. Because of Atkinson's pressure, the SAT I banned word analogies and added an essay section in an attempt to appease the UC.[47]

How are word analogies biased? I don't get it. For example, the following question will no longer be allowed on the SAT I:

> DETECTIVE is to CLUES as
> (A) student : school
> (B) deer : trail
> (C) bloodhound : scent
> (D) merchant : receipt
> (E) sleuth : mystery[48]

This is biased? If you're black, do you see this question differently than if you're white? (The answer for both blacks and whites is C.)

But apparently more than just word analogies are tilted against minorities. Here are some examples of phrases or ideas deleted from standardized texts to avoid "bias": references to marital status, grandmothers in rocking chairs, men as doctors and women as nurses, teen-aged rebellion, and hamburgers, birthday cake, and soda. In their places are: one-parent homes, one-child families, grandmothers jogging, gender-neutral occupations, obedient kids and fruit juice and vegetables.[49] What a strange world we live in.

SPECIAL TREATMENT

In California, affirmative action is banned by Proposition 209, which prohibits the use of race or gender preferences in state hiring or admissions. That referendum passed easily, with 54 percent of the public vote. However, that doesn't stop the universities from attempting to "increase diversity" in different ways.

UCLA education Professor James Catterall called for new measures to put those of different races into the UC system. He "proposed admitting students on criteria other than just academics to ensure classrooms where students excel in different areas."[50] In short, ignore grades and SATs so that we can ensure access to those who are great at finger-painting.

UCLA took Professor Catterall's suggestion to heart. The new admissions policy takes into account "life challenges." Of course, the admissions boards who read the "life challenges" will grant more credit to those of minority races (excluding Asians). A front-page *Wall Street Journal* article detailed this policy: "Starting this spring, all applicants were weighed under a process known as comprehensive review, which awards extra credit for surmounting a wide range of personal, family, or psychological obstacles—what UCLA calls life challenges." The article also contrasted the cases of Stanley Park, a Korean, and Blanca Martinez, a Latino. Park and Martinez had virtually identical "life challenges," and Park scored a 1500 out of 1600 on his SATs, 390 points higher than Ms. Martinez. Strangely, Park was not admitted to UC Berkeley or UCLA, while Martinez was admitted to both.[51] It's not that hard to figure this one out. If you're black or Hispanic, you're in. If you're white, Asian, or Jewish, you're out. It's as simple as that.

When the race-based admissions policy of the University of Michigan Law School was challenged in court, the courts upheld the policy. Professor Gary Orfield of Harvard applauded the decision, stating: "We must compliment the leaders and scholars from the University of Michigan for providing a very vigorous and intellectually rich defense of their affirmative action policies." Harvard President Lawrence Summers concurred: "I applaud the Sixth Circuit opinion that supports Harvard's [and Michigan's] approach to admissions that race may properly be considered as one among many factors in a well designed and competitive admissions process. This is welcome news."[52] Perhaps this is welcome news to Summers, but it sure isn't to qualified students sure to be rejected in favor of unqualified minorities.

The UC faculty generally opposed UC Regent Ward Connerly's "Racial Privacy Initiative." RPI would bar the state from seeking or keeping records of race-based data. This would, of course, have had enormous ramifications for college applicants, who would not have to state their race. It would also have ended questions about "non-proportional representation" in schools.

Fellow UC Regent William Bagley inanely asserted, "The banning of the [ethnic check] boxes would be counterproductive and deleterious to our effort to recruit qualified minorities."[53] Yeah, right. Qualified minorities won't apply because the application doesn't ask their race? If that drives them away, they're frankly too stupid to get in anyway.

Chicano studies Professor Paule Takash self-righteously stated, "You do not achieve a color-blind society by hiding the problem or by not addressing it."[54] Apparently according to Takash, the solution must be to continue thrusting race in everyone's face and calling everything discriminatory.

The final result of "diversity goals" in admissions: underqualified candidates make it into some of the most highly regarded schools in the country. The Fall 2002 admittees at UCLA included seven students with SAT scores between 700 and 800 (you get 400 points just for writing your name on the answer sheet), 106 students with scores between 800 and 900, 412 students with scores between 900 and 1000, 762 students with scores between 1000-1100, and 982 with scores between 1100 and 1200. Meanwhile, 191 students with SAT scores between 1500 and 1600 were rejected from UCLA, as were 1455 students with scores between 1400 and 1500, 4667 students with scores between 1300 and 1400, and 7609 with scores between 1200 and 1300. Simply put, lower scoring students got slots that should have gone to the people with better credentials.[55] The story was the same at UC Berkeley, where the Fall 2002 admittees included 381 students with SAT scores between 600 and 1000. Meanwhile, 641 students with near perfect scores on the SAT were rejected.[56]

The universities push affirmative action, "life challenges," and racial classifications in order to admit minorities—not because they're smarter than their white or Asian counterparts, but solely *because they're minorities*. In so doing, they look for ways to admit *underqualified* students in place of qualified ones. Why not instead push for better achievement from minority students? Isn't it racist to imply that minorities can't live up to the challenge?

"THAT'S OFFENSIVE!"

In recent years, universities have become so sensitive to "insensitivity" that many have instituted speech codes prohibiting students from speaking about certain topics. Best-selling author and commentator David Limbaugh reports that "as many as 90 percent of American universities have adopted such codes in one form or another."[57] Since everything offends *someone*, universities may soon resemble silent monasteries.

At Bucknell University, students are barred from "bias-related behavior," defined as "any action that discriminates against, ridicules, humiliates, or otherwise creates a hostile environment for another individual or group because of race, religion, ethnic identity, sexual orientation, gender, language, or beliefs."[58] That just about covers everything, doesn't it? By this definition, Mr. Rogers is as offensive as Al Sharpton.

Meanwhile, at Shippensburg University, students must "mirror" university policy regarding "racial tolerance, cultural diversity and social justice." Social justice? So if you oppose minimum wage, you're committing a hate crime? The code continues: students must not "provoke, harass, intimidate, or harm another."[59] Provocation is not clearly defined. Somehow I doubt that railing against Bush would be considered provocation. For some reason I think that railing against Clinton could be.

Tufts University bans "demeaning or derogatory slurs, name-calling and using words or negative images associated with a group on signs to create a publicly hostile environment." Tufts goes on to ban students from "attributing objections to any of the above to the 'hypersensitivity' of others who feel hurt."[60] This last clause is amazing. If my shoes offend you, you can cry about it, but if I say that you're a crybaby, I can be punished by the university administration.

Hendrix University students are expected not to participate in "conduct which leads to embarrassment, physical harm, or indignities to other persons."[61] Don't go pointing out that someone's socks don't match. If you live in the dorms at UCLA, don't make "derogatory remarks about one's clothing, body, or sexual activities based on gender" or "disparaging remarks, jokes, and teasing based on gender"—that might be "sexual harassment."[62] Sexual harassment at the University of Missouri-Rolla extends further than UCLA's policies: even "ogling and inappropriate staring" can be considered sexual harassment.[63]

Harvard students are required to refrain from "Behavior evidently intended to dishonor such characteristics as race, gender, ethnic group, religious belief, or sexual orientation"; such behavior "is contrary to the pursuit of inquiry and education."[64] Similarly, at Colby College, "Harassment, which can run the gamut from verbal abuse to physical assault, directly conflicts with a commitment to human dignity and will not be tolerated."[65]

Dartmouth President James Wright sums up the attitude of the universities with regard to free speech: "In a community such as ours, one that depends so much upon mutual trust and respect, it is hard to understand why some want still to insist that their 'right' to do what they want trumps the rights, feelings, and considerations of others. We need to recognize that speech has consequences for which we must account."[66] For the vast majority of college students, the consequences for free speech could be punishment by the administration.

RACE-BAITING

University faculties love racial tension. They can't bear the idea that conservatives might be right about creating a color-blind society in place of a special treatment one. These professors espouse views that bear no resemblance to the views of mainstream America.

On October 31, 2001, another protest took place, this time for affirmative action. The crowd was much smaller, since the University of California had implemented de facto affirmative action policies, and there wasn't much to fight about.

I stood above a crowd of about a hundred protesters; each person in the crowd had a bandanna tied about his/her mouth in silent protest. I had been standing with another anti–affimative action sign for about forty minutes when I was approached by a young, well-dressed Latino student. He looked at my sign, then back at me, and said: "I'm so glad you're here holding that sign. Otherwise people would think that everyone on this campus is for affirmative action. I am against affirmative action because I made it into this university on my own merit, and everyone thinks I made it here because I am Latino. I don't want everyone thinking that whatever I do in life, I got the opportunity to do it because of my race. It's insulting."

About half an hour after my conversation with the young man, one of my TA's saw my sign and stopped by. I had developed a good rapport with the TA and smiled as she came up. She strode up, questioned me about the sign for a minute, and then said, a note of anger in her voice, "I'm going to leave now. I don't want to be associated with that sign." She became noticeably less friendly for the duration of the quarter.

I don't want to say that all people who believe in affirmative action are malicious or hostile, because I'm sure there are one or two of them who aren't. But what I can say with certainty is that the universities poison their students regarding race relations. Universities do not strive to make their students color-blind, but instead encourage an acute awareness of color. And that is the tragedy of the situation.

5

SEX IN THE CLASSROOM

During the "sexual revolution" of the 1960s, college campuses were a hotbed for wild, immoral sexual behavior. Sleeping around became a mainstream practice; homosexuality leapt out of the closet; students around the country yelled "make love, not war," then did it. Professors cheered them on, often even participating in the fun.

Things haven't changed all that much since then. Sex is promoted non-stop in the classroom. All types of sex are deemed natural and fulfilling. Homosexuality is perfectly normal. Pedophilia is acceptable, if a bit weird. Statutory rape is laughed off. Bestiality is fine.

Taking a contrary position means getting lambasted by both professors and the students who "learn" from them. For example, I wrote an article for the *UCLA Daily Bruin* explaining why a United Nations pamphlet excusing sexual promiscuity in refugee camps should be opposed. The pamphlet promoted adultery, pre-marital sex, and homosexuality. Professor Robert Watson responded to my piece by calling me a stick in the mud: "Ben Shapiro . . . spent a previous column complaining that the UN lets children have too much fun in refugee camps."[1]

I wrote another column opposing "National Coming Out Week," a week sponsored by the university that encourages homosexual/bisexual/transvestite students to "come out of the closet." The response to my piece was loud and vicious. *TenPercent*, the homosexual magazine on campus, labeled me a "self-righteous homophobe."[2] Every letter printed in the *Daily Bruin* in response to the column was loaded with personal insults. From student to staff member, they couldn't resist demonizing their opposition. I was called "small-mind[ed]" and "ignorant," a person who uses "emotional appeals to spew forth [his] loosely-veiled, blindly-conceived hatred of an entire group,"[3] one who "need[s] some help"[4] and is "prejudiced and callous."[5] And those are just the responses that were printed.

DOWN AND DIRTY WITH THE ENGLISH DEPARTMENT

Professors and other members of university faculty constantly inject sex into their lesson plans. This is most obvious in English classes, where any subject can be deliberately misinterpreted to bring sex into the conversation.

I took an English class at UCLA during Fall 2001, taught by Professor Luke Bresky. He taught virtually every story as an allegory about gender roles or homosexuality. Some of this sexual discussion was called for, as when he taught poems of Walt Whitman. But much of it was not. Professor Bresky assigned Henry James's *The Aspern Papers*, where he attempted to profile the narrator as a closet homosexual. When I searched google.com for any other literary criticism describing *The Aspern Papers* as a homosexual allegory, I could find none. Needless to say, by the end of the course, my classmates and I were fed up with the professor's constant harping on sex and gender.

Dartmouth University Professor Brenda Silver seems to do the same thing: she turns everything into a metaphor for sex. The independent student paper, the *Dartmouth Review*, describes Silver: "An avid feminist critic, Professor Silver reads literature with the firm belief that anything longer than it is round must be a phallus. Silver is a vehement addict to anything anti-male, and holds out androgyny as the human ideal."[6]

An unnaturally acute focus on sex is extremely common in English Departments across the country. Many have devoted entire classes to sexual topics.

- UCLA: M101A—Lesbian and Gay Literature before Stonewall; M101B—Lesbian and Gay Literature after Stonewall[7]

- California State University at Northridge: Erotic Literature, Male Sexuality, Gay Literature, and Lesbian Literature and Poetry[8]

- University of Arkansas: Literature and Eros[9]

- Dartmouth College: Topics in Literary and Cultural Theory: Feminist Theories, Queer Theories[10]

- University of Chicago: Problems in Gender Studies[11]

- Williams College: Queer Literatures in English: An Introduction[12]

- University of Colorado: Introduction to Lesbian, Bisexual, and Gay Literature; Queer Theory; Studies in Lesbian, Gay, Bisexual, and Transgender Literature[13]

- Truman State University: Representations of Gender and Sexuality[14]

- University of Wisconsin at Milwaukee: Same-Sex Desire in Modern Literature[15]

- Stanford University: Orientations: Sex, Self, and Subterfuge in Fiction[16]

- Boston College: Literary Themes: Queer Literary Traditions[17]

- Georgetown University: Unspeakable Lives: Gay and Lesbian Narrative[18]

- Illinois Wesleyan University: Bad Girls; Sex, Text, and Tradition in Black Women's Fiction[19]

- Carnegie-Mellon University: Gay and Lesbian Theory[20]

- Bryn Mawr College: Thinking Sex: Representing Desire and Difference[21]; Queer Literature/Queer Theory[22]

- University of Michigan: How to be Gay: Male Homosexuality and Initiation[23]

Some English professors go beyond the classroom to "teach" their students. Professor Richard Burt of the University of Massachusetts posted dirty pictures of himself with bare-breasted women on his university-registered Web site. Later, he "voluntarily" took them down after students began complaining.[24] Strangely, Burt was not fired. Can you imagine an employee at a company who posted pornography on his company Web site still retaining his job? But that's how it works at the universities.

Professor Christina Hauck of Kansas State University is spending her research time looking into the life of one Marie Stopes, a woman credited with writing the first "sex manual." "I just think she's so cool and interesting," she said. "She also made herself unpopular in the same way that women who have drive, power and have a vision they want to see accomplished are unpopular. . . . No one calls Winston Churchill pushy."[25] Yes, you read that correctly. She just compared a sex therapist to Winston Churchill. Makes you wonder where Hugh Hefner stands on the list of all-time important figures.

Perhaps some of these professors will eventually find their true calling, as did Professor Gloria G. Brame. She was an English professor before eventually switching tracks and getting her PhD in Human Sexuality. She's now an expert who gives advice on various important topics including bondage, sadomasochism, fetishes, and cross-dressing.[26] If she wanted, she could probably still chair an English Department somewhere.

"IT'S NOT SEX, IT'S ART"

Liberal professors consider art and sex inextricably linked. All sexual expression is a form of art, and all art is good. While no one would consider Michaelangelo's David pornographic, sex-as-art on campus goes far beyond the bounds of good taste. Portrayal of sexual objects or the sex act itself no longer has any element of higher beauty or holiness. Professors use art as an excuse to make all sorts of sick actions legitimate.

In October 2003, Paula Carmicino, a film student at the New York University Tisch School, came up with a brilliant idea for her project: intersperse film of sex acts with film of everyday activities. So Carmicino found two actors willing to have sex on camera, before a class full of students. Why not just simulate the sex on film? "That's censoring the sex part. My thing is how we censor ourselves during the day when we're not having sex." Carmicino's professor, Carlos de Jesus, thought this was terrific. But before giving his go-ahead, de Jesus asked the administration. The administration refused. All hell broke loose.[27]

The *Washington Square News* condemned the film school's decision-making process: "The Tisch's School of the Art's decision to stop junior Paula Carmicino from including sexual penetration in her student film was made in the total absence of any written policy. It is preposterous that in such a sexualized time—when the Paris Hilton sex tape makes top national news—Tisch did not have a policy regarding films of this nature beforehand."[28] Christopher Dunn of the New York Civil Liberties Union criticized the decision: "Students should be able to make films, write books or compose paintings without their university acting as a moral censor."

The administration, while standing by its decision, was contrite. Richard Pierce of the Tisch School called Carmicino a "serious and valued student," and explained that "the history of art is replete with examples of artists producing great art under limitations."

Meanwhile, the administration refuses to do anything about the rampant sexuality in the film school as a whole, despite the fact that Carmicino's graphic filmmaking is more the rule than the exception. NYU student Lisa Estrin made a film depicting stuffed dolls of Minnie Mouse and Lamb Chop having sex. Vera Itkin described another class film including graphic pornographic images, and recalled two class scripts, which involved hardcore sex scenes including necrophilia.[29]

"Since Burlesque, there's always been a long tradition of art and sex," says PhD candidate Annie Sprinkle. Sprinkle is a self-described whore, artist, and filmmaker. "Annie Sprinkle would say that her feminist mother would come into her room and tell her she was either going to be a whore or an artist," states Professor Linda Williams of UC Berkeley. "That's what sets her apart. She is both. . . . There are some exceptional porn makers who care about art. And Annie Sprinkle is one of them."[30] Sprinkle's "art" includes photographing her breasts and her buttocks and other such garbage. A modern-day Van Gogh.

At the San Francisco Art Institute, Professor Tony Labat's students were told to create a performance art piece for his class. One student, Jonathan Yegge, created what many leftists would call a masterpiece. Yegge got a volunteer and brought him out into a public campus area. After binding and blindfolding his little helper, the two engaged in oral sex and defecated on each other. "It's about pushing the notion of gay sex, pushing the notion of consent, pushing the notion of what's legal," Yegge explained.

Labat, in a weak condemnation, called the piece "bad art." But Yegge claims he had run the idea for the piece by the professor, and he had approved.[31] So what was Labat doing while the "performance" was going on? Was he just sitting around, enjoying the show?

The university responded to the incident not by firing the instructor or by condemning the performance piece, but by angrily denouncing the fact that Yegge had *unprotected* sex, which carried the risk of AIDS. "It is considered a serious violation for you or any individual to participate in any activity, sexual or not, which involves exposing yourself or others to any bodily fluids or excretions including but not limited to feces, urine, semen, saliva and blood," said a letter from Larry Thomas, vice president and dean of academic affairs for the university.[32] Apparently, it's okay to have oral sex and excrete into the anal cavities of others in public, as long as you're both using protection. Comforting to know there are people like Thomas looking out for America's students.

Perhaps Yegge best explains the universities' view of art: "They say you can do whatever you want as long as you can justify it artistically."[33]

THE JOY OF LGBT

At universities, homosexuality is normal. It's as American as apple pie. Lesbians, gays, bisexuals, and transsexuals all have equal if not superior lifestyles compared to straights. It's starting to look like San Francisco in little pockets of higher education all over the United States.

I remember sitting in my Geography 5 class in Winter Quarter 2001. The professor, Joshua Muldavin, decided to tell a personal story.

"Class," he said, "I recollect one time I was in a southern state with one of my friends. He's French, by the way. I was talking to him, walking down the street with my arm over his shoulder, when we were accosted by some religious fanatic carrying a sign that said 'AIDS is a plague from God.' We were going to keep walking, but the guy ran up to me and said 'Take your arm off that man!' So naturally, I turned around and gave my friend a big kiss, right on the lips." The students sat stunned for a moment, not sure exactly what to do. Then they burst into laughter and applause.

That's the usual response to homosexuality on campus. In one political science class I took, Professor Lynn Vavreck showed two separate polls. One demonstrated that Americans opposed discrimination against homosexuals. Another poll showed that Americans also opposed openly gay people holding job positions of authority, in teaching and religious leadership, for example. Said Vavreck: "The fact that Americans support gay rights, but don't want gays to be teachers—that's the kind of thing the founding fathers would have disapproved of."[34] Huh? Thomas Jefferson, a supposed liberal, proposed that sodomy be punishable in Virginia by castration.[35] The founding fathers weren't exactly gay rights activists.

The perspective of Princeton University professor Anthony Appiah is even more shocking. At a panel meeting of the United Nations Gay, Lesbian, or Bisexual Employees, Appiah suggested that religion should be limited since it poses a "challenge" to the homosexual agenda.[36]

Gay rights are equated with civil rights and women's rights by professors. "The advances in civil rights over the past half-century have been extraordinary . . . For example, in addition to women and gays the disabled have won significant victories,"[37] gushes one assigned political science reading at UCLA. "It is theoretically possible to make peace with ourselves and with our environment, overcome racial and religious prejudice, reduce large-scale cruelty, and increase economic equality . . . A utopian notion? Maybe. But considering the progress that already has been made in areas such as . . . women's and gay rights . . . it's worth a try,"[38] spouts another assigned reading in a UCLA biology course.

Then there are the openly gay courses. Almost all major universities have Lesbian, Gay, Bisexual and Transsexual (LGBT) Departments that offer majors or minors to students. "In the last five years, just about every podunk college in the United States has established something," says Professor John Yunger of Duke. "It's very mainstream."[39]

One course offered at UCLA was taught by Cal State Northridge Professor Jacob Hale. Hale is a transsexual who recently "transitioned" from female to male. The course focuses on answering questions about the meaning of gender and sex and the history of transgendered people.[40] Valuable information, to be sure. And taught by one who would obviously know so much about the meaning of gender and sex.

Some more of the LGBT courses at UCLA, as described by *TenPercent*, UCLA's magazine for homosexuals:

- M101A Intro to LGBT Studies: "To a closeted gay boy soon to shed the cocoon and emerge a winged Nubian Princess, this class was all that and a box of press-on nails . . . The two professors were the perfect Yin-Yang combination: Professor Schultz's bright fairy flame lit the fires of pride in my soul and Professor Littleton's Uber-Dykeyness slapped me with reason and political reality."

- M101A Lesbian and Gay Literature Before Stonewall: "Greeted every day by a sassy Professor Little . . . this class gives a sometimes foggy, but always thought-provoking look at gay literature . . . Finally, a class that encourages having a queer desire within texts has never been so utterly titillating . . . Who knew assigned reading could be so fun and so 'GAAAAYYYYY!'"

- M101B Lesbian and Gay Literature After Stonewall: "If ever there was a class that shocks you with radical queerness, this is the one. This class now brings you literature about angry Asian bottoms, crunchy granola lesbians, a ghetto-fabulous gay hip-hop princess and a vagina jungle."

- M147 The Social Psychology of the Lesbian Experience: "'Dyke Psyche' is a must for every single queer student on campus, regardless of gender or sexual orientation. Culture, history, and psychology converge in this unique forum."

- M197D Creating Queer Performance Art: "Performance artist and comedienne Monica Palacios helps you create your very own piece of queer performance art."[41]

Campus administration treats gay couples just like straight ones. The UC Regents voted unanimously in May 2002 to give full-pension benefits to same-sex "domestic partners." "Families with children and their partners need the secure sense that their personal lives they spent years to plan will come through," explained Thomas Wortham, chair of the English Department at UCLA.[42]

Same-sex "domestic partner" benefits are also available at Indiana University, University of Iowa, University of Michigan, Michigan State University, University of Minnesota, Northwestern University,[43] Carnegie Mellon University,[44] University of Pennsylvania, all the Ivy League schools, Stanford University, MIT,[45] and scores of others.

Gay professors' views of the world are superior to those who are straight, or so they claim. Dr. Rose Maly of UCLA said, according to *TenPercent*, that "the relative ease with which professors can be open about their sexuality is due in part to the positions of power they hold within a very liberal environment . . . she feels that her homosexuality has helped her to relate better to the marginalized populations she studies, like the elderly."[46] Are all elderly people gay, or is there some other reason only a gay woman can relate to them?

Professor Arthur Little of the UCLA English Department said that being black and gay has helped him "gain deeper perspective on his scholarship," according to *TenPercent*.[47]

"Transgendered folk are perhaps the people that have the most to teach us about the relationship between gender and sexuality because they endure a tremendous amount of pain to be truly who they are, and I think that is very admirable. They have a lot to teach us about courage," says Professor Peter Hammond of UCLA, who teaches a course on same-sex erotic behavior in foreign cultures.[48] I disagree with the professor. Courage is saving a child from a burning building; getting your genitalia surgically altered is merely strange.

SEX WITH CHILDREN

Many professors excuse and even encourage pedophilia—sex between adults and children.

"Though Americans consider intergenerational sex to be evil, it has been permissible or obligatory in many cultures and periods of history," says

Professor Harris Mirkin of the University of Missouri. Mirkin uses "intergenerational sex" as a euphemism for pedophilia in order to imply some similarity between the coupling of a sixty– and thirty-year-old and sex between a twenty-year-old and a ten-year-old. "Children are the last bastion of the old sexual morality,"[49] he declares. According to the *Kansas City Star*, Mirkin believes "there needs to be a more real, open discussion of pedophilia and adult-child sex, not just emotional reactions that call all such relationships 'evil.'"[50]

"The category 'child' is a rhetorical device for inflaming what is really an irrational set of attitudes" about pedophilia, concurs Professor Gilbert Herdt of San Francisco State University. Herdt is also co-author of a book called *Children of Horizons: How Gay and Lesbian Teens Are Leading a New Way Out of the Closet.*[51] Of course, Herdt is wrong. The category "child" is not a "rhetorical device"; it describes those in a lower age range, incapable of fully giving consent. And it is not "irrational" to want to stop adults from molesting children—it's called basic human decency.

Still, there is no "inherent harm in sexual expression in childhood," states an article released by the Institute for Advanced Study of Human Sexuality in San Francisco.[52] Those who oppose pedophilia are motivated by "self-imposed, moralistic ignorance," says Professor John Money of Johns Hopkins University.[53]

Professor Bruce Rind at Temple University agrees. Negative effects on the child-victims of pedophilia are "neither pervasive nor typically intense," he said in a study published by the American Psychological Association.[54]

This is the highest form of evil. To rip away the purity and innocence of childhood is the most brutal of acts; to excuse it intellectually is a sign of moral depravity so low that it boggles the mind.

Professors also see statutory rape as normal and acceptable, just another way of "expressing love." Statutory rape is generally defined as sex, consensual or otherwise, between a minor aged twelve to eighteen and a person over eighteen years of age. It is considered a felony, and carries with it heavy jail time. Professors don't think that's right.

Professor Philip Jenkins, formerly of Pennsylvania State University, believes that society should draw a distinction between pedophilia and what he calls ephebophilia, or love of teenagers. He thinks ephebophilia is fine; according to the *New York Review of Books*, he also advocates that "statutory rape laws should not outlaw such youth-love, since there is nothing in nature (as opposed to local custom) to deny the power of consent to even very young teenagers." Jenkins also believes that such acts as pedophilia, incest, and rape are "social constructs." Jenkins' idea of ephebophilia, or sex with teenagers, is often used to justify cases of man-boy sex in the Catholic clergy.[55] It should be legal for a fourteen-year-old girl to have sex with a thirty-year-old man? These children are damaged for life. Is that acceptable to Jenkins?

In 2001, the movie *Tadpole* premiered. It is a film about a fifteen-year-old boy who is sexually attracted to his stepmother; he ends up having sex with his stepmother's best friend. Conservatives attacked the movie as morally corrosive. According to Professor Gerald Baldasty of the University of Washington, the conservative uproar over the movie's exoneration of statutory rape was over-the-top: "The media are pretty conservative in many ways . . . [conservative antagonism amounts to] a Chicken-Little–the sky is falling attitude."[56]

At the universities, the sky *is* falling.

STRANGE, STRANGE BEHAVIOR

A few professors have interesting perspectives on bestiality as well. It's fine, as long as you're not too cruel to the animal.

Ugh.

The strangest of the strange is Professor Peter Singer of Princeton University, who wrote an essay for *Nerve Magazine* in which he lauded that noblest of human activities, bestiality. "Sex with animals does not always involve cruelty," writes Singer. "Who has not been at a social occasion disrupted by the household dog gripping the legs of a visitor and vigorously rubbing its penis against them? The host usually discourages such activities, but in private not everyone objects to being used by her or his dog in this way, and occasionally mutually satisfying activities may develop."[57] Um . . . *what?* Maybe Professor Singer thinks it's "mutually satisfying" to make mad, passionate love to Fido, but we in the real world call that disgusting.

And there are many more who do more than walk their dog. Harvard

Professor Marjorie Garber, director of the university's Center for Literary and Cultural Studies, wrote an entire book on puppy obsession, entitled *Dog Love*. "Animal contacts . . . have had a long and honorable history in sexual *fantasy life*," Garber notes. "Behavior that appears (in practice) as a primary violation of boundary between humans and animals turns out to be (in figure) foundational to received notions of 'culture' and 'civilization.'"[58]

With the "honorable history" of bestiality in mind, Garber gleefully recounts literary and real-life cases of bestiality in her chapter "Sex and the Single Dog." Perhaps the most egregious example is her account from Laura Reese's *Topping from Below*, describing a "love scene" with a Great Dane.[59] Every woman's fantasy—making out with Marmaduke. Revolting? Disgraceful? Absolutely. But what else should we expect from Professor Garber, the author of such great works as *Vice Versa: Bisexuality and the Eroticism of Everyday Life* and *Vested Interests: Cross-Dressing and Cultural Anxiety*?

PROMOTING PROMISCUITY

College is supposed to be a learning experience. And there's no better learning experience than sleeping with everyone in sight, right? The universities think so. They'll try as hard as they can to make sure that everyone reaches a minimum quota of one hundred sexual partners. Just make sure you use a condom, okay?

At UC Berkeley, they have all sorts of naughty fun in class. One especially wet 'n' wild Berkeley course concerning male sexuality made national headlines. All the students in the co-ed class publicly discussed their sexual fantasies. Porn stars guest lectured. An early exercise in the class involved each of the students photographing his/her own genitals. The photographs would then be exchanged, and everyone would try to match each set of genitalia to its owner. As one student put it, things shockingly devolved into an "orgy." During another class assignment, students went to a gay strip club, where they watched one of the instructors have sex on the stage. What fun! And everyone in the course got two credits.[60]

The fun's not restricted to Berkeley. At Mount Holyoke, a small, supposedly straight-laced school, similar action is taking place. Professor Susan

Scotto teaches a non-accredited stripping course on university grounds. Scotto, married with two children, enjoys stripping at nudie bars in her off-time. She's been stripping since *her* college days, when she was putting herself through school. As Salon.com describes, "The girls got into it immediately. A few started to slowly gyrate their hips, raising their arms over their heads belly dancer-style. . . . The next song that came on was faster, with a sexy bass beat. A few of the girls had loosened up enough by then to take off a few pieces of clothing. . . . Within the next fifteen minutes, all but a few of the girls had shed their outer layers of clothing and were wriggling around in their underwear."[61] Ah, the benefits of a quality education.

During the 1999-2000 school year, Wesleyan students enjoyed the sexual titillation taught by Professor Hope Weissman. She taught College of Letters 289, a course on pornography as a political and cultural practice.

From the course description: "The pornography we study is an art of transgression which impels human sexuality toward, against, and beyond the limits which have traditionally defined civil discourses and practices . . . Our examination accordingly includes the implication of pornography in so-called perverse practices such as voyeurism, bestiality, sadism, and masochism."[62] Course reading material included the Marquis de Sade, Susan Sontag, and *Hustler Magazine.*

The final course assignment was, in Professor Weissman's own words, "Just create your own work of pornography." And so the students did. A student who earned an "A" on the final filmed a male masturbating; the background music was a recording of Ella Fitzgerald. One female student videoed a man's eyes while he masturbated. Another female student acted out a scene of sexual bondage before the class, wearing black pants, harness-like leather straps that left her nearly topless, and calling for a male to whip her with a cat-o'-nine-tails. "I think [Weissman is] a very brave woman," says Professor Constance Penley. Sick is more like it.

Kansas University has its own version of Professor Weissman: Professor Dennis Dailey. Dailey's class, entitled "Human Sexuality in Everyday Life," shows students three hours of "explicit" videos; most of the videos graphically depict heterosexuals, gays, and lesbians in the act of sex.

When State Senator Susan Wagle (R-Wichita) asked to see the videos to determine whether Dailey's class was a useful way to spend tax dollars,[63] KU faculty immediately demonstrated their support for Dailey and his highly educational class. KU's College of Liberal Arts and Sciences (CLA&S) posted a letter on its Web site backing Dailey. The signatories included Kim Wilcox, the dean of the CLA&S and thirty-seven associate deans, directors, and chairs of various academic departments. "We the undersigned . . . join our colleagues in the School of Social Welfare in expressing our unreserved support for Professor Dennis Dailey," the letter read. "We deplore Senator Wagle's relentless attack on the teaching, the professionalism, and the character of one of KU's most highly regarded teachers. . . . We are also disturbed by the wider implications of Senator Wagle's efforts to impose a form of censorship on what is taught and how it is taught at the University, with legal and monetary punishment for non-compliance. The principle of academic freedom exists precisely to protect those engaged in the pursuit and exchange of knowledge . . . from the arbitrary external imposition of belief and ideologies held by individuals and groups in the larger society."[64] The moral relativism here is stunning. Instead of condemning a professor for showing pornography in the classroom, professors attack a state senator for opposing the use of tax dollars for the perversion of students. Incredible.

Wesleyan and Kansas University aren't alone. Emerson College, New York University, Northwestern University, Arizona State University, and several campuses in the University of California system all offer classes on pornography. "To not study pornography is to ignore an absolutely pervasive phenomenon in our culture," explains Professor Linda Williams of the University of California at Berkeley.[65]

Professors are major advocates of "sexual experimentation," which includes "hooking up" – no-strings-attached sexual encounters ranging from kissing to sex. Professor Lyndall Ellingson of California State University-Chico, says that college students should have lots of sexual partners and avoid long-term relationships: "That's what they are supposed to be doing, experimenting and risking and finding who they are."[66] Dr. Ruth Westheimer of New York University, told a crowd of students at Brown University to become sexually literate, explore their bodies, and avoid limiting their sexual habits.[67]

It's working. Research conducted by the Institute for American Values' Courtship Research Team shows that 40 percent of undergraduate women had "hooked up" at least once, and 10 percent had "hooked up" six times or more.[68] So much for the purity of youth.

GETTING IN ON THE ACTION

For obvious reasons, professors oppose university bans on teacher-student sex. Such bans restrict rights of sexual expression . . . and well, why can't the professors have fun too?

"In the olden days when I was a student (back in the last century) hooking up with professors was more or less part of the curriculum," writes Laura Kipnis of Northwestern University. "Whether or not it's smart, plenty of professors I know, male and female, have hooked up with students, for shorter and longer durations."[69]

Professor Barry Dank of California State University at Long Beach feels that he has the God-given right to sleep with his students. Dank founded a group dedicated to preserving this crucial liberty: Consenting Academics for Sexual Equity. He calls restrictions on such relationships "an attack on young women," and claims that if universities ban student-teacher playtime, young women will lose the "freedom to decide what they want and what they don't want."[70] Dank married one of his former students, twenty years his junior.[71]

At William and Mary College, student-faculty relationships were finally prohibited after two incidents. First, a former creative writing teacher wrote an article for *GQ* claiming that he had an affair with a married student, whose husband committed suicide after finding out. A few months after the *GQ* article, an anthropology professor resigned his position after allegations surfaced that he had impregnated a student who worked for him; the professor then made a series of threatening phone calls to the student after discovering her pregnancy.[72]

Many students oppose a ban as strongly as do professors—after all, how else can they pull up their grades? "It might not be the classiest thing to sleep with a teacher to improve your grade," explains University of California at Santa Barbara political science major Andrea Bravo, "but I'd definitely say that there are far worse things that go on at this campus."[73]

SEX-EDUCATION PREDATORS

"The majority of young people coming to . . . college have no basic sexuality education, even human anatomy, how to protect themselves, let alone what's the meaning of sexual practice," says Professor Gil Herdt of San Francisco State University, which offers a master's degree in human sexuality.[74]

Universities feel "obligated" to teach students about sex. To that end, they teach about intercourse with members of the opposite sex. They teach about intercourse with members of the same sex. They teach about intercourse with children of either sex. They even teach about intercourse with members of a different species. And they say everything's natural. This is what they're teaching. And they're doing it on our tax and tuition dollars.

6

SAVING THE EARTH

Professors have a mission, one so dangerous and terrifying that Superman would flinch: They're out to save the world—with environmentalism. And not the wholesome, green-thumb brand of environmentalism that encourages conservation, but the extremist environmentalism that calls for bans on SUVs, blames American enterprise for all pollution, and tries to prevent all lumberjacking (as if that would prevent forest fires). As Professor Robert Nelson of the University of Maryland says, environmentalism is a "secular religion" to the professors.[1]

Professors teach that every environmental problem is a crisis. Global warming will burn us all to a crisp. Drilling for oil in Alaska will kill every caribou on Earth. Use of pesticides will create giant superbugs that will rise up and rule the planet. Biotechnology will create new and more horrible problems, like people with nine arms. And so on.

It filters down to the students. A Gallup poll conducted in 2000 shows that 80 percent of college students feel that the environment is already deteriorating.[2] I can't even count the number of times I have spoken to classmates on the subject and been screamed at for suggesting that the environment isn't in terrible shape.

It's a terrifying thought, but there it is. The professors are creating a whole new generation of Ralph Nader clones, who will see the Earth as a wonderful place, except for man, the scourge of the universe. Man creates pollution; man promotes environmental degradation; man is greedy, corrupt, and evil.

"You should be friendly to the microorganisms—it's really their world," said a UCLA biology professor in one Life Science class I took. "We're just interlopers."[3] And this is how professors feel—man should live in a mud hut, drink rainwater, and eat vegetables so as not to harm his "natural environment."

The needs of Mother Nature above the needs of mankind, they say. And, if need be, let man die rather than affect his surroundings.

IS IT HOT IN HERE?

Global warming, which professors say is caused by man, is a hugely popular issue on campus. It's not a question, it's a certainty, they declare. And the consequences could be disastrous.

"Global warming is a real issue and a serious threat to future generations," says Professor Charles Weiss of Georgetown University.[4] Michael E. Mann, a professor at the University of Virginia, claims that there is a scientific consensus that significant human-caused global warming exists.[5] "You screw around with the climate, you can expect [deserts, growth areas] to move around substantially," concurs Professor Brunk of UCLA.[6]

Jane Lubchenco, a professor of zoology at Oregon State University, does not tolerate dissent on this issue: "The evidence is overwhelming that the climate is warming and the vast majority of scientists are in agreement . . . It's no longer possible to say we don't have a scientific basis for taking action." Lubchenco continued: "Climate change is with us, the issue is urgent and it needs immediate attention. The sooner we take action, the more options we will have. Because carbon dioxide lingers in the atmosphere for 100-150 years, there is a long, long time between when we start fixing the problem and when we'll see results. We have a moral obligation to act now."[7]

According to Professor William Moomaw of Tufts University, combating "climate change" is as important as defeating slavery, advocating the women's vote, marching for civil rights, and fighting against the Vietnam War.[8] But he's not overstating the case. Really.

The only solution, they state, is for the US government to re-sign the Kyoto Protocol, a treaty that would severely limit carbon dioxide emissions. President Clinton signed the treaty in 1997; President Bush rejected the treaty in 2001.

When Clinton signed it, the professors were ecstatic. "I think the Kyoto agreement will come to be viewed as a watershed whether or not it is ratified by Congress," exclaimed Professor Weiss of Georgetown University.[9]

They were ready to fight hard for congressional approval. "If you don't fight for this one, I don't know what you're going to fight for," said Harvard Professor Eric Chavian.[10] Professor Jane Lubchenco of Oregon State University, along with five other scientists, wrote a letter to then-President Clinton asking him to consider extreme actions to prevent global warming; the letter was signed by over twenty-five hundred scientists, many of them professors.[11]

After Bush's rejection, the professors were fit to be tied. "There's a pattern in the current Bush administration of pulling out of treaties we've already signed," sneered UCLA Professor Kenneth Schultz.[12] Professor Robert Percival of the University of Maryland snarled, "He's had a pretty abysmal record" (referring specifically to Bush's rejection of Kyoto).[13]

"There's something dismissive about the way he approaches [policy]. Kyoto is a serious issue," cautioned Professor Roger Wilkins of George Mason University.[14] In criticizing President Bush's rejection of Kyoto, Professor Huck Gutman of the University of Vermont claimed, "In its rush towards isolation, the United States has abdicated the mantle of leadership in the post-modern world."[15]

In reality, Clinton was wrong to sign the treaty, and Bush was right to reject it. Signing the Kyoto treaty would do virtually nothing to end global warming, since developing countries like Mexico, China, and India are exempt from making cuts in CO_2 emissions. According to the median estimates of temperature increase due to global warming, America's signature to Kyoto would only avert a climate change of a mere 0.06 degree Celsius over the next half-century. And it would cost the US about one hundred billion to four hundred billion dollars per year to sign the treaty.[16]

But professors don't let facts get in the way of a good story. Students only get the wacko environmentalist side of the issue. Sitting in an upper-division political science class at UCLA, I heard Professor Kenneth Schultz remark repeatedly that "disagreements about global warming are largely vanishing among scientists" and that "the science is becoming increasingly clear."[17] After class, I talked to one of my friends in the class.

"I can't believe the stuff he said today," I remarked.

"What?" she said.

"Well, he's acting as though man-made global warming is a certainty. Thousands of prominent scientists disagree. There are books on the subject, showing that global warming is not significantly linked to man's creation of carbon dioxide."

"Really?" she answered. "I've never heard that before here. You should tell the class that."

"Isn't that the professor's job?" I replied.

"CAN'T WE JUST RIDE BICYCLES?"

During Winter 2001, in my geography course with Professor Muldavin, we were assigned a project. We created a poster explaining an environmental issue to our classmates. I chose drilling in the Arctic National Wildlife Refuge (ANWR) as my environmental topic, and designed a poster-board explaining the pros and cons. In the end, I said, it was in the best interest of the United States to drill for oil, because it would help both our economy and our national security.

From the back of the class, I saw a girl's hand shoot up into the air.

"Yes?" I asked.

"Well, I don't understand," she said. "Why can't we just get rid of cars, and like, all ride bicycles and stuff? Then we wouldn't need oil, and we wouldn't need to like, kill caribou and stuff."

I was stunned. This was a first-grade question coming out of the mouth of a college student at a highly respected university.

"Bicycles aren't going to cut it," I answered. "We would never get to where we want to go, our economy would plummet, and our national security would be jeopardized. If the Chinese were to attack us with tanks, could we fight them with bicycles? And we live in a free country, don't we? Why shouldn't a US citizen be able to decide he or she wants to drive an automobile?"

"Oh," she said, "I hadn't thought of that."

And it was true—she hadn't considered that. Because the professors would never in a million years say out loud in class that US citizens have a right to buy automobiles if they so choose. Rather, the government should regulate, regulate, regulate.

Professors want to ban "gas-guzzling" SUVs, despite the fact that millions of Americans will pay big bucks to own them, and that SUV production keeps thousands of people working.

"It is indeed uncomfortable for Americans to realize that it is their gas-guzzling habits that are responsible for so much violence hurled in our direction. . . . Look in the mirror and ask yourself, honestly, if you really need a 15-mile-per-gallon SUV or van," advises Professor William Moomaw of Tufts University.[18]

During the summer of 2001, when Californians were paying more per gallon of gas than people of any other state, Professor Richard Gilbert of UC Berkeley blamed "the popularity of gas-guzzling behemoths."[19]

After then-Governor Gray Davis of California signed far-reaching emissions legislation, professors couldn't contain their glee. "The auto industry has been constantly making improvements to engines using onboard computers," says UC Berkeley Professor Robert Harley. "If they put those technology advances toward fuel efficiency instead of building sport utility vehicles, it would make a difference."[20] "If you look at history, legislation is the way to go," agrees Professor Mark Jacobsen of Stanford.[21] Yes, restrict those corporate fat cats who use technology for profit rather than making fuel-efficient cars no one wants.

They also want to place high taxes on use of gasoline to force down consumption, ignoring the thousands of jobs which would be lost in the process.

Professor Lawrence Goulder of Stanford feels that a carbon tax, designed to raise gas prices, "wouldn't be a free lunch, but it may be a lunch worth buying."[22] France's high tax on oil is wonderful, said Professor Brunk in his UCLA Life Science 15 class, because "it pays for itself."[23] Georgia should raise gasoline taxes, states Professor Michael Meyer of Georgia Tech: "If the case can be made to taxpayers . . . I think people will buy it."[24]

"When people consume gas," explains Professor David Romer of UC Berkeley, "they impose harms on other people that they aren't paying for otherwise. They crowd the freeways and pollute"[25]—therefore, we need a higher federal gas tax. "This federal tax should be higher than some other tax," nods University of Michigan Professor Joel Slemrod.[26] Professor Michael Golay of MIT believes in "heavy restrictions and taxes on fossil fuel use."[27]

When in doubt, let big government come to the rescue.

CARIBOU ARE PEOPLE, TOO

The issue that raises the most professorial ire is drilling in the Arctic National Wildlife Refuge (ANWR). Professors feel America shouldn't do it. It will hurt the caribou and destroy a "pristine wilderness." Besides, they whine, there's probably not that much oil there anyway.

Professor Alan Richards of UC Santa Barbara calls drilling in ANWR "egregiously stupid."[28] Professor Karl Francis, an official in local Alaskan government, derides those who want to drill as "urban wilderness buffs" with an "odd lust" for ANWR. "Indeed, we see these people as dangerously naïve with a strange religious fanaticism that is both weird and frightening," writes Francis.[29]

Professors ignore all the facts that indicate drilling is a good idea. They deny that vast stores of oil in ANWR could provide an alternative to reliance on foreign oil. Professor Albert Bartlett of Colorado State University at Boulder said before the US House Subcommittee on Energy, "The proposal for rapid drilling in the Arctic National Wildlife Refuge . . . appears to be a short-term energy fix that seems to ignore the real-world reality of resource availability."[30] Boston University Professor Andrew Hoffman states that the amount of oil in ANWR "is not in any way . . . significant enough to enhance our oil security."[31]

"If we could eliminate the need for imported oil by drilling at ANWR, that would be one thing," concurs Professor Richard Alley of Penn State. "But drilling at ANWR won't greatly change the equation."[32]

Wrong. Right now, the United States imports about 58 percent of its oil.[33] If ANWR were opened to drilling, that number would fall substantially. According to Secretary of Energy Spencer Abraham, the amount of oil in the ANWR would be enough "to replace oil imports from the Persian Gulf region for ten years, or from Iraq for fifty years."[34]

They ignore that the section of ANWR that would be drilled is vast tundra, with little life and less beauty, and that it is less than one half of one percent of the total area in ANWR. They say that it is a pristine area, America's last true wilderness. In 2000, two hundred and forty scientists signed a letter to this effect, stating, "Five decades of biological study and scientific research have confirmed that the coastal plain of the Arctic National Wildlife Refuge forms a vital component of the biological diversity of the refuge."[35]

They discard Alaskan public opinion, which overwhelmingly supports drilling, instead pointing to minority groups that oppose drilling. The classic example is the Gwich'in Indian tribe, who oppose drilling on environmental grounds—professors constantly cite the Gwich'in as the final authority on drilling. They completely ignore the Inupiat Indians, another tribe which steadfastly supports drilling and actually lives in ANWR. "While past injustices to American Indians can't be undone, the threat to [the Gwich'in] culture can be stopped" by refraining from drilling, writes Professor Steven Dinero of Philadelphia University.[36] "Sacrificing a place like the Arctic Refuge and a culture that has endured for thousands of years is simply wrong," urges Professor Khalil Zonoozy of Portland State University.[37]

They disregard actual caribou population statistics, instead proclaiming that drilling will kill the caribou. "Caribou will move away from oil fields as disturbance increases," speculates Professor David Klein of the University of Alaska at Fairbanks. "The pipeline and [nearby] haul road [at Prudhoe Bay] have essentially fractured the Central Arctic herd into two groups," he says,[38] ignoring the fact that the Central Arctic herd has grown more than five-fold in the last thirty years.[39] And even if drilling did kill some caribou, do dead caribou take precedence over national security?

TOO MANY PEOPLE

The planet is overpopulated, according to university faculty. We've filled up all our space. We're eating all our food. We're destroying our environment. So it's time for a change: we need to promote birth control (including forced abortion) in Third World countries, and we need to redistribute our wealth.

Do you sense a bit of alarmism here?

In 1974, Professor Garrett Hardin of UC Santa Barbara wrote the cult environmentalist wacko classic essay "Living on a Lifeboat," in which he suggested that society look at population in terms of "lifeboat ethics." Imagine that each nation (and by extension, the entire world) is a lifeboat, he says, and that if too many people get on, the entire boat sinks. The only solution is to let some people drown.[40]

Professor Paul Ehrlich has been preaching Chicken Little demographics for decades. In his 1968 book *The Population Bomb*, Ehrlich wrote: "Too many cars, too many factories, too much detergent, too much pesticide, multiplying contrails, inadequate sewage treatment plants, too little water, too much carbon dioxide—all can be traced easily to *too many people*." He predicted that in the 1970s, overpopulation would lead to massive famines and hundreds of millions of deaths. Oops. But facts don't stop Ehrlich from teaching his philosophy years after being proven wrong.[41]

"We're within an ant's eyebrow of being overpopulated right now," warned Professor Brunk in my Life Science 15 course at UCLA.[42] "There are very substantial numbers of reasonable biologists who feel we have already reached our carrying capacity," he reiterated later in the quarter.[43] And then again, two days later: "My guess is that the carrying capacity of the Earth is below six billion, probably somewhere between three and six billion. I'm almost sure it's not nine billion. I'm willing to bet you any amount of money that the population will reach nine billion in your life-times."[44] And again, a week later, he stated: "Population growth is going to come back and bite you in so many ways."[45] I guess if you repeat something enough, it becomes true.

Brunk's assigned biology textbook follows his line of thinking: "Imagine a world where people must share a room with four to twelve others. A room of one's own is a rare luxury. In fact, people who have any housing at all consider themselves fortunate, because so many people have none. . . . Beggars crowd every street, and each garbage can is searched through time after time by starving people looking for something to sustain them. . . . a future like this may be in store for all of us unless something is done soon, and on a massive scale, to control population growth."[46] Flash to scene from *Blade Runner*.

And there's no solution other than to cut population growth, by any means necessary, they say.

Don't bother trying to grow more food. "Just growing more food is too simplistic," declares Brunk. "We increased food production and population increased, so now the percentage of people who don't have enough food is the same as before. It's kind of discouraging."[47] Not exactly. In fact, it's downright encouraging that population can grow rapidly and still the same percentage of people can be fed.

And they say new technology isn't the answer either. "Some believe, and many hope, for a technological fix during the coming decades, one that will set civilization back on a course towards ever greater prosperity," pens University of North Carolina Professor Allan Combs. "I call this general view the *Star Trek Solution*. . . . we have been waiting for the technological utopia for many years, and there is no good reason to think it is finally coming just in time to save us."[48]

Professor Ehrlich agrees. "Large-scale technologies take a long time to deploy. It is crazy to think some magic bullet will save us," states Ehrlich in his own inimitable style. "And we've invented a lot of technological rabbits out of hats but they have toxic droppings."[49]

The only answer is global socialism combined with forced population control. "It is not too late for humanity to avert a vast ecological disaster and make the transition to a sustainable society," pontificates Professor Ehrlich, "but the task will not be simple . . . Population growth should be halted and a slow decline begun . . . Wasteful consumption in rich countries must be reduced to allow for needed growth in poor countries."[50] Because as we all know, if you stop yourself from buying those extra bananas at the grocery store, they will magically appear in Nigeria, allowing Nigeria to grow.

RETURN OF THE LUDDITES

The Luddites were an anti-technology group in England in the eighteenth century who revolted against the Industrial Revolution by roaming around the countryside breaking machinery. That group died out a century ago, but it's experiencing a revival on college campuses, where professors rip technology as anti-environment.

Professor Chet Bowers of the University of Oregon calls computers "a colonizing technology . . . computers profoundly alter how we think and inevitably reduce our ability to understand nature."[51] Apparently, the best way to commune with nature is to carve term papers out of stone.

And go back to hunter-gatherer means of agriculture. "The plow increased soil erosion," stated Professor Joshua Muldavin in a UCLA geography class. Muldavin labeled the plow as a "harmful policy."

Professor Neil Postman, a media and technology critic and chair of the New York University Department of Culture and Communications, told an audience at a Regent University Journalism Conference that "*All* technological change is a Faustian bargain . . . You can go as far back as the invention of the phonetic alphabet, the printing press with the movable type, or the invention of telegraphy and photography. And you will find that for every problem such an invention solved, it raised a problem that we did not have before."[52] For Postman, this means that "computers in learning are a problem and not something to celebrate."[53]

Professors hate pesticides. They believe that all the gains in productivity due to pesticides are of no value, and that pesticides only cause environmental degradation.

The saint of the anti-pesticide movement is Rachel Carson, who, as Professor Paul Licht of UC Berkeley put it, "shocked us, scared us and galvanized a generation into a new kind of environmental activism."[54] Carson's book, *Silent Spring*, proposed banning DDT, a pesticide that kills mosquitoes, because of its alleged harmful effects on humans, and because it thinned the egg shells of bald eagles.

The Environmental Protection Agency went along with Carson and dramatically restricted the production and use of DDT on US soil. Because of Carson, between thirty and sixty million people have died from malaria.[55] As the *Wall Street Journal* editorial board put it, "proponents of a ban on DDT should be forced to answer the question about which is more important: the life of a bird that might be harmed by DDT, or the life of a Third World child who might be saved."[56]

Professors' answer: the life of a bird. Professor Muldavin touted a worldwide ban on DDT in his Geography 5 class at UCLA, citing *Silent Spring*.[57] Professor Ehrlich suggested that US life expectancy would be diminished by ten years if DDT were used on American soil.[58] Dr. Mark Hermanson of the University of Pennsylvania teaches a class called "Searching for Rachel

Carson: DDT and the Comeback of the American Eagle." The course description reads: "Students will learn about the biology of tertiary and quaternary [sic] bird species, the effects of DDT and other pesticides on the food chain, and learn about Rachel Carson's research concerning the effects of DDT in the environment."[59]

Biotechnology is also under attack, from human genetics to genetically modified foods. I vividly recall one teacher's assistant who couldn't stand biotechnology. He derided all the success stories of biotechnology as "due to media bias" in favor of biotechnology.[60] Of biotechnology's advances, he stated, "So you extend your life five or ten years, but you'll die anyway. Other diseases will come."[61] It's easy to shrug off five or ten years when it's not your life on the line.

REVOLUTION AGAINST THE GREEN REVOLUTION

The Green Revolution of the 1960s and 1970s revolutionized food production, creating new types of high-yielding crops and increasing use of pesticides and fertilizers. These new strategies increased crop yields so much that food supplies were able to keep pace with skyrocketing world population. But if it's good for the populace, the professors must hate it.

And they do. "There's a lot of uneasy feelings about the Green Revolution," says Professor C.F. Brunk of UCLA. "In just over a decade, population growth overcame the gains of the Green Revolution," he told the class.[62] Only one problem: it didn't. No one said that the Green Revolution would feed everyone; proponents only said that the Green Revolution would revitalize the agricultural sector. In fact, food production has kept pace with population—there is more than enough food on earth to feed everyone.

Professor Muldavin lectured that the Green Revolution "ignored distribution of food," and that the main effects of the Green Revolution were soil erosion, water degradation, chemical inputs, genetic erosion, and social calamity.[63] He skipped right by the part where the Green Revolution fed millions of people. But maybe it's asking too much for him to teach that. Soil erosion takes priority.

Professor Ravi Batra of Southern Methodist University rips the Green

Revolution. "[F]ar from alleviating poverty, the Green Revolution has actually increased it," writes Batra, "and instead of bridging the gap between the rural rich and poor, it has widened it."[64] Unfortunately for him, Batra is wrong. Due to the Green Revolution, absolute poverty in the Indian region was cut by half.[65]

Professors who hate the Green Revolution also hate genetically modified (GM) crops, which have higher yields than ordinary crops. And though they can't prove that GM crops actually have negative effects, speculation is good enough.

"There is no evidence at all of deleterious effects of genetically modified (GM) foods on human health," admitted Professor Brunk. "But the step from potential problems to actual problems is a very short step."[66] That's rather paranoid. If there's no evidence that something is a problem, why worry about it? Unless you're an alarmist college professor, that is.

Professor Jane Rissler, head of the Union of Concerned Scientists, which represents hundreds of university faculty members, opposes GM foods. "Our point of view is that we're skeptical of many of the benefits. We're worried about the uncertainties and the risks. This leads us to believe that for the most part these products will not be useful in a sustainable agriculture," she states.[67]

Professors decry the Green Revolution because it saved human lives and gave man the ability to increase population. At root, the fight of the radical environmentalists is a fight against human progress, and the fight against human progress is a fight against the existence of humanity itself.

BIODIVERSITY, EXCEPT FOR HUMANS

The university faculty constantly preaches "biodiversity" —the preservation of all species—even at the expense of human endeavors. They ignore that man is part of his environment, and that extinction of various species has been an ongoing process for millions of years. They drastically exaggerate the damage being done to biodiversity by humanity; their goal is to stop humanity from progressing in new and more efficient ways.

"The driving force in this extinction period is human activity, pure and simple," averred Professor Brunk. "Whenever humans are introduced to the environment, you can usually expect biodiversity to go down."[68] The implication? Stop human expansion, by any means necessary. Why? Because we love moths.

"Species are disappearing at an accelerating rate through human action," reiterates Professor Edward O. Wilson of Harvard, "primarily habitat destruction but also pollution and the introduction of exotic species into residual natural environments."[69] Wilson and Professor Paul Ehrlich of Stanford actually asked President Clinton to sign legislation "to reduce the scale of human activities . . . every new shopping center built in the California chaparral . . . every swamp converted into a rice paddy or shrimp farm means less biodiversity."[70]

The agenda-driven professors quote astronomical extinction rates in order to alarm the students. "The numbers are grim. . . . half of all living bird and mammal species will be gone within two hundred or three hundred years," Professor Donald A. Levine of the University of Texas solemnly warned. Even Levine admitted, though, that these statistics were "crude."[71]

Such overblown estimates are not uncommon. "[A]ccording to our data," says Professor Ehrlich, "the loss of mammal populations actually may be much more severe [than current estimates], perhaps 10 percent or higher."[72] Professor Wilson puts the extinction rate at "crisis proportions— perhaps one hundred to one thousand times higher than it was before humanity came along."[73]

All of this is false. Professor Julian Simon of the University of Maryland, one of the most widely known and respected scientists of the last century, explains, "A fair reading of the available data suggests a rate of extinction not even one-thousandth as great as doomsayers claim. If the rate were any lower, evolution itself would need to be questioned." In his writings, Simon shows where the exaggerated figure originated, and he demonstrates that the figure was "pure guesswork."[74]

Professor Bjorn Lomborg of the University of Aarhus in Denmark, author of the controversial book, *The Skeptical Environmentalist*, agrees with Simon. He estimates the extinction rate at "0.7 percent over the next 50 years," or 0.014 percent per year, one hundred times smaller than the rate suggested by environmental alarmists.[75]

Lomborg is hardly a right-winger: he admits that he has the same basic goals as the environmentalists, but he sees that environmental problems aren't as severe as the Greens say they are. But standing up against the mean, green, lying machine in any way means coming under heavy fire. Professor Wilson of Harvard leads the anti-Lomborg crowd. He refers to the publicity surrounding Lomborg as "the Lomborg scam," calls Lomborg a "contrarian" and a "parasite," and rips Lomborg's research ability as "characterized by willful ignorance, selective quotations, disregard for communication with genuine experts, and destructive campaigning."[76] Is that what passes for a scholarly critique of a fellow scientist these days?

BOW TO MOTHER NATURE

In the end, all of the environmental alarmism at universities is really a cover for a nihilistic anti-human tilt. Without man, the world would be a glorious Garden of Eden, they think. There would be no global warming. No automobiles. No oil. What a wonderful place!

Rutgers University ecologist David Ehrenfeld believes the smallpox virus should not be destroyed since it kills only human beings.[77] "[T]he ending of the human epoch on Earth would most likely be greeted with a hearty 'Good Riddance,'" spits Professor Paul Taylor of City University of New York.[78]

The deep Greens desire the destruction of mankind as we know it. These extremists are not rare or hard to find. All you have to do is check your local university.

7

THE WAR ON GOD

In Genesis, Chapter Eleven, the Bible tells of a time when the entire earth was of one language and one common purpose. All of mankind settled in a place called Shinar. And the people said, "Come, let us build a city, and a tower with its top in the heavens, and let us make a name for ourselves." So they began to build a tower that would reach into the heavens, hoping to challenge God Himself.

And God looked at the city, and at the tower, and He said, "Behold, they are one people with one language for all, and this they begin to do?" And God dispersed them from there over the face of the whole earth; and they stopped building the city. The name of the city and of the tower was Babel.

The university system is the new city of Babel. Professors hope to build an intellectual tower that reaches into the heavens, to challenge God. They drag organized religion through the mud and then shoot arrows at its dirtied carcass. And once they've done that, they make moral judgments for all of mankind, as if obtaining a PhD conferred upon them some sort of supernatural moral wisdom.

They wish to tear down biblical morality and place in its stead a morality of their own choosing. It is a degraded morality they seek to promote. Without God, there is no right and wrong, no good and bad. Anything goes. Life itself loses value, and with that loss of value comes a loss of societal strength. In short, America becomes France.

What these professors want is a jihad against God, a crusade against traditional morality. And their battlefields are lecture halls full of innocent civilians.

A DARK AND GODLESS PLACE

It's terrific to have professors around to enlighten students to the purpose-lessness of their own existence. God doesn't exist, they say. Or if He does, He is uninvolved in the world. Life has no meaning, and there are no rules. Man takes the place of God.

Spouts Professor Peter Singer of Princeton University: "If we don't play God, who will? There seem to me to be three possibilities: there is a God, but He doesn't care about evil and suffering; there is a God who cares, but He or She is a bit of an underachiever; or there is no God. Personally, I believe the latter."[1] *Someone's* going to Hell.

Professor John McCarthy of Stanford University, one of the nation's leading experts on artificial intelligence, feels that "the evidence on the god question is in a similar state to the evidence on the werewolf question. So I am an atheist."[2] The evidence on Professor McCarthy's arrogance is in, and it's definitive.

"I think in many respects religion is a dream—a beautiful dream often. Often a nightmare," says Professor Steven Weinberg of the University of Texas. "But it's a dream from which I think it's about time we awoke. Just as a child learns about the tooth fairy and is incited by that to leave a tooth under the pillow—and you're glad that the child believes in the tooth fairy. But eventually you want the child to grow up."[3] That's rather high and mighty of him.

Professor James Wright of Hunter College calls Jesus a "half-crazed logi-cian," and states "I don't believe in God. He hurts too much."[4] Professor Corey Washington of the University of Maryland agrees: "I am simply say-ing that it is more probable that God does not exist."[5]

Then there are the professors who foul the waters with New-Age garbage. "If God is understood from monotheistic traditions, it could be problematical for me," explains Professor Tu Weiming of Harvard University. "If God is understood as creativity itself, as a generative force, as a transformative power, as the source of all values, all our truths, all our ideas of human self-realization, then I certainly have faith in God."[6] Whatever happened to plain old monotheism? Too boring?

Professor Camille Paglia, who lectures at the University of the Arts in Philadelphia, believes that society should return to pagan worship. "The public realm is not *owned* by Judeo-Christianity. It is *shared* by people of all cultural and religious backgrounds. Therefore, I'm arguing for the Greco-Roman or pagan line, which is very tolerant of homosexuality and even of man-boy love." Paglia also says she's for "the abolition of all sodomy laws. I'm for abortion rights. I'm for the legalization of drugs—consistent with alcohol regulations. I'm for not just the decriminalization but the legalization of prostitution."[7] Does she want to legalize prostitution because professors are underpaid?

DAMNING ORGANIZED RELIGION

As early as 1951, William F. Buckley was pointing out in his landmark work, *God and Man at Yale*, that "if the atmosphere of a college is overwhelmingly secular, if the influential members of the faculty tend to discourage religious inclinations, or to persuade the student that Christianity is nothing more than 'ghost-fear,' or 'twentieth-century witchcraft,' university policy quite properly becomes a matter of concern to those parents and alumni who deem active Christian faith a powerful force for good and for personal happiness."[8]

If fears of anti-religious universities were well-founded then, those fears are a thousand-fold more legitimate now. Professors hate God, and they hate organized religion even more. They see it as outdated, a danger to modern society, and the cause of thousands of pointless deaths. Religion is a childish plaything that man uses to blind himself to his own mortality, they say. Only one out of every five professors attends religious services once a week,[9] as opposed to about 40 percent in the general public.[10] Forty-eight percent of professors say they rarely or never attend a religious service.[11]

Professor Thomas Sugrue of the University of Pennsylvania states that among academics, religion is "the subject of distrust and even derision . . . much of the academic skepticism about organized religion is warranted."[12]

Diana Chapman Walsh, president of Wellesley College, made the same distinction between spirituality and religion to a group of UCLA students. "Religion is something we can perhaps do without," she told the students. She defined spirituality as love, compassion, and forgiveness—and she said that spirituality does not involve faith.[13] Thank you, flower-child.

Professor Peter Singer is at it again, calling Judeo-Christian values the biggest obstacle to animal rights: "One of the things that causes a problem for the animal movement is the strong strain of fundamentalist Christianity that makes a huge gulf between humans and animals."[14] This is hardly a surprise coming from the famous lecturer who backs bestiality and the murder of severely disfigured infants.

So how does fellow leftist Professor Paul Ehrlich, who sometimes morphs into a religious expert, explain religion's role in the world? "Religion . . . continues to play a role in maintaining the status of elites today, for instance in justifying poverty and wealth as expressions of God's will."[15] Actually, I use religion to justify mental acuity as an expression of God's will. I'm sure God *must* have a reason for making Ehrlich such a babbling idiot.

UCLA Professor Joshua Muldavin made a similarly anti-religious remark in his Geography 5 class, where he labeled Christianity as a "harmful policy" because it said the earth was to be used.[16] Perhaps he's right: We shouldn't use the earth; we should worship it and nourish it with human sacrifice.

Professor Brunk of UCLA stated in our biology class that Charles Darwin's *Origin of Species* was the most influential book ever written by one author. When a student asked him about the Bible, he responded: "Religious texts don't count, because they are *invariably* by multiple authors."[17] Last time I checked, God is not "multiple authors."

Biola University Professor Richard Flory and University of Southern California Professor Donald Miller cooperated to create an exhibition about the future of Christianity. Flory and Miller came to the conclusion that focusing on biblical truths would lead Christianity down the path to doom. "The idea is, you need to reinvent the church to be adaptable to contemporary culture," Miller says. The section of the exhibit concerning conversion attempts through Biblical teachings is characterized by marked disdain. Even the far-left *Los Angeles Times*, which mocks Christianity at every turn, calls the section of the exhibit concerning biblical teachings "judgmental."[18] If the *L.A. Times* calls an anti-Biblical exhibit "judgmental," you can bet your life the exhibit is a wildly anti-Christian screed.

"RELIGION OF PEACE"

Unlike the Judeo-Christian tradition, Islam is tolerant and peaceful, professors say. Islam means peace, after all, right? Actually, not really—the literal translation is "submission." But professors like to think so.

"Islam means peace," explains Professor Aly Farag of the University of Louisville.[19] Islam means peace, agree Professors Mustafa Suwani of Truman State University,[20] Nadira K. Charaniya of Springfield College,[21] Zeki Saritoprak of Berry College,[22] G.A. Shareef, formerly of the Bellarmine College.[23] Scores of others concur.

Islam means peace, agrees Professor Ali Asani of Harvard. "If you look at it this way," Asani continued, "a Christian or a Jew is Muslim as well; any who submit to the one God is already Muslim."[24] Really? What happened to that whole bit about Christians and Jews being non-believers, and non-believers sitting in everlasting fiery torment?[25]

Not only does Islam mean peace, Islam is the "religion of peace." "Islam is a religion of peace," states Professor John Berthrong of the Boston University.[26] Professor Ahmed Asker of Florida A&M University calls Islam a religion of peace, love, mercy, compassion, and forgiveness.[27] "Islam is a religion of peace," concurs Dr. Tayyib Rana of the University of Buffalo. "It wants to liberate men and women to live life to its fullest." Then why does it fail to liberate men and women wherever it is tried?

Islam is just misunderstood, professors maintain. "The level of understanding of Islam is abysmally low in this country, even among educated people," scolds Professor David Mitten of Harvard.[28] Professor Akel Kahara of the University of Texas blames anti-Islam sentiment on "ignorance, prejudice and intellectual racism."[29] Sure, that must be it. It couldn't have anything to do with the fact that most terrorists are Muslim and that Muslim terrorists have killed thousands of Americans.

"Although the Quran and the teachings of the Prophet Muhammad . . .

have given Muslims a general understanding of Judaism and Christianity," writes Professor Nimat Hafez Barazangi, "Jews and Christians usually have little, if any, knowledge about Islam."[30] The Quran teaches that Jews think Ezra was the son of God (false), and warns Muslims not to be friends with Christians or Jews, both of whom will suffer in the everlasting flames.[31] Is that what Professor Barazangi considers a general understanding of Judaism and Christianity?

Islam isn't stagnant, either—in fact, Islam means progress. Or something like that. Islam is "moving forward and increasing in self-awareness," says Professor Gerhard Bowering of Yale.[32]

Professor Akbar Ahmed of Princeton calls Islam "the third great religion of America," and says that it is "one of the most misunderstood religions in the world." "How many people," he asks, "know the greatest names of God in Islam are compassion and mercy?"[33] That's good to know when Christians and Jews are burning in Allah's eternal flames.

SCIENCE VS. RELIGION

Most Christians and Jews feel that there is no implicit conflict between science and religion. Gregory Mendel was a priest. Maimonides was a doctor. Sir Isaac Newton was a religious man. It was Albert Einstein who said that God does not play dice with the universe. Science and religion bolster one another. The more we learn about the world in which we live, the clearer it becomes that there must be a divine Planner.

Professors don't think so. Science and religion are completely at odds with one another. God is not a master designer; everything is an accident. As Professor David Krupp of Winward Community College puts it, "The minute you start bringing in religious concepts, it messes up science."[34]

Perhaps the perceived dichotomy between science and religion explains the lack of faith among scientific faculty. While the percentage of Americans who believe in God remains between 85 and 95 percent, the percentage of scientists who believe in God is less than 40 percent.[35]

The main battle between science and religion takes place in the field of evolutionary biology, where professors demonize creationists as archaic relics of the Dark Ages. Creationism isn't just wrong, it's intellectual sin, they say, despite the fact that 45 percent of Americans believe in intelligent design.[36]

An assigned textbook in a UCLA biology course reads: "Many adaptations seem more easily explained by natural selection than by God's design because God presumably could have 'done better.'"[37] The text also derides creationists as people who "tr[y] to portray themselves as scientists, calling their new approach 'creation science.'"[38]

"American neoconservatives promote creationism because, as their own statements reveal, they apparently fear an educated population and see the theory of evolution as a threat," writes Professor Paul Ehrlich.[39] Did it ever occur to Ehrlich that perhaps many neoconservatives believe in the word of God? Probably not, since Ehrlich believes conservatives are out to lynch blacks and enslave the poor.

Teaching creation science is foolish, professors believe. "They could just as well talk about Kumulipo," the Hawaiian creation chant, scoffs Professor Pauline Chinn of the University of Hawaii.[40] "Creationism isn't science, it's faith," nods Hawaii Institute of Geophysics and Planetology Professor Gerald Fryer.[41] "The big lie is that there's something to (creationism)," sneers Professor Victor Stenger, also of the University of Hawaii.

In Cobb County, Georgia, creationism is a hot topic. The school board there is attempting to clarify its policy with regard to teaching creationism in the public schools. The professors are livid. Professor David Jackson of the University of Georgia maintains that while he does not tell students what to believe, "I make it clear what Cobb County is doing is pretty clearly illegal."[42] Professor Norman Thomas, also of the University of Georgia, is more blunt: "We're dealing with science, and we don't deal with issues that aren't scientific," he says. "I think the state needs to tell Cobb County what should be in the science classroom."[43]

Patrick Henry University, in Virginia, was denied accreditation by the American Academy of Liberal Education because it teaches creationism. Despite meeting all of the criterion for accreditation and openly stating that it is a Christian college, the AALE dismissed its accreditation. University President Mike Farris calls the ruling "discrimination on the basis of viewpoint and ideology," and states that the AALE "want[s] to force us to teach what they want us to teach."[44] And he's right. If you don't teach it the liberal way, the liberal education establishment will shut you down.

Professor Kevin Haley of the Central Oregon Community College was fired from his post for allegedly teaching creationism *as well as* evolution. Haley denied the charges. "I am a creationist and I'm also a scientist, and I have no trouble teaching evolution," explains Haley, but "[a]s far as teaching creation in the classroom, not on a bet."[45] Let's assume for the moment that Haley actually did teach creationism as well as evolution. What's so wrong with that? Professors are allowed to teach homosexuality, Marxism (a secular religion), and anti-Americanism, but mention God and you're out of a job.

CHRISTIANS NEED NOT APPLY

The receivers' coach for Nebraska's football team, Ron Brown, was interviewed in 2002 for the position of head coach at Stanford. Brown has a stellar record in his seventeen years at Nebraska: in that time, twenty-six of his pupils have gone on to play in the National Football League.[46] Brown is black. It seems he would have fit perfectly into the system.

There was only one problem: Brown is a religious Christian. And that was the deal-breaker. The assistant athletic director at Stanford, Alan Glenn, said that Brown's religion "was definitely something that had to be considered. We're a very diverse community with a diverse alumni. Anything that would stand out that much is something that has to be looked at."[47]

In specific, it was Brown's commitment to the biblical ban on homosexuality that Stanford found objectionable. As Brown described the discrimination against him, "If I'd been discriminated against for being black, they never would have told me that. They had no problem telling me it was because of my Christian beliefs."[48]

Brown's story isn't unusual. Christians are turned away from university jobs and ridiculed in the classroom for their religious views.

Dr. Troy Thompson tells a story about his time at Wayne State University, where he went to medical school. As Thompson relates: "Our class asked Dr. Jack Kevorkian to come and speak to us about his practices— at the time he was calling it 'medi-cide' . . . He asked us to raise our hands if we thought abortion wasn't ethical. I was the only one in the class of three hundred to raise my hand. Kevorkian pointed right at me and told the class, 'Raise your hand if you think that man is a religious fanatic who will never be a true physician.'"[49] Where was the professor during all of this? Euthanizing one of the students?

At Depauw University, a Methodist college, Professor Janis Price was the victim of another anti-Christian attack at the hands of the administration. Price brought in the James Dobson–sponsored magazine, *Teachers in Focus*, and placed it on the back table of one of her classrooms. At the end of lecture, she told the students that they were free to take a copy of the magazine if they were interested. No article was ever discussed in class. One of the articles in the magazine discussed how public schools should handle the touchy subject of homosexuality. One student was offended by the article and reported Professor Price to the administration.

Busted.

Vice President of Academic Affairs Neal Abraham sent Price a scathing letter calling her actions "reprehensible," the magazine "intolerant," and accusing her of creating a "hostile environment" in the classroom. He put Price on probation, cut her pay 25 percent and barred her from teaching at the university, saying that the college "cannot tolerate the intolerable."[50] It is a frightening era in which the administration of a Methodist university considers Christianity intolerable.

"WHAT WAS YOUR NAME AGAIN?"

Each year, usually during summer, movies about college life premiere. Most of them include some sort of "life-lesson" learned by the main character; for many, the climax of the movie occurs during finals week. But each and every one shows risqué sexual behavior taking place on campus. Is it an exaggeration? Perhaps. Is it occurring frequently? Assuredly.

Religious groups have protested this kind of behavior for years, and they have specifically targeted co-ed dorms as the cause of much of this promiscuity. But the universities maintain that co-ed dorms are good, and that the promiscuity that often results from close contact between the sexes is normal and healthy.

An Independent Women's Forum survey of more than one thousand college women showed that 40 percent of them admitted to having engaged in a "hook-up"—an impersonal sexual encounter, ranging from kissing to intimacy, in which the woman did not expect further contact with her partner. Ten percent of the women admitted to having "hooked up" more than six times. Associate director of the McCosh Health Center at Princeton, Janet Finney, said that she was surprised by the number of "college students who become friends with people because of proximity" rather than shared interests. The same could probably be said for sexual relationships. Instead of being shocked by the statistics, Professor Fernandez-Kelley of Princeton was pleased, since she "disagrees with moralists" who feel that young people should not experiment sexually.[51]

In 1998, five Orthodox Jewish students sued Yale University for the right to live off campus after they were forced to live in co-ed dorms where most students used co-ed toilets and showers, sex manuals and condoms were openly available, and freshmen were required to attend "safe sex lectures." Dubbed the Yale Five by the media, their story made national headlines.

Yale would not capitulate, stating that living in the dorms was a "a central part of Yale's education,"[52] despite the fact that Yale does not require juniors and seniors to live in the dorms. Richard Levin, president of the Yale Hillel (a campus Jewish organization), ripped the Orthodox students as close-minded, stating that they didn't belong at Yale if they weren't willing to live in the obscenity-filled world of the co-ed dorms: "Why come to a university like this one if you won't open your mind to new ideas and new perspectives?" he said. "This is not a place where people who close themselves off to the world can thrive." In essence, the university asked the students to either choose their morality or a Yale education. Morality won. The students paid for campus housing and lived off campus.[53]

A conversation I had with a female acquaintance on campus comes to mind. Both of us were at a meeting with some other Jewish students. For some reason, she decided to announce before the entire group that she had recently dated a Muslim (remember, she is Jewish). Since Jewish law forbids intermarriage, her unprompted comment irritated me.

"Why were you going out with a guy who's not Jewish?" I asked.

"Well, I didn't know he wasn't Jewish," she answered.

"How long did you go out with him?"

"About three months."

"And you didn't know that he wasn't Jewish?"

"Yeah."

"Why?"

"Well, you know, we met in the dorms, and we became really close, and then we kind of, you know, it just happened . . ."

By this time, the conversation had grown rather heated. "So you slept with the guy, not even knowing his religion? Next time it might behoove you to find out his name first," I chided.

"Well, that's the way it works in the dorms, you know," she answered.

"KEEP YOUR HANDS OFF MY BODY!"

On June 5, 2002, a pro-life group came to UCLA campus. They went to BruinWalk, the main campus pathway, and set up gigantic twenty-foot-high posters containing horrific photos of aborted fetuses. I normally don't use BruinWalk to get to class, but I was intrigued enough to walk down to the posters and observe the reactions of the people who passed by, both students and faculty. A few gasped in horror; some simply walked by the posters without looking back; most slowly shook their heads as they walked by, ridiculing the audacity of those radical pro-lifers who would dare to bring their conservative political views into the middle of this pristine campus.

It was about the reaction I expected. College faculty is overwhelmingly and militantly pro-choice, and it rubs off on the students. Fully 99 percent of Ivy League professors oppose a legal ban on abortion.[54] The effect on the students? A 1996 Gallup poll showed that while 47 percent of women were pro-life when they finished high school, that number dropped to 24 percent by the time the women finished college.[55]

Professor Sarah Weddington of the University of Texas is probably the leading pro-choice advocate in the country. In 1967, Weddington wrote about her own abortion experience in Mexico in her book, *A Question of Choice*. Six years later, in 1973, Weddington successfully argued *Roe v. Wade* before the Supreme Court, the case in which abortion was deemed a "woman's right to choose." Now, she's out proselytizing for abortion: "[W]e have to have a new generation of younger women [supporting abortion rights]. . . . we can't win it without them. We've got to have their help in organizing people to vote pro-choice, protecting clinics, working with Planned Parenthood."[56] Weddington uses her podium as a weapon.

Professor James Lindgren of Northwestern University, who is pro-choice, did a study examining reasons for the extremely pro-abortion tilt of the law school professoriate. He concluded that the population groups most likely to be pro-life—Hispanics, Catholics, and Republicans—are among the most underrepresented on law school faculties. Republicans compose only 32 percent of the law school faculty, according to the study.[57] No wonder most lawyers are leftists.

At the University of Illinois, pro-choice Professor Eileen McDonagh of Northeastern University pulled out of a debate with pro-life speaker Scott Klusendorf of Stand to Reason after McDonagh's supporters refused to allow her to speak. Said one of McDonagh's supporters, Chrissy Trilling of Campus for Choice: "We don't want to give [the pro-life side] a forum for their extremist views."[58] Women's Studies Professor Sonya Michel of the University of Illinois attacked Klusendorf as unlearned, calling his academic record insufficient.[59] Debates are acceptable as long as there are no right-wingers. That's the intellectual's way.

Professors are willing to go out on a limb to kill babies. Many professors even support the gruesome D&E (dilation and evacuation) and D&X procedures (dilation and extraction). A D&E is a late-term abortion wherein the doctor crushes the baby's skull in the uterus with a forceps, then dismembers the baby and extracts it. A D&X is also a late-term abortion, but in this one, a doctor pulls the baby through the birth canal by its feet, then cuts a hole in its skull and sucks out its brains, afterward removing the corpse.

To *ban* D&X is cruel, claims Professor Susan Frelich Appleton of Washington University in St. Louis. "Would you want the Legislature deciding whether some other option is safer or better when that is a medical issue?"[60] she asks. Dr. Ann Davis of Columbia University is involved in pro-choice group Medical Students for Choice; she calls both D&E and D&X procedures "very safe."[61] Safe for whom? Certainly not the baby.

Professor Mary Mahowald of the University of Chicago feels that Americans' views on D&X are clouded by outside influences: "The media has totally exaggerated the incidence and evoked perceptions that informed and experienced clinicians would challenge."[62] A woman's right to choose takes precedence over all—even if that means crushing the skull of a living child and sucking its brains into a sink.

UNALIENABLE RIGHT TO DIE

Judeo-Christian tradition says that euthanasia is inherently wrong. God gives life, and God takes it away—it is not up to the individual to decide when he should die. In Jewish ritual, in fact, Jews are required to say a blessing when they hear of another's death: "Blessed is the True Judge," to show that the question of life and death is always in the hands of God.

For professors, however, human life is not divine, and therefore man should be able to take it when he sees fit. Without a higher authority to answer to, life belongs only to the one who possesses it, and he or she can decide to end it.

Sidney Wanzer of the Harvard Law School Health Services and Harvard Professor James Vorenberg teamed up to create a piece of model legislation that advocated permitting physician-aided suicide. "I've felt for a long time that anyone has a right to be released from life if life has become a trap," explains Vorenberg. And Wanzer says, "I would look at physician-assisted suicide as part of the spectrum of treatment that should be available to the patient." Wanzer and Vorenberg agree that euthanasia should be available to those who are not even terminally ill.[63]

One of the leading advocacy groups for euthanasia is the Hemlock Society. As of September 2003, the chairman of the society was Professor Paul Spiers of MIT and Boston University. Other members of the board included Professor Fred Richardson, who formerly taught at Ohio Wesleyan University, and Professor Alan Meisel of the University of Pittsburgh.[64]

Another of the major groups supporting euthanasia is Death With Dignity. As of September 2003, the board of directors included Professor David Orentlicher of Indiana University School of Law, Professor Charles

Baron of Boston College Law School, and Professor David J. Garrow of the Emory University School of Law. The board also included Professor David Mayo of the University of Minnesota, Professor Timothy Quill of the University of Rochester, Professor Margaret Battin of the University of Utah, Dr. Ivan Gendzel of the Stanford School of Medicine, Professor Samuel Klagsbrun of Albert Einstein College of Medicine, Professor Sharon Valente of the University of Southern California, Professor James Werth of the University of Akron, Professor Irvin Yalom of Stanford University, and Professor Charles McKhann, formerly of the Yale School of Medicine. Also Professor Alan Meisel, whom you may remember from the Hemlock Society.[65] Detecting a trend here?

Professor William Curan of Harvard, who earned the title of "Father of Health Law" and the praise of the *New York Times*, was a staunch backer of euthanasia.[66] Professor Lawrence Tribe, also of Harvard, is one of the main proponents of "a right to die with dignity."[67] Professor Robert Sedler of Wayne State University was one of the lawyers for Dr. Jack Kevorkian;[68] Kevorkian has been personally involved in at least sixty-nine euthanasias, only seventeen of which were patients with terminal illness.[69]

If public opinion were as solidly pro-euthanasia as the universities, America would be full of suicide clinics already.

LET THERE BE DARKNESS

Polls show that while students who just finished high school believe in an active God at a rate of 77 percent, once students reach the level of post-graduate education, that rate drops to 65 percent.[70] This may be due to youthful arrogance; more likely, it is due, at least in large part, to the anti-God bias of the universities.

Higher education undermines religion, not because knowledge inherently threatens religion, but because professors wish for religion to be undermined. As role models and teachers for their students, professors openly proclaim their atheism. They discard organized religion as foolishness, except for Islam, which they enshrine. They teach that science and religion must come into conflict, and that when they do, science is assuredly correct. The universities themselves discriminate against religious Christians and

Jews; their tolerance extends only to non-Judeo-Christian cultures. They promote abortion, and they advance the cause of euthanasia.

God is no longer welcome on campus. Unless He disguises himself as a professor.

8

BURNING THE FLAG

On the morning of September 11, 2001, I was with my father, driving my younger sister's carpool to school. My father and I had just dropped off the carpool when his cell-phone rang.

"Hello?"

"Do you see what's going on?" It was the mother of one of the girls in the carpool.

"What?"

"They just bombed the World Trade Centers."

"*Again?*"

"No, you don't understand. *The World Trade Centers are gone. They've collapsed.*"

"Oh my God . . ."

In the aftermath of September 11, Americans came together like no time since World War II. There were massive prayer meetings. Impromptu memorials went up. The people of the United States saw the enemy, and they gave President Bush their unconditional blessing in the War on Terror.

So naturally, when I got back to school, I expected some kind of campus-wide solidarity. I thought the professors would discuss the greatness of this nation. I thought that the students would hold vigils for the victims of the attacks and attend rallies for the war.

Boy, was I naïve.

Professors immediately blamed America for 9/11. It was caused by foreign policy failings. It was our wasteful consumption that led to Third World anger. It was our lack of respect for Islam. It was America's "cowboy style," our arrogance. It was slavery, oppression, brutality against American Indians and Africans.

America's reaction to the attacks was disgusting, the professors growled. Simplistic displays of patriotism only bred resentment against Arab Americans. The War on Terror was a misguided attempt to create an enemy where President Bush could find none. Continuing support of Israel made Arab countries even less likely to ally with us. America's "go it alone" attitude was unconscionable. Saddam Hussein was not an enemy, but a strong and principled leader.

Victor Davis Hanson, a conservative commentator and professor at Cal State Fresno, describes the professors at his university: "Maybe 90 percent of the faculty sympathizes with boutique anti-Americanism."[1] It's no exaggeration, and the pattern holds nationwide. There is no flag-waving. There is no mourning for American victims without using the word "but." There is no pride in being American on campus.

THREE CHEERS FOR OSAMA!

Many professors felt pangs of joy as they saw three thousand Americans dying in Washington DC, New York, and Pennsylvania. To hear these professors talk about 9/11, it sounds as if they must have danced around the room, or wept in honor of the occasion as they watched men and women jumping from hundred-story buildings to their deaths.

On September 11, Professor Richard Berthold of the University of New Mexico stepped up to the microphone to speak to his class about the events transpiring on the East Coast. "Anyone who bombs the Pentagon has my vote," he proclaimed.[2] Berthold's statement was the opening salvo for all the anti-American professors to begin speaking their minds. Scores of professors strode to lecterns across the country and blasted away.

In a philosophy/political science class I took, Professor Dan O'Neill, a self-described "bleeding-heart leftist,"[3] suggested that "the people who caused September 11 might fit into Locke's definition of justified resistance."[4] I looked around to see the class' reaction; most were nodding their heads in silent assent, like puppets manipulated by the strings of the professor.

The Middle East Studies Association, MESA, held a meeting in November 2001 in San Francisco. As the *New Republic*'s Franklin Foer relates, "[P]resenter after presenter referred to 'so-called terrorism' or 'terrorism in quotation marks.' In one typical panel, the University of Arkansas's Gwenn Okruhlik defended the fundamentalist opponents of the Saudi regime as slightly perturbed Marxists: 'They're calling for redistribution of wealth and social justice. They want rule of law.'"[5] Those Saudi extremists, always striving for social justice.

A University of North Carolina teach-in included William Blum, author of the book, *Rogue State: A Guide to the World's Only Superpower.* At the teach-in Blum blithely stated, "There are few if any nations in the world that have harbored more terrorists than the United States."[6] At the same teach-in, Professor Catherine Lutz of UNC stated, "If one [of the perpetrators of September 11] is Osama bin Laden, send the international police for him and pick up Henry Kissinger and Augusto Pinochet on the way home."[7]

The "America as terrorist" sentiment is extremely popular. "We have not shown that our actions differentiate us from those who attacked us," pontificates Georgetown University's Michael Hudson. For example, he states, "We ought to be reminded of our responsibility for Hiroshima and Nagasaki and understand that we're not so good."[8] Adam Goldstein, the former campus relations committee chairman for the University of Wisconsin at Madison, wrote a letter to the editor of the University of Wisconsin *Badger-Herald*: "before you preach at us about the evil terrorists, why don't you try getting your facts straight and face up to the reality that our leaders are war criminals just as much as people like Hitler, Stalin, and other monsters of the 20th century."[9]

University of Texas Professor Robert Jensen feels that September 11 "was no more despicable than the massive acts of terrorism . . . that the US government has committed during [his] lifetime."[10] "My anger on this day," he writes, "is directed . . . at those who have held power in the United States and have engineered attacks on civilians every bit as tragic."[11] I can't remember the last time United States Marines hijacked passenger aircraft and flew them into buildings full of working civilians, can you?

There is no living professor who can match the anti-American record of

Professor Noam Chomsky of MIT. In 2002, Chomsky's *9/11* became an international hit. Globally, people loved it because it ripped America as a terrorist state. Chomsky is always careful to say that nothing can justify the attacks of September 11 in his book; then he proceeds to justify them. "[T]he World Court was quite correct in condemning the United States as a terrorist state," states Chomsky. America is responsible for "massive terrorism . . . and it continues right to the present."[12] Next time, Professor Chomsky should volunteer to fly the suicide missions.

UCLA offered seminars for students based on the September 11 attacks. One of them was called "Terrorism and the Politics of Knowledge." The course description reads, "While the world rightfully stands united in its condemnation of the bombings of September 11, the American mainstream media has remained impervious to those critical voices which have also drawn attention to America's own record of imperialistic adventurism and the relation of the WTC bombings to American excesses in Iraq, Sudan, and the Middle East. This seminar asks fundamental questions about how we constitute "terrorism" and its agents . . . Should the continuing sanctions against Iraq also be considered a form of terrorism? . . . What is the relationship of the bin Ladens of this world to 'Western state terrorism'?"[13] Could this possibly get any more disgusting?

Yes. Professor Roxanne Dunbar-Ortiz of Cal State University at Hayward teaches a course entitled—no kidding—"The Sexuality of Terrorism." She says that military conflict is caused by masculine sexual aggression. "Armed conflict is not necessarily a hell for those who fight it, but a form of eroticism," she states. Her course also emphasizes Taliban suffering at the hands of the American aggressor. "In [President Bush's] administration are some of the most documented terrorists on the face of the earth."[14]

On July 1, 2001, students at the University of Texas opened up copies of the *Daily Texan* to find an anti-American diatribe by Professor Dana Cloud. "It seems very strange to pledge loyalty to a scrap of cloth representing a corrupt nation that imposes its will, both economic and military, around the world by force," she wrote. "I pledge allegiance to the people of Iraq, Palestine and Afghanistan, and to their struggles to survive and resist."[15] It's people like Cloud who need to be in buildings when terrorists hit them. It's only fair, since Cloud and her ilk so willingly support terrorist actions.

"IT'S ALL OUR FAULT"

If the reaction of the universities wasn't "America deserved it," it was "we must ask why." Professors sought to understand the terrorists, to deny that their actions were evil by justifying them. Usually, this meant blaming American foreign policy for "Muslim anger."

Professor William Beeman of Brown University begged students to look deep into the terrorists' souls and try and relate to them. "[I]nstead of rushing to judgment and seeking vengeance against those responsible for the terror . . . understand the more difficult question of 'why did they do it?'"[16] he told them. At UCLA, understanding comes in the form of seminars: Professor John Agnew teaches a seminar titled "Understanding the Taliban."[17] St. Lawrence University in New York offers a course called "Why Do 'They' Hate 'Us'?"[18]

"We need to understand their grievances to create political reforms to deal with these movements, rather than military actions," agrees Paul Lubeck of UC Santa Cruz.[19] Appease, appease, appease.

"I am skeptical that we have even learned anything from this attack," declared Professor Aamir Mufti of UCLA at a teach-in about September 11.[20] What America had failed to learn, of course, was that its foreign policy created hatred in the Arab street. Solution? Change our foreign policy.

Apparently being part of a death cult isn't a good enough reason for people to murder Americans. It must be something we did.

Students at Georgetown University were treated to a debate titled "Resolved: America's Policies and Past Actions Invited the Recent Attacks."[21] The terrorist acts were "the predictable result of American foreign policy," stated Bill Israel of University of Massachusetts.[22]

Tom Pettigrew of UC Santa Cruz said that US actions and policies were to blame for the September 11 attacks, especially the $2 billion a year the United States provides in foreign aid to Israel. Forget the fact that Israel is America's closest ally. Forget that America gives nearly $2 billion a year to Egypt, as well. Forget that the total amount of American money going to Muslim states dwarfs the amount going to Israel. "Around the world, the US is seen as a huge, aggressive superpower that has no rival," Pettigrew maintains.[23]

Professor Mazier Behrooz of San Francisco State University agrees with Pettigrew: "The [international] resentment comes from factors such as sanctions against Iraq, US support for unpopular regimes, US presence in the Middle East, and the Palestinian-Israeli conflict."[24] So does Professor Donald Quataert of Binghamton University in New York; he says the attacks were the reflection of twenty-five years of "failed US policies in the Middle East."[25]

Echoing the "America is arrogant" argument, UCLA Professor James Gelvin excused the terrorists for slaughtering three thousand Americans. "They hate us because of our freedom, arrogance, and hypocrisy," he declared to an audience of UC Irvine students.[26] Professor James McCormick of Iowa State University concurs, asking: "[I]s the US too arrogant and should it not use its power but [work] with other countries, or should it just use its military power?"[27] Let's think about this one. Okay, done thinking. I choose military power.

A UCLA seminar reflecting on September 11 was entitled "America as Hyperpower," and was taught by Professor Geoffrey Garrett. The course description reads: "People in the US, on the street and in Washington, believe that American power has been used benevolently, for the good of all the world. But reactions tend to be very different outside America, running the gamut from polite disgruntlement to mass protests, and finally to the tragic events of September 11."[28] Because we're so cruel to the Muslims, they want to come over here and kill our civilians. Never mind that the United States government has placed its soldiers in harm's way to save Muslims, as in Yugoslavia. It must be our fault.

Rutgers University Professor Barbara Foley: "Whatever [September 11's] proximate cause, its ultimate cause is the fascism of US foreign policy over the past many decades."[29] Fascism? Has this lady ever lived in a truly fascist country? If she had, she'd know that it is the foreign policy of the Arab world that is fascistic.

Professor Ayad Al-Qazzazz of Cal State University at Sacramento insists that Arabs do not hate Americans, only American foreign policy. And, he says, President Bush's policies will create more terrorists. "If Bush refuses to address the causes of terrorism, I can guarantee the problem is going to be with us for a very long time," Al-Qazzazz states. What are the causes of terrorism? "They just hate American foreign policy. From their perspective, it's based on dictation, interference and supporting corrupt regimes, particularly the Israelis." The solution, Al-Qazzazz suggests, is to "educate yourself and keep an open mind about Arab people and the situation in the Middle East."[30] To end terrorism, just keep an open mind about the terrorists and their agenda. Sounds like sympathy for the terrorists to me.

There must be something uniquely psychotic about the University of North Carolina. A panelist at a University of North Carolina teach-in suggested that the US government apologize to "the tortured and the impoverished and all the millions of other victims of American imperialism."[31] A University of North Carolina professor required students to read a book lauding the Koran, and gave assignments based on the readings. The book ignores Surahs four, five, and nine, all of which encourage Muslims to kill infidels.[32]

Professor Sarah Shields of UNC calls Osama bin Laden "the result of misguided US policies," and says that "new misguided US policies will create dozens, perhaps hundreds more bin Ladens."[33] No, idiots like Shields block the US government from targeting terrorists like bin Laden by whining about US foreign policy.

"DON'T BLAME ISLAM"

The professors' first reaction was to blame America. Their second was to defend Islam from all culpability. And they've done a fantastic job. While 39 percent of Americans say they have an unfavorable impression of Islam and 47 percent say they have a favorable impression, a whopping 61 percent of college students say they have a favorable impression of Islam, and only 24 percent are unfavorable toward Islam.[34]

"This is not about religion, it's about economics and politics," insists Professor Donald Quataert of Binghamton University.[35] Using the old intellectual formula, moral relativism, Professor Jamal A. Badawi stated to University of Connecticut students that: "Throughout history, people have done the most horrendous things in the name of religion," and therefore we shouldn't blame Islam.[36]

To justify their violent opposition to safety measures like racial profiling, professors cite "domestic terror." Abortion bombers and white male Christians like Timothy McVeigh pose as much danger to Americans as Islamic terrorists, professors maintain. The September 11 bombers were only fanatics, and there are American fanatics too, so let's not crack down on Muslims, okay?

Law professor Khaled Abou el Fadl says there is a double standard with domestic terrorists.[37] "There's a double standard when acts of terror are committed by people of Islamic background," nods Professor Jamal A. Badawi in a lecture to students from the University of Connecticut.[38] Not exactly: McVeigh and the Unabomber both got the death penalty.

"Judging Islam based on the acts of Osama bin Laden would be like condemning all Christians for the acts of Timothy McVeigh," asserts Professor Mark Berkson of Hamline College.[39] This is deliberately misleading the students. McVeigh was an avowed atheist, while bin Laden is a devoutly religious Muslim.

"It was most unfortunate that our president declared war on terrorism, which is a military tactic," says UC Santa Cruz Professor Alan Richards. "I would much prefer that he had declared war on fanaticism. That's what killed people in New York and Washington. . . . Muslims have no monopoly on fanaticism. We have it in the United States, too."[40] Not in the same numbers. Timothy McVeigh killed 168 people, and anti-abortion bombers have killed six people since 1993.[41] That's not much in comparison to the huge numbers of Americans killed around the world by Islamic terrorists. Muslim terrorists killed more than seventeen times as many Americans on September 11 alone, and they're clearly planning more murder and mayhem.

"Just as most [Americans] would regard bombers of abortion clinics to be outside the pale of Christianity, so the actions of these terrorists should not be accepted as representing Islam in any way," nods Professor Alan Godlas of the University of Georgia.[42] Except that a large percentage of Muslims do not see suicide bombings as contrary to Islam.

Professor Diana Eck of Harvard also goes the route of moral relativism.

"My sense is that in every religious tradition, we have fanatics," she states. "We have people who are willing to kill and destroy for their vision of justice and their vision of truth."[43] Then why don't Jews and Christians blow themselves up along with innocent civilians in the name of their religion, Professor?

"Islam did not cause the events of September 11. Islam is not inherently violent, and the vast majority of Muslims are peaceful people who had nothing to do with this," maintains Professor Paul Powers, lecturing at Lewis and Clark College.[44]

Professor David F. Forte of Cleveland State University characterizes the attacks as a perversion of Islam, and then tries to lump together Muslims and the West as dual victims of bin Laden. "[Osama bin Laden's] war is as much against Islam as it is against the West," Forte writes. "[I]n its modern form, bin Laden's kind of extremism has much more in common with Stalin, Hitler, and Mao than it does with Islamic tradition. Like those state terrorists, bin Laden is at war with his own people."[45] Not exactly. Most Arab nations support bin Laden, if not openly then secretly, and America has yet to see major Muslim imams condemning both the 9/11 attacks and suicide bombings in Israel. Islam isn't exactly non-violent.

THE WAR ON THE WAR ON TERROR

Nine days after the September 11 attacks, President Bush addressed Congress. "Every nation in every region now has a decision to make," Bush declared. "Either you are with us or you are with the terrorists. From this day forward, any nation that continues to harbor or support terrorism will be regarded by the United States as a hostile regime."[46] So began our War on Terror. America defeated the Taliban rapidly, built the Office of Homeland Security, shut down funding for terrorist groups, and looked to Iraq as a source of terror.

And the professors had a hissy fit.

The War on Terror is a nightmare, according to the universities. Fighting back is a sin. It will contribute to a "cycle of violence." Besides, if we kill our enemies, how are we any different than they are?

Soon intellectuals banded together to form the "Not In Our Name" group, opposing the war. They released a "Statement of Conscience," printed in the *New York Times*, which calls "the people of the US to resist the policies and overall political direction that have emerged since September 11, 2001, and which pose grave dangers to the people of the world." The petition calls "all Americans to RESIST the war and repression that has been loosed on the world by the Bush administration. It is unjust, immoral, and illegitimate." It compares the events of September 11 to American bombing of Baghdad during the Gulf War and events of the Vietnam War; it lauds Israeli soldiers refusing to monitor the West Bank and Gaza, as well as Vietnam Draft evaders. "What kind of world will this become if the US government has a blank check to drop commandos, assassins, and bombs wherever it wants?" the statement asks. The statement also pledges solidarity with those hurt by current US policies— the terrorists.

The revolting "Statement of Conscience" is signed by many professors: Professor Joel Beinin of Stanford University, Professor Paul Chevigny of New York University, Professor Noam Chomsky, Professor David Cole of Georgetown University, Professor Kimberly Crenshaw of Columbia University and UCLA, Professor Roxanne Dunbar-Ortiz of Cal State University at Hayward, Professor Leo Estrada of UCLA, Professor Sondra Hale of UCLA, Professor Christine Harrington of New York University, Professor David Harvey of CUNY, Professor Susannah Heschel of Dartmouth, Professor Fredric Jameson of Duke University, Professor Jesse Lemisch of CUNY, Professor Richard Lewontin of Harvard University, Professor Rosalind Pecheskey of Hunter College, Professor Peter Rachleff of Macalaster College, Professor Saskia Sassen of the University of Chicago, Professor Edward Said, Professor Juliet Schor of Boston College, Professor Ron Takaki of University of California at Berkeley, Professor Michael Taussig of Columbia University, Professor Immanuel Wallerstein of Yale University, and Professor Howard Zinn.[47] They must have been flattered to sign the document next to the likes of intellectual giants Mos Def, Eve Ensler, Gloria Steinem, Susan Sarandon, and Oliver Stone.

Those are just a few of the professors who believe the War on Terror is misguided. A Cal State University-Chico professor, apparently unrelated to Cynthia McKinney, stated that President Bush sought to "kill innocent people," "colonize" the Arab world, and grab "oil for the Bush family."[48] That's a lot of work for one war.

"I believe there is a fear that we will lose our moral compass," explained Monsignor Stuart Swetland, head of the Newman Center at the University of Illinois at Urbana-Champaign, during a panel discussion about September 11. "It has never been accepted as a just case to pursue a war for the sake of vengeance alone." Swetland called on the United States to "break the cycle of violence."[49]

The war is "morally, legally, and strategically unsound," agrees Professor Anne McClintock of the University of Wisconsin. "If the deaths in Afghanistan should be described as collateral damage," Professor Anne McClintock of the University of Wisconsin said, "then we should see those who died on Sept. 11 as collateral damage as well."[50] Not exactly. Civilians killed in Afghanistan are killed accidentally. Civilians killed on 9/11 were killed purposefully. But it's just like the professors to equate the two.

"Certainly Bush made some of the right noises after Sept. 11 by saying that this was not a war against Muslims," said Professor Michael Herb of Georgia State University. "But since then, by proposing to attack Iraq and by ignoring the Arab-Israeli conflict, he's created a polarization that is quite stark. I don't think most Americans realize that much of the rest of the world sympathizes with the Arabs rather than the US."[51] So because much of the world loves the Arabs, we should abandon our moral position?

It will lead to the ever-cited cycle of violence, professors say. "Our misguided 'war on terror' has made the US more vulnerable to future attacks," predicts Professor Behrooz Ghamari of GSU.[52] Professor Dane Archer of the UC Santa Cruz cautioned against "buying into the spiral of retaliation."[53] "Revenge is almost surely going to increase the probability of terrorist attacks happening again," said Tom Pettigrew of UC Santa Cruz.[54] Notice the use of moral equivalence here. If we target terrorists, they might get mad and retaliate—by killing civilians. Does that make September 11 a retaliatory attack as well?

Any confrontational political language is immediately attacked by the professors. The best example of this is the opposition to President Bush's "axis of evil" declaration, in which he stated that Iraq, Iran, and North Korea were all members of an axis of evil.

Bush's "axis of evil" phrase was "rhetorically a step in the wrong direction, and gave tremendous support to the opposition," Professor Michael Intriligator of UCLA spouted.[55] "The implication of this language is a sort of insight and ultimate judgment that most Christians are a little uncomfortable with," says Professor James Dunn of Wake Forest University in North Carolina. "When that sort of ultimate certainty comes along, you have the Crusades, the Inquisition, the Puritan hangings."[56] Look out—if we draw a clear moral line in the sand, all of a sudden we might be burning witches at the stake!

"The reward that Iran got for helping out was to be labeled a part of Bush's axis of evil," whimpered Professor Jalil Roshandel of UCLA, an Iranian.[57] Iran helping the United States? Where do they get this stuff?

Then there are the professors with a Vietnam hangover. In their eyes, every conflict America enters will become a "quagmire." "[The terrorists] want to suck Americans into another quagmire," declared UC Santa Cruz Professor Paul Lubeck about Afghanistan, a country America brought to its knees in a mere three weeks.[58] At UCLA, Professor Deborah Larson discussed how the Gulf of Tonkin Resolution from the Vietnam War might compare to President George W. Bush's current actions in the war on terrorism.[59] At Brown University, Professor James Blight teaches a course entitled "The Vietnam War and the War on Terrorism."[60]

Professor Michael Intriligator of UCLA said that the War on Terror would surely wreck the United States. "I don't think Osama bin Laden was capable of doing it. I think it was a part of a larger plot—getting us in a war with Afghanistan is a great way to destabilize the country. It's a big mistake. They've got the wrong guy."[61] It's Intriligator who made the big mistake—bin Laden did it, and America wiped the Taliban off the map.

Finally, there are those who hate Bush and will use any excuse to rip him. "The [Bush] administration is in disarray, on both foreign and domestic policy," states Professor Dan Franklin of Georgia State University. "[I]f September 11 hadn't happened, he'd be in a real crisis of power right now."[62]

Fellow University of Georgia Professor Loch Johnson is angry that Bush is keeping information under wraps, as any good president would do. "We as taxpayers and citizens have a right to know the details," he said.

"There's been far too much going on behind closed doors. I've never seen such a secretive administration."[63] Perhaps he forgets the Clinton administration, which handed military secrets to the Chinese, sold presidential pardons to the highest bidder, and gave terrorists free passes, among others.

"I'm not sure which is more frightening: the horror that engulfed New York City or the apocalyptic rhetoric emanating daily from the White House," states Professor Eric Foner of Columbia University.[64] I'm not sure which is more frightening: Foner's idiocy, or the fact that he actually teaches students.

THE PHANTOM BACKLASH

More prevalent than mourning for the victims of September 11 was an immediate outcry from the intellectuals to protect Arab Americans from attacks by the unwashed masses of American racists.

"We have to all stand up and say we are all Arab Americans. We cannot stand for this. The fanatics are a minority. Unless we start from that premise and stand together as a society, we're not going to go very far," urged Professor Edmund Burke of UC Santa Cruz.[65] "Whenever there's a war or conflict, there's a tendency to turn upon 'the other,'" warned Professor Daryl Thomas of Binghamton University.[66]

The backlash against Muslim Americans never materialized. As syndicated columnist Ann Coulter puts it, "The only backlash by actual Americans . . . consists of precisely one confirmed hate crime. Some nut in Arizona murdered a Sikh thinking he was a Muslim. Current hate crime tally: Muslims: 3,000 (and counting); White Guys: 1."[67]

But the professors wouldn't let go of the "Arabs as victims" idea. They manufactured widespread terror among Arab Americans out of thin air, as though there were brigades of renegade white men running about the countryside murdering Muslims.

"Trust is gone," weeps Professor Karen Jehn of the University of Pennsylvania. "People are looking at their [Arab or Muslim] colleagues and saying: 'We could be best friends, and you could be involved in some way.'"[68]

"[R]ecognize from the standpoint of American Muslims and Sikhs, how they themselves have felt suddenly afraid in what is by now their own country, the attack on mosques within hours of the tragedy here in New York and in Washington," mourns Professor Diana Eck of Harvard University. "We begin to see Muslim parents taking their kids home from school and Muslim schools like the New Horizon School in Los Angeles closing. Sikhs begin to be mistaken for Muslims, a Sikh gentleman hauled off a train in Providence because he looked a bit like Osama bin Laden."[69]

Arab-American Professor Ibrahim Syed of Bellarmine College in Kentucky feels insecure about his safety. "There is fear because we are singled out (as Muslims)," Syed says. "Anything can happen at anytime." He shouldn't feel too unsafe; there was only one documented hate crime against Arab Americans in the entire state of Kentucky from September 11, 2001 until September 11, 2002.[70]

THE ATTACK ON PATRIOTISM

On campus, anyone who dares to love America is criticized as a flag-waver: a patriotic racist buffoon who believes in American imperialism. Patriotism is seen as a hallmark of stupidity.

At Florida Gulf Coast University, staff members put stickers on their desks reading "Proud to be an American," in honor of the September 11 victims. Their supervisor ordered them to take down the stickers at the risk of being fired, because the stickers could offend international students. After intense media scrutiny, the president of the university rescinded the order and disciplined the supervisor.[71]

The University of California at Berkeley wanted to hold their one-year anniversary memorial for the September 11 attacks without God, flags, or patriotism. They were going to omit the "Star-Spangled Banner," "God Bless America," and red, white, and blue ribbons, in order not to offend foreign students. The president of the Berkeley Graduate Assembly and an admitted hater of the American flag and the US government, Jessica Quindel, evaluated the planned ceremony: "We are trying to stay away from supporting Bush. We don't want to isolate people on this campus who disagree with the reaction to Sept. 11. . . . The flag has become a symbol of US aggression towards other countries. It seems hostile."[72] Berkeley later decided to allow students to pass out red, white, and blue ribbons after national outrage at the original ceremony plan.

Professor Cecilia Elizabeth O'Leary doesn't attack patriotism head-on; rather, she attacks what she calls "conservative" patriotism. "Patriotism can be mistaken for conformity," she avers. "Today, a conservative patriotism led by those who display indiscriminate, biased, racial criteria has come to dominate." O'Leary mentions people like Attorney General John Ashcroft as practitioners of this "racist" patriotism.[73]

Professors Frank Lentricchia and Stanley Hauerwas of Duke University are composing an essay collection disparaging patriotism as simplistic. "We've had wall-to-wall, unreflective patriotism in this country—we're trying to crack through it," proudly states Lentricchia. In the collection, Hauerwas writes: "Do I forsake all forms of patriotism, failing to acknowledge that we as a people are better off because of the sacrifices that were made in World War II? To this I can only answer, 'Yes.'"[74]

Professor Vijay Prashad of Trinity College in Connecticut derides patriotism as "jingoism," a simplistic and superficial support for the United States. "It is as if the acts of terror from the 11th of September must be washed away or else exorcised with an excessive display of nationalistic jingoism," he sneers.[75] Professor Todd Eisenstadt of the University of New Hampshire went further, comparing nationalistic Americans with the September 11 suicide bombers. "A certain jingoism accompanies excessive devotion to any cause, inducing suicide hijackers to pilot commercial jets into our nation's very foundations," he wrote. "And blind patriotism surely fits that description."[76]

"Patriotism can be very exclusionary," cautions Professor Eric Foner of Columbia University. "There is a sense that you have to rally around the flag."[77] Oh, no, anything but that!

IN TATTERS

"[T]he United States claims it has its reasons [for the War on Terror]," states America-hating Professor Noam Chomsky. "And the Nazis had reasons for gassing the Jews."[78] Many professors agree—the modern-day United States and President George Bush are identical to World War II Germany and

Hitler. So we deserved what we got on September 11. And the men and women vaporized in airplanes, or pulverized into the ground after jumping from flaming skyscrapers, or plummeting thousands of feet into an empty field in Pennsylvania got what was coming to them.

Those who don't believe America had it coming still believe that America's foreign policy was to blame for the attacks. "The ultimate responsibility [for the attacks] lies with the rulers of this country, the capitalist ruling class of this country," says Professor Walter Daum of City College of New York.[79] If we would only capitulate to the desires of the Arab street, they would love us. Let Israel be overrun by its Arab enemies. Tell India to let the Pakistanis walk into New Delhi. Back the Chechens against the Russians. Then they won't ever attack us, they say.

The professors blame American foreign policy, but never Islam, which has only been perverted by extremists. And all religions have extremists, right?

When America finally does respond in a rational, justified way, the professors condemn *that*. For example, 166 intellectuals, including 66 Berkeley professors, signed a *New York Times* ad that rebuked President Bush for the War on Terror, which they called "unacceptable."[80] It's brutal, shocking, and obscene, they cry. If we attack the terrorists, are we no more than terrorists ourselves?

It's no shock that the professors think Americans are terrorists; they already think we are racists. They consistently hearken back to non-existent hate crimes against Arab Americans that other Americans supposedly executed. The race card has always been a favorite tactic of the professors, and it was played to the hilt with regard to September 11.

In the end, it all comes down to patriotism. Professors hate America, and Americans are patriots. So professors insult patriotism as simplistic. They compare patriots to terrorists.

The professors are the intellectual terrorists. May they reap what they sow.

9

TEACHING FOR SADDAM

Professors like terrorists, and they *love* Saddam Hussein and his Iraqi regime. Since Day One they have opposed any war on Iraq to rid the world of his murderous government or to assure the security of America and American interests. While they pay lip service to the idea that Saddam is a "bad guy," professors press students to take up the anti-war banner, bash George W. Bush, and rally to Saddam's defense.

"Put these [anti-war] signs in your yards when you get home. Get on the Internet," University of Kentucky professor Nikky Finney urged a group of student protesters. "Don't just preach to the choir."[1]

At an anti-war protest, Professor Judith Frank of Amherst College vowed to use her classroom as a podium to express her views: "We can teach, that we can do at least, even if we don't know how effective it will be. Because if you wait until you know it's effective, nothing will get done."[2]

At Citrus College, Professor Rosalyn Kahn told her students in Speech 106 to write anti-war letters to President Bush for extra credit. When several of her students asked if they could write pro-war letters, Kahn told them that pro-war letters would not be accepted.[3]

At Wayne State University, professors rushed to brainwash students to oppose war and President Bush. Two hundred and ten faculty members signed a petition calling for a university-wide day of reflection on the war. "The WSU academic community should undertake a variety of opportunities to raise questions about this war drive and its potential consequences," the petition stated. "We must, as scholars, teachers, and citizens, assume our responsibilities to engage in constructive discussion and action." Professor

Francis Shor, co-chair of the committee responsible for the petition, said that the goal was for students to become increasingly knowledgeable on the topic of war and more involved in the anti-war movement.[4]

Professor Brian J. Foley of the Widener University School of Law wrote that it was his duty to teach his students "as the bombs kill and maim innocent people in Baghdad. I will teach my class in the hope that the skills my students learn will make them better citizens, who will ask questions and demand answers before they let their country be led into war. It's the most patriotic protest I can make."[5]

Is indoctrinating students patriotic?

"NO BLOOD FOR OIL"

Many professors, believing that there was no moral justification for a war against the Saddam Hussein regime, attribute scurrilous motives to the Bush administration's desire for regime change in Iraq. As with anti-war protesters in general, the most common motive professors ascribed to the Bush administration was "war for oil." Since Iraq holds the second largest petroleum reserves in the world (after Saudi Arabia) and untapped fields of hydrocarbon fuel, and since America could *never* be attacking Iraq for moral or self-defense purposes, these professors argue that President Bush is putting American lives on the line to preserve lower gas prices. It makes no difference to the professors that America could save time, money, and lives by merely dealing with Saddam Hussein, or that America could just as easily attack Saudi Arabia. No, American capitalist imperialism is the root of this conflict.

"This could prove to be the biggest oil grab in modern history, providing hundreds of billions of dollars to US oil firms," writes Professor Michael T. Klare in the *Nation*. "But is oil worth spilling the blood of American soldiers and Iraqi civilians who get caught in the way?"[6] "[P]eople everywhere know that if not for oil, the United States would not be pursuing a war," nods Professor Robert Jensen of the University of Texas.[7]

Professor Hugh Gusterson concurs. He told an MIT student anti-war crowd of about six hundred that war in Iraq is "about oil, about Israel, about American global dominance." Apparently the fact that America does not want to occupy Iraq but instead wants to set up a democracy there in place of a brutal dictatorship does nothing to persuade Gusterson, who insulted the Bush administration's attempt to fight terrorism as a "squalid, inhumane vision."[8]

Winthrop Professor Stephen Smith echoed the despicable "blood for oil" canard at a rally in South Carolina. "Would the United States attack Iraq if its main export were broccoli?" Smith asked before hundreds of cheering students. "The only peace [Bush] wants is a piece of Iraqi oil, if not all of it."[9] Hilarious. If only Smith's take on foreign policy were half as clever as his oh-so-witty puns.

At a Karl Rove speech at the University of Utah, English professor Tom Huck carried a "No Blood for Oil" sign, and told reporters, "This is about imperialism. Iraq does not represent a threat to the United States. They've been trying to prove that for years."[10] If Iraq truly wanted to persuade the world of its non-violent intentions, refusing to provide proof of disarmament even in the face of war is a funny way of doing it.

In an inarticulate, rambling letter to the editor in the *Auburn Plainsman*, Auburn Professor Yehia El Mogahzy called on Americans to open their eyes to Bush administration perfidy: "Wake up America, spend some time watching the war game that we are about to play, over $300 billion dollars of our money is about to be spent on a war game. Against one person and thousands of children and innocent people. Blood for oil."[11] A "war game"? Since when is toppling a regime and freeing millions of Iraqis a war game? And exactly when did war on Iraq become a war against "thousands of children and innocent people"? The US military has taken amazing steps not to harm the civilian population, and the Bush administration has threatened to prosecute Iraqi officials who harm Iraqi civilians. This isn't blood for oil—it's blood to save civilians and preserve American security.

HEGEMONY

If it's not about oil, it's about hegemony, the professors declare. Any war in Iraq is just another American power-grab, an attempt to set up a US empire. In much the same way that the American intellectuals condemned

Ronald Reagan as an imperialist for his fight against communism, they now condemn George W. Bush for his fight against terrorism.

Howard University's Harold Scott Jr. observed that "This [war] is not international leadership; it is an imperialist position worthy of Napoleon—or the Roman Empire at the start of its decline."[12] Professor emeritus Richard Falk of Princeton University sees war in Iraq as an attempt by the US to "dominate the world," and portrays the War on Terror as a conflict between "two essentially fundamentalist visions," Islamic fundamentalism on one hand and economic liberalism on the other.[13] Maybe the professors are uncomfortable about exporting democracy, but the rest of us aren't.

Michael Hardt, a professor at Duke University, also casts aspersions on any American attempt to install democracy in Iraq. "The ultimate hubris of the US political leaders is their belief that they can not only force regime change and name new leaders for various countries, but also actually shape the global environment—an audacious extension of the old imperialist ideology of mission civilisatrice [a mission to civilize]. Regime change in Iraq is only the first step in an ambitious project to reconstruct the political order of the entire Middle East."[14] God forbid that the United States should try and improve the lives of millions in the Middle East! Let those brutal dictators alone, you fool imperialists!

For Professor Ronnie Lipschutz of the University of California at Santa Cruz, American policy has been power-oriented since September 11. His conclusion: "If the United States does succeed in going it alone—or substantially alone—it will mark the beginning of a new geopolitical era after hegemony, that of American Empire."[15] If the goal is American Empire, why would the goal of the Bush administration be to set up a democracy in Iraq rather than a friendly dictatorship? Paul Wolfowitz, assistant secretary of defense, stated on *Meet the Press* on April 6, 2003, that even if the Iraqi democracy elected an Islamist government, the US would not act against it. Is that empire?

Professor Jim Rego of Swarthmore College expressed his views on the war. "I think we've run out of people's butts to kick and that we essentially want to keep the butt-kicking going," he stated at a panel discussion.[16] How articulate. And how wrong. There are plenty of butts left to kick.

Predictably, the late Professor Edward Said, formerly of Columbia

University, jumped on the "hegemony" bandwagon. But when he got bored riding the bandwagon, he got down and pushed it. US policy in Iraq, he said, was a "grotesque show" based on desire for "oil and hegemony." The policy, he claimed, was forwarded by a "small cabal" of unelected government officials who sought to wage war on behalf of an "avenging Judeo-Christian god of war." This kind of US-led evil was nothing new according to Said, who then said that the US has a long history of "reducing whole peoples, countries and even continents to ruin by nothing short of holocaust."[17] An "avenging Judeo-Christian god of war"? We're not the ones yelling "Allahu akhbar" and flying civilian airliners into skyscrapers.

BUSH'S REVENGE

In their quest to portray George W. Bush as stupid and petty, many professors say that Bush wanted a war on Iraq to avenge Saddam Hussein's assassination attempt on Bush's father and to finish the job George H.W. Bush started in 1991. The very idea that President Bush would put Americans in harm's way and spend billions to rebuild Iraq because Hussein's agents planned to kill his father is absurd, to say the least. But absurdity has never stopped professors before.

"It's a simple story of father to son: 'I'm doing your work, Daddy. Are you proud of me?'" Professor Becky Thompson of Duke informed an antiwar protest mainly composed of Duke students. "To me it seems like [the United States] missed a really early lesson on how to play in the sandbox."[18]

Professor Alon Ben-Meir of New York University agrees with Thompson: "I can understand [Bush's] anger and the hatred he must feel toward the Iraqi leader, but I never imagined that a personal vendetta would influence his decision to wage war against Iraq. But I have come to believe it has, for why else did he mention the assassination attempt in the same breath as when he spoke about the need to get rid of Saddam? The recognition that Mr. Bush is acting from personal reasons, at least in part, explains the growing skepticism of our allies and many congressional leaders concerning his efforts in making the case for war."[19] But President Bush never explicitly mentioned the assassination attempt as a rationale for war. When facts are not at Ben-Meir's disposal, he makes them up as he goes along.

Ben-Meir only accuses Bush of putting American soldiers in danger for personal vengeance. Professor Walt Brasch of Bloomsburg University goes even further, accusing the president of trying to convince the American people that "as many as twenty-four million Iraqis need to be wiped off the earth in order to destroy Saddam Hussein and avenge the uncompleted work of George the Elder."[20] Twenty-four million Iraqis? The implication: Bush wants to nuke Iraq and kill every citizen of that country. By essentially accusing Bush of genocide, Brasch places him on a par with Stalin, Hitler, and Mao.

Some Bush-haters get even more twisted when they set foot on a college campus. When Representative Maxine Waters (D-Calif.) spoke to a crowd at the University of Southern California, she railed against Bush's Iraq policy: "Some of us, maybe foolishly, gave this president the authority to go after the terrorists. We didn't know he was going to go crazy with it. Now we know he has a problem with Saddam Hussein. We know that. We know that he's got to take revenge for what Saddam did to his daddy."[21]

WAG THE DOG?

If invading Iraq wasn't about oil, hegemony, or revenge, there must be yet another ulterior motive for the Bush administration. Harkening back to the Clinton administration, the professors came up with an idea. If Clinton could fire some missiles into Afghanistan to deflect attention from a burgeoning sex scandal, the Bush administration *must* be pursuing war with Iraq to deflect attention from domestic issues, specifically the economy.

Professor Stephen Walt, dean of the Kennedy School of Government at Harvard University, questioned the timing of President Bush's move toward war. "The timing is being driven primarily by domestic politics," he told the press. "Iraq is the next step in extending his wartime presidency," agreed Professor Constantine Spiliotes of Dartmouth College.[22] The economy hit a mild recession in the middle of 2000, but Bush made no mention of an attack on Iraq until after September 11, 2001. If war were a diversion from the economy, why wouldn't Bush have pushed for war, even before September 11?

Bush-hating Temple University government professor James Hilty acerbically stated: "Bush has almost no domestic legs so he has to be commander-in-chief. There's definitely a political agenda here. If the war on terrorism stops, people will wake up and see the effects of the humongous tax cut Bush engineered last year."[23] If Bush were so concerned about the public "discovering" his tax cuts, why would he try and ram through some more tax cuts, as he did before, during and after the war in Iraq? Bush is hardly embarrassed about his supply-side ideology, and for Hilty to suggest otherwise is ludicrous.

"It has been suggested that, whether the US ultimately goes to war with Iraq or not, the campaign against Saddam Hussein was meant to influence domestic American politics and the November 2002 election," suggests former University of California at San Diego professor Chalmers Johnson. "Faced with 2002 midterm elections, the leaders of the Republican party were desperate to deflect discussion from issues like the president's and vice-president's close ties to the corrupt Enron Corporation, the huge and growing federal budget deficit, tax cuts that massively favor the rich, a severe loss of civil liberties under attorney general Ashcroft."[24] H.L. Mencken said a person could never go wrong underestimating the intelligence of Americans. Looks like Johnson was taking him at his word—and then some. He thinks the public is too slobberingly stupid to see through a misdirection ploy by its president. Then again, is it possible that the public isn't nearly so stupid and there wasn't any misdirection?

Professor Brian J. Foley of the Widener University School of Law in Delaware feels that President Bush has deceived the nation. "Certainly, Bush has much to distract us from," Foley writes, citing economic policy and the War on Terror as Bush "failings." Then Foley goes to the limit, accusing Bush of an "enormous abuse of presidential power," "[endangering] our nation's security" with his "war talk."[25] For a man who believes that war talk can do so much to endanger Americans, does Foley realize the value his pacifism could hold for enemies of America?

"REGIME CHANGE" IN AMERICA

On April 2, 2003, Democratic presidential nomination candidate John F. Kerry stated to a crowd of Democrats in New Hampshire: "What we need now is not just a regime change in Saddam Hussein and Iraq, but we need a regime change in the United States."[26] Naturally, the comment triggered a firestorm of protest from the Right. Tom DeLay (R-Texas), the House majority leader, called the remark "desperate." Denny Hastert, House speaker, added that the statement was "not what we need at this time."[27] Of course, professors beat Kerry to the punch a long time ago; they've been counseling American "regime change" since the 2000 election. With the war on Iraq, criticism of the Bush administration has kicked into even higher gear.

Professor Francis A. Boyle of the University of Illinois at Urbana-Champaign proposes bringing an article of impeachment against the Bush administration. "[W]e don't want a police state in the name of an oil empire," he calmly explains.[28] I hope that Boyle is using the royal "we," because not many people stand behind him in his desire to let terrorists and murderers roam free.

Ayida Mthembu, associate dean of Counseling and Support Services at MIT, told an ecstatic anti-war crowd of students, faculty, staff and administrators: "With this war, we are witnessing the effects of a coup d'etat. But by coming out here, we can be renewed. Bush and his White House Negroes want us to be confused and passive and afraid. They want us to watch TV and doubt our common sense. But common sense says, war is horrible. Being here says, we love the world enough to struggle together to make America the place we want it to be."[29] Aside from the blatant racism of the statement (calling Condeleezza Rice and Colin Powell house negroes hardly gains points for good taste), it is incredibly naïve. If America could live in a world without war, we would surely do so. But sometimes war is necessary to ensure the security of our citizens and the growth of freedom around the world—something a vast number of professors either do not understand or appreciate.

But according to Professor Gene Burns of the University of Montana, the Bush administration is hardly a force for freedom. In fact, Bush and his cronies are fascists. "Don't ever think America is free from tyranny," he warned an anti-war crowd composed mainly of students. "Let your voices be heard."[30]

Professor Wythe Holt Jr. of the University of Alabama School of Law fully agrees. He stated that the strongest reason against going to war is that American freedom would be "trampled" by the war itself. "We not only oppose war, but we oppose shutting us down," Holt said. "You have to be brave in order to say these things today."[31]

Drake University law professor Sally Frank was even more flamboyant in her protests for "free speech": she ripped the Bill of Rights out of a copy of the US Constitution and threw it into a toilet to assert that civil liberties, immigrant rights, health care, and jobs are being "flushed down the toilet." "That's what (Attorney General John) Ashcroft and Bush have done to our civil liberties," Frank said.[32]

These professors are extremely loud for people whose freedom of speech is supposedly being silenced. The Ashcroft/Bush/Rumsfeld Gestapo must have missed them this time around.

"THE CASE HASN'T BEEN MADE"

Ever since President Bush began talking about war in Iraq, professors have complained about the Bush administration's failure to make a "convincing case" for going to war. Even after Secretary of State Colin Powell, the Left's favorite cabinet member, made his highly-regarded speech at the United Nations on February 5, 2003, peaceniks whined that they needed more evidence.

"We believe that the false evidence that the US president has peddled regarding Iraq's imminent threat to the US, together with the US government and media's manipulation of the American public's grief over last year's 9/11 tragedy, mask a deceptive and wholly undemocratic campaign to coerce the American people and the peoples of the world into accepting the unlawful and unwarranted US invasion of other countries." This statement was signed by forty Filipino US university educators, including professors, lecturers, or other staff members from the University of California at San Diego, the University of Michigan, the University of Oregon, the University of California at Riverside, the University of California at Irvine, the University of Texas at Austin, San Jose State University, the University of Hawaii at Manoa, Sonoma State University, the University of California at Berkeley, the University of Massachusetts, the University of California at

Santa Cruz, San Francisco State University, the University of Denver, Old Dominion University, the University of Connecticut at Storrs, New York University, Bloomfield College, the University of Miami, City College of San Francisco, DePaul University, and the University of Washington.[33] Strong language, but completely unfounded. Invasion of Iraq was indeed warranted, and the Bush administration's push for war was not "wholly undemocratic"—at the beginning of the war, a vast majority of the country supported war in Iraq, even without the approval of the United Nations.

Bruce Ackerman, professor of law and political science at Yale University, held the Bush administration to a higher standard than the United Nations. "To justify an invasion," he wrote, "it is not enough for the United States to insist that it already has enough evidence of a material breach" of UN resolutions. Ackerman did not give a concrete standard of justification for the Bush administration to reach.[34] It must be his opinion.

Finally, the Bush administration decided to risk its intelligence sources and let Secretary of State Colin Powell present evidence of Iraqi non-compliance on February 5, 2003. For professors, that wasn't good enough. "[I]t was striking how weak was the case Powell offered; the charts, maps and phone intercepts were more impressive than the underlying evidence or conclusions. Even if his claims were all true, nothing he said makes the case for war," sneered Professor Robert Jensen of the University of Texas.[35] Professor As'ad Abukhalil of California State University at Stanislaus concurred, snorting that despite Powell's presentation, "the claims of terrorism links remain hollow."[36] Wrong.

Even the anti-war *New York Times* acknowledged the power of Powell's presentation, writing: "Secretary of State Colin Powell presented the United Nations and a global television audience yesterday with the most powerful case to date that Saddam Hussein stands in defiance of Security Council resolutions and has no intention of revealing or surrendering whatever unconventional weapons he may have."[37]

DEFYING INTERNATIONAL LAW

The professorial elite, devoid of respect for traditional morals and values, find their moral guidance in international law. And if the Bush administration transgressed international law by attacking Iraq, they feel it is just as wrong and evil as Saddam Hussein.

While the US pursued diplomacy in the United Nations, professors proudly spoke of their Neville Chamberlain-esque foreign policy ideals. Professor John E. Lillich of Purdue University encouraged President Bush to stop talking about Saddam's bad qualities, for the sake of negotiations. "Even if a guy is as bad as Hitler, he's a human being, and you have to do negotiations with human beings," Lillich stated, somehow forgetting that negotiation with Hitler didn't end in triumph. "What the president may not realize is that he can be a bigger winner by negotiating a settlement than by winning a war. If he could settle this without a war, he'd win the Nobel Peace Prize."[38] Wow, a Nobel Peace Prize? Like that great president Jimmy Carter? Now *there's* an achievement.

After the US withdrew its request for a second UN resolution authorizing use of force in Iraq because of French and Russian threats to veto the resolution, Professor Balakrishnan Rajagopal of MIT hysterically declared, "I'm a lawyer, and I am here to tell you, the US has just trashed international law and our own laws."[39] Professor Marjorie Cohn of the Thomas Jefferson Law School in San Diego similarly stated, "There is no legal justification for a preemptive attack on Iraq."[40] On legal grounds, perhaps they are right. On moral grounds, they are wrong to the most extreme degree. There could not be a more moral goal than freeing the people of Iraq from brutal tyranny, democratizing the region, and ensuring American security.

Of course, none of these goals matter to anti-war professors. Professor Scott Cawelti of the University of Northern Iowa bashed the Bush Iraq policy and appealed to European sensibilities. "[O]ur go-it-alone policy has created worldwide disdain, if not contempt," he penned. "Europeans, who know real war far better than Americans, see our president's insistence on making war to ensure peace as an impossible trap. They see our president as a cowboy superhero, obsessed with fighting evil."[41] Europeans know real war, all right. Every time they have one, the US has to come save them. We *are* cowboy superheroes—if we weren't, the whole continent would be speaking German right now.

With the Bush administration embarking on a new strategy of preemptive warfare against our enemies, including Iraq, professors are going out of their gourds. "It's not a just war!" they continue to scream, in classic Jimmy Carter fashion.

"[W]e side with the principled opponents of war against Iraq, relying not only on international law, including the UN Charter, but also on the moral and religious guidelines contained in the just war doctrine," declared Professor Richard Falk of Princeton University, along with his *CounterPunch* co-author, David Krieger.[42]

NYU law professor Philip Alston asserted to the Associated Press that ignoring the UN, "opens the door for every country to take the law into its own hands and launch preemptive military strikes without any universally binding restraints."[43] "It is utterly irresponsible," agrees Professor Srinivas Aravamudan of Duke University. "We are embarking on a new imperial era of carnage."[44] September 11 is carnage. Gassing Kurds and murdering Shi'ites is carnage. Removing Saddam Hussein from power is justice.

The case can be made that the United States did work in accordance with international law, but the truth is that it really doesn't matter. We have a higher moral obligation than resolutions from the UN, and if France insists on blocking resolutions, we have the duty to ignore the UN.

USEFUL IDIOTS AND AMERICA-HATERS

Some professors cross the line between free speech and useful idiocy or flat-out treachery. While each professor has the right to speak out under the First Amendment, some provide comfort and aid to the enemies of the United States.

Professors advocated the "human shield" movement, which sent hundreds of Western civilians to protect Saddam's assets from the American military. "A number of groups have been choosing to do this," smiled Joseph Elder, a professor of sociology at the University of Wisconsin. "They call themselves witnesses for peace or witnesses of suffering . . . I think the fact groups are doing this is a reflection of the fact there are a lot of Americans who are very opposed to any action of war on the part of the [United States]," Elder said. According to Elder, the scale of the human shield movement dwarfs any comparable movement in the past.[45]

Former Harvard professor Helen Caldicott also got in on the act, imploring Pope John Paul II to go to Baghdad and act as a human shield. Since the Bush administration has "no reservations about slaughtering up to 500,000 innocents in Iraq, there is one person whose life they absolutely will not risk. That person is Pope John Paul II," she wrote in a letter to the pontiff, whom she also called "the ultimate human shield."[46]

When not fighting for the human shield movement, professors were busy traveling to Baghdad to act as Saddam's propaganda patsies.

In November 2002, Professor Bill Quigley of the Loyola University New Orleans School of Law traveled to Iraq as a member of the Iraq Peace Team, a project of Voices in the Wilderness, a joint US/UK program to protest economic sanctions against Iraq. In a series of obviously contrived events, Quigley was given the impression that the Iraqis living under Saddam's brutality wanted to prevent his removal. Quigley was approached by an Iraqi soldier, who welcomed him to Iraq, and then said: "America, Yes!" followed by a thumbs-down and "Bush, no!" He was approached by a man who gave him a picture of his eight-month-old daughter, with a message on the back of the picture reading: "Dear American administration mems. I am Sala Adil. I am 8 months. I am an Iraqi. I would be very grateful if you let me live peacefully away of bombing and sanctions like all the children of the world. Sala." Like the useful idiot he most certainly is, Quigley bought into the whole act, observing, "I am using my freedom to try and stop our government from paying for regime change with the lives of Iraqi sons and daughters, especially the lives of innocent civilians like little Sala."[47]

On January 12, 2003, a thirty-five-member delegation mainly comprised of academics touched down in Baghdad for a "fact-finding" tour. The tour was sponsored by the University of Baghdad, a tool of Saddam.

Dr. James E. Jennings, a former Illinois University professor, led the delegation, which visited Iraqi schools, hospitals, and other sites in order to promote peace. "Not in Hanoi or Panama or Baghdad last time, or anywhere else for that matter, has there been this many people to a city that probably will be bombed to bits saying, 'Don't do it. It doesn't make sense,'" the noble professor told the *Washington Post*. Fellow delegate and Le Moyne College professor Keith Watenpaugh added, "We're going to go back to our schools and our communities to tell them what's happening here. People in America need to see people who think it's okay to oppose this war."[48]

It is difficult to tell whether all the professors on the tour realized how Saddam would manipulate their tour and use it for anti-American propaganda. But Professor Michael Rooke-Ley of the University of Oregon School of Law certainly did. "Yes, our visit was carefully choreographed by the Iraqis, and initially we saw only what they wanted us to see. . . . Did we risk being used as propaganda tools for the Iraqi government? Of course— just as others have served the Bush administration's public relations efforts here at home," Rooke-Ley wrote.[49] Except that in America, you have the choice of what to say and what to see, and in Iraq, you don't.

While on Saddam Hussein's home field, Rooke-Ley made a speech in which he lambasted the Bush administration's War on Terror, which he said "is free-wheeling and unrestrained and will set us on a dangerous path of retaliation and mass destruction such as the world has never seen." At the end of the trip, the delegation had the "extra-ordinary good fortune to meet with Iraq's foreign minister, Naji Sabri, an impressive articulate intellectual whose analysis of the political situation merits our attention." When Sabri suggested that the reason the United States was considering war in Iraq was "number one, Iraq's traditional support for the Palestinians and, two, oil," Professor Rooke-Ley nodded his agreement.[50]

Professors also gave aid and comfort to Saddam by providing him with excuses and moral equivocation to commit war crimes or kill Americans.

"We sentenced Nazi leaders to death for waging a war of aggression," states International Law Professor Francis A. Boyle of the University of Illinois at Urbana-Champaign. "It's very clear," he adds, "if you read all the press reports, they are going to devastate Baghdad, a metropolitan area of 5 million people. The Nuremberg Charter clearly says the wanton devastation of a city is a Nuremberg war crime."[51] By morally equating George Bush with Adolf Hitler, Boyle surely belongs in the category "America-hater."

Professor Mark Lance of Georgetown University, said that US policy toward Iraq was "hypocrisy," since America has committed the same crimes on a larger scale than Saddam Hussein. "The United States," Lance argued, "has done more than any country historically to develop and spread technology of mass destruction . . . including nuclear [technology], biotechnology and nerve gas . . . including to Saddam long after his crimes had become known."[52]

Erwin Chemerinsky, a professor of law at the University of Southern California, wrote a piece for the *Los Angeles Times* in which he argued that the United States was hypocritical in protesting Iraq's execution of prisoners of war, since America was detaining terrorists at Guantanamo Bay. "The United States cannot expect other nations to treat our prisoners in accord with international law if we ignore it," Chemerinsky wrote. He did not even bother to refute the claim that Iraq would be justified in violating international law regarding POWs.[53] When radio talk show host Hugh Hewitt asked Chemerinsky if he realized that Iraq could use pieces like his to excuse their war crimes, Chemerinsky protested that Hewitt was questioning his loyalty. Chemerinsky refused to condemn Jane Fonda's Hanoi trip to North Vietnam during the Vietnam War which resulted in the torture of US prisoners of war. Chemerinsky also refused to condemn a sign at a rally that read, "We Support Our Troops When They Shoot Their Officers."[54]

Professor Michael Ballou of Santa Rosa Junior College urged his students to think about assassinating President Bush. In his Summer 2003 course, he assigned his students the task of composing an e-mail message utilizing the phrase "kill the president." The goal of the assignment, Ballou said, was "to bring our underlying fear of government into the open." When one of his students actually sent the e-mail to Rep. Mike Thompson (D-California) and another told his parents, both the FBI and Secret Service showed up at the university. Ballou took shield behind the First Amendment, claiming that the words "kill the president" could be interpreted to mean someone other than President Bush.

Amazingly, Santa Rosa Junior College refused to fire Ballou for "unprofessional speech." In fact, Janet McCulloch, incoming president of the college's All Faculty Association, said that Ballou "has the right to say what he wants in the classroom," although that liberty "doesn't go to the point of asking students to jeopardize their futures."[55] Ballou defended himself this way: "I'm not going to take any flak from the 60 percent of the American people who don't vote anyway. For them the President and the Presidency are already dead."[56] Any more questions about which president he was talking about?

The most blatant case of treachery emanated from Columbia

University, where Assistant Professor Nicholas De Genova told a crowd of students at a teach-in that "The only true heroes are those who find ways to help defeat the US military," and stated that he "personally would like to see a million Mogadishus." At Mogadishu, eighteen US servicemen were killed; De Genova is calling for the deaths of eighteen million Americans. "If we really believe that this war is criminal," De Genova explained, "then we have to believe in the victory of the Iraqi people and the defeat of the US war machine."[57] De Genova deserves a one-way ticket out of this country he so despises.

"HOW DARE YOU CALL US UNPATRIOTIC?"

After all is said and done, many of these professors are just plain unpatriotic. It's one thing to protest a war, but to demonize the president of the United States as another Hitler, to tell students to think about assassinating the president, to travel to enemy soil and criticize our government, to pray for the deaths of US soldiers, is un-American.

But just try saying that to professors' faces. They go off the deep end if anyone so much as suggests that they dislike America, calling anyone who says so McCarthyistic, a witch hunter, a fascist, and a totalitarian to boot.

"To brand anti-war activism as anti-American is offensive and dangerously anti-democratic. Such attempts to silence dissent also do a profound disservice to our nation," complains Professor Peter Cannavo of Hamilton College. "If it is 'anti-American' to raise these issues, then someone had better save our country from its 'friends.'"[58] "War time seems to make people feel that they can use patriotism as a stick," mourns Professor Darlene Boroviak of Wheaton College. "It's unfair to criticize people as being unpatriotic. They have the right to express different viewpoints."[59]

"[It] is really a contradiction in saying that this is a war to liberate another country but people who are opposed at home are supposed to stifle their criticism," concurs Professor Gerald Turkey of the University of Delaware.[60] Criticism is most definitely not being stifled. Those of us who disagree with the anti-war activists have the same right of free speech as peaceniks do, and we can use it to criticize the peaceniks if we want.

"Patriotism is not a neutral term," states Professor Robert Jensen of the

University of Texas at Austin. "It comes with a history, and it's been used as a weapon. I can always tell when somebody has exhausted his own thought process, because that's when they call me unpatriotic and un-American."[61] Actually, the thought process doesn't have to be exhausted before calling Professor Jensen unpatriotic. He is the same man who proclaimed weeks after September 11 that the terrorist attacks on the World Trade Center and Pentagon were "no more despicable than the massive acts of terrorism . . . that the US government has committed during my lifetime."[62]

Professor Sheila Peters of Fisk University states, "I don't think people who are antiwar are less patriotic than those who are pro-war. I just think they deal with issues facing their country in different ways."[63]

Those few honest people in the anti-war movement know better. Professor Nicholas De Genova, the same professor who hoped for "a million Mogadishus," admitted in a rare moment of truth: "Peace is not patriotic. Peace is subversive, because peace anticipates a very different world than the one in which we live—a world where the US would have no place."[64] Straight from the horse's . . . mouth.

IT AIN'T OVER 'TIL THE PROFESSOR PROTESTS . . .

After major military operations in Iraq were over, the UCLA Academic Senate, composed of thirty-two hundred professors (only a few of whom actually vote—quorum is two hundred eligible voters present at some time during the meeting), decided to do something about the war. They condemned it. After Iraqis had cheered the downfall of Saddam Hussein. After mass graves had been uncovered. After children had been released from Hussein's prisons.

None of it mattered. A resolution was brought before the Academic Senate condemning President Bush for his "preventative war," opposing the establishment of an American "protectorate" in Iraq, affirming the Academic Senate's "commitment to addressing international conflicts through the rule of law and the United Nations," and calling for post-war Iraq to be placed under UN jurisdiction.

Exactly 196 professors voted. The vote was surprisingly close. The measure passed, 180-7. Nine professors abstained.

It was not the place of the Academic Senate to deal with this issue. The purpose of the Academic Senate is to deal with matters in the curriculum, matters of standards and tenure. But the professors thought differently.

I interviewed Professor Karoly Holczer, a member of the senate who voted in favor of the resolution. Holczer stated that "the few academic senates in the country are the *only organizations* who should take a stand on human morals. It's more than our right, it's our obligation." But isn't this a political statement? I asked. Isn't this outside the purview of the Senate? "This is not a political statement," he answered. "It's a statement about those kinds of human values that every single person believes in . . . This is an example that I really hope every successful teacher shows for his students."

Holczer also stated that a US protectorate might be worse than a Saddam Hussein regime. "It's not a great idea to see a national library burning, a national museum destroyed," he remarked. But now that the US had toppled Saddam, Holczer suggested that we turn over control of Iraq to the UN, suggesting that the UN would be fairer than the United States.

Then I asked Professor Holczer the key question: Do his opinion, and the opinions of his colleagues, enter the classroom? "I really hope so," he replied.

The brainwashing continues. Each day, students hear about how the US has entered a quagmire, is bungling the reconstruction, is cheating the Iraqi people. The war is over, but not for the professors.

A DEFEAT FOR THE PROFESSORS?

Professors have had quite an impact on student opinions when it comes to the war in Iraq. At New York University, twelve hundred students ditched class in a show of anti-war solidarity. At University of California at Berkeley, fifteen hundred students rallied at Sproul Plaza as the war in Iraq began and demanded that Baghdad University be declared a "sister school." Both NYU and Berkeley were awarded a slot in *Mother Jones*' "Top 10 Activist Campuses."[65]

As the mass media has noted, much of the anti-war movement gained its strength from college students, hundreds of thousands of whom have participated in protests around America. But the conversion wasn't complete. At universities like Yale and Berkeley, professors state that vast majorities of the faculty oppose war in Iraq. Yet students polled by the Yale Daily News were split right down the middle about the war. Professors haven't gained a complete success, and they're fighting mad about it.

"We used to like to offend people," Professor Martha Saxton of Amherst College told the *New York Times*, who is disappointed with the lack of student anti-war activism. "We loved being bad, in the sense that we were making a statement. Why is there no joy now?" Professors like Saxton feel that students are missing out on the college experience if they refuse to protest, 1960s style.

At Amherst, the Progressive Students Association requested that the student government ask professors to discuss war in Iraq for fifteen minutes in class. The student government refused. In the Amherst dining hall, forty professors paraded in to protest the war, where they were greeted by a strong negative reaction from the students, one of whom came to physical blows with a professor.

Students at the University of Wisconsin at Madison are also disappointing their professors. "In Madison, teach-ins were as common as bratwurst," lamented Professor Austin Sarat of UW. "There was a certain nobility in being gassed. Now you don't get gassed. You walk into a dining hall and hand out information pamphlets." Apparently provoking the police into throwing tear gas is a badge of honor for these faculty members.

"My job is not to get my students to agree with me," insists Professor Barry O'Connell of Amherst. But "there is a second when I hear them, and my heart just falls."[66]

There is still hope for American youth. Just keep them as far as possible from their professors.

10

"ZIONIST PIGS"

During August 2001, my family and I traveled to Israel for the first time. We went with a tour group, and we journeyed across virtually the entire country, from the scenic and lush greenery of the Shomron to the barren desert of the Negev. The Bible came alive; these were real places. We saw the spot where David slew Goliath. We prayed near the Temple Mount, the holiest site in Judaism, and we explored the tunnels dug next to the massive surrounding wall, a section of which is known as the Western Wall.

We stopped in Efrat, an American suburb planted in the disputed territories; it looked like Beverly Hills transported to Israel. We went to the beautiful city of Haifa in the North. We visited the gigantic Ramon Crater in the South. We saw dingy Arab villages surrounding cosmopolitan Jewish outposts—the difference was marked and stark.

There were places we could not go. We could not go to Hebron, the second holiest site in Judaism, to visit the tomb of the Patriarchs. Many of the roads were surrounded by cement barriers to prevent Palestinian snipers from shooting at tourists. We walked through East Jerusalem surrounded by Israeli armed guards so that we would not be killed by Arabs living in that part of the Old City.

And we were at the Knesset in Jerusalem when the tour guide got a phone call. A Palestinian terrorist had blown himself up at Sbarro's pizza restaurant in Jerusalem. My family and I were to have been on that corner two hours later that day. Others weren't so lucky. Fifteen people were slaughtered, and another 132 were wounded, many seriously—bolts in their bodies, nails in their brains, limbs blown off. A Los Angeles teacher, Shoshana

Greenbaum, and her unborn child were murdered that day—the teacher was an only child, the only hope for her parents to have grandchildren.

The rest of the trip was solemn. Everyone was on edge. My father and I were constantly on the lookout for Arab-looking men carrying bags or wearing heavy coats. Every time we saw an Israeli Defense Force soldier carrying a gun, we sighed with relief. When we went to eat at Burger King on Ben-Yehuda Street, we sat on the top level of the restaurant, just in case a bomber detonated on the bottom level.

Being in such close contact with a country under siege made me acutely aware of the one-sided anti-Israel sentiment among the college professors when I returned. Since September 11, anti-Semitism on campus has spun out of control. Criticizing Israel does not make someone anti-Semitic. Criticizing Israel's very existence and advocating measures that will lead to its destruction—criticizing Zionism—does make someone anti-Semitic. Singling out Israel, holding Israel to a higher standard, forcing Israel to act with no regard for self-preservation, is anti-Semitic. As Martin Luther King so succinctly stated to an audience at Harvard University in 1968, "When people criticize Zionists, they mean Jews. You are talking anti-Semitism."[1]

Anti-Semitism on campus is getting so bad that on September 17, 2002, Harvard President Lawrence Summers addressed students at a morning prayer service at the Memorial Church. "I speak with you today not as president of the university but as a concerned member of our community about something I never thought I would become seriously worried about—the issue of anti-Semitism," Summers declared. He continued,

Indeed, I was struck during my years in the Clinton administration that the existence of an economic leadership team . . . that was very Jewish passed without comment or notice. Without thinking about it much, I attributed all this to progress—to an ascendancy of enlightenment and tolerance. A view that prejudice is increasingly put aside. A view that while the politics of the Middle East was enormously complex, and contentious, the question of the right of a Jewish state to exist had been settled in the affirmative by the world community.

But today, I am less complacent. Less complacent and comfortable because there is disturbing evidence of an upturn in anti-Semitism globally, and also because of some developments closer to home. . . . Of course academic communities should be and always will be places that allow any viewpoint to be expressed. And certainly there is much to be debated about the Middle East and much in Israel's foreign and defense policy that can be and should be vigorously challenged.

But where anti-Semitism and views that are profoundly anti-Israeli have traditionally been the primary preserve of poorly educated right-wing populists, profoundly anti-Israel views are increasingly finding support in progressive intellectual communities. Serious and thoughtful people are advocating and taking actions that are anti-Semitic in their effect if not their intent.[2]

"OCCUPATION"

Professors believe that all problems in the Middle East started with the Jews. Many believe that Israel is an illegitimate state to begin with, despite a consistent Jewish presence on the land for three thousand years and the complete lack of any government called "Palestinian." But the biggest problem is the "occupied territories," land won by Israel in the 1967 Six Day War, in which Israel was attacked by Egypt, Jordan, and Syria.

Professor M. Shahid Alam of Northeastern University explains the false professorial version of Israeli history: "Increasingly, the world outside the United States understands that Israel is not a 'normal' country. . . . Israel emerged in 1948—through the conquest and ethnic cleansing of 800,000 Palestinians. Yet this was not enough. . . . In 1967 this shortfall was corrected when Israel, after defeating Egypt, Syria and Jordan, occupied the West Bank and Gaza. Another, smaller campaign of ethnic cleansing was introduced into this second round of conquests."[3] Ethnic cleansing? Where were the mass graves, the gas chambers? And why do hard facts say otherwise—that 539,000 Arabs left,[4] that Arab leaders told Arabs within Israel to leave,[5] and that 68 percent of those Arabs never even saw an Israeli soldier?[6]

But the myth of the "brutal occupation" remains, even despite the fact that since the Oslo Accords, Palestinians in the West Bank and Gaza have lived primarily under the rule of Yasser Arafat and his Palestinian Authority.

While discussing Frederick Douglass's *Narrative of the Life of Frederick Douglass*, one UCLA English professor compared Israel's possession of the West Bank to the enslavement of blacks during eighteenth and nineteenth century America.[7] Maybe I missed it, but I don't see Palestinians toiling in cotton fields, being whipped by their Israeli masters. The comparison is a true insult to the travails of the black slaves.

"There are 149 substantive articles of the Fourth Geneva Convention that protect the rights of every one of these Palestinians living in occupied Palestine. The Israeli government is currently violating, and has since 1967 been violating, almost each and every one of these," sniffs Professor Francis Boyle of the University of Illinois School of Law.[8]

"Israel looks increasingly like South Africa to the rest of the world," sneered Professor Fouad M. Moughrabi of the University of Tennessee at Chattanooga.[9] "Did the Black South Africans immigrate or did they leave South Africa because they suffered a great deal under the ugly Apartheid white regime?" asks Professor Mouyyad Hassouna of Valdosta College in Georgia. "Jordan belongs to the Jordanians, South Africa belongs to Black South Africa, and the Palestinians belong to their country, Palestine. . . . Israel is the belligerent occupant of Palestine."[10] Palestine, by the way, stretches from the Jordan River to the Mediterranean Sea. Professor Hassouna is advocating the complete destruction of the State of Israel.

"[Israel] must stop abusing the rights of Palestinians . . . because they are endangering themselves with the brutal occupation," advised Professor Nancy Kanwisher of Harvard University at a Harvard/MIT teach-in. "And it is not crazy to think that current Israeli policies are also endangering us here in the US."[11] Did you catch that language? Israel is "endangering" itself—provoking Palestinian bombings. And Israel's self-defense is "endangering us here in the US."

At UC Berkeley, Snehal Shingavi caused a national uproar after he began a class, English R1A, entitled "The Poetics of Palestinian Resistance." The course description originally read: "The brutal Israeli military occupation of Palestine, [ongoing] since 1948, has systematically displaced, killed, and maimed millions of Palestinian people. And yet, from under the brutal weight of the occupation, Palestinians have produced their own culture and poetry of resistance. This class will examine the history of the [resistance] and the way that it is narrated by Palestinians in order to produce an understanding of the Intifada. . . . This class takes as its starting point the right of Palestinians to fight for their own self-determination. Conservative thinkers are encouraged to seek other sections."[12]

After criticism began pouring into Berkeley, the university altered the course description—but only by dropping the last line. The rest remained virtually the same.[13]

Quite even-handed.

"SHARON IS A TERRORIST"

Professorial opponents of Israel often blame the lack of peace between Israelis and Palestinians on one man: Ariel Sharon. They call him a butcher, a baker, a candlestick maker, and just about every other epithet under the sun. They blame him for a 1982 attack by Christian Phalangists (a Lebanese Christian group persecuted by Yassar Arafat's terrorist Palestine Liberation Organization) on Sabra and Shatilla, Palestinian refugee camps in Lebanon. As Israeli defense minister, these Sharon-haters say, Sharon should have known and prevented the attacks (Sabra and Shatilla were hotbeds of terrorist activities, widely considered the home base for global terrorist training). Now, the professors lie, he is continuing "bloody policies" against the Palestinians. They set him up as a foil for the man with true blood on his hands, Yasser Arafat. They ignore that Sharon was elected only after the start of the latest Palestinian Intifada, and that Arafat had negotiated with Yitzchak Rabin, Shimon Peres, Benjamin Netanyahu, and Ehud Barak before Sharon was even prime minister.

Professor Rashid Khalidi of the University of Chicago compares Ariel Sharon's elected Likud coalition government with the murderous Palestinian terrorist group Hamas. "Both the extremes, the extremists who rule Israel and the current Israeli government and Hamas believe deeply in an eye for an eye and a tooth for a tooth. So we will have more bloodshed," he averred on Jim Lehrer's *NewsHour*.[14]

Sharon bears "criminal responsibility" for targeting and killing known terrorist leaders, according to Professor Richard Falk of Princeton University. Falk goes even further—he also calls former Labor Prime Minister and knee-jerk appeaser Ehud Barak a war criminal.[15] Isn't there *any* way to please Professor Falk?

Professor Colin Flint of Penn State plays the moral equivalency game, pretending that Arafat's record of terrorist activity is comparable to Sharon's military record. "It's pretty one-sided to focus on Arafat's past as a terrorist," he sniffs, "given Sharon's alleged involvement in past war crimes."[16] Did he ignore the word "alleged," or did I miss something?

"There is virtually no likelihood of any progress in the peace process between Israel and Palestine. As long as Yasser Arafat and Ariel Sharon are in charge, you are not going to see any progress," declares Professor Donald Snow of the University of Alabama.[17]

Professor Louis Kriesberg of the University of Syracuse also blames both Sharon and Arafat. "They're useful enemies for each other," he states.[18] Arafat's been in charge of his constituency for thirty-nine years. Sharon's been in charge for less than three. In thirty-nine years, there has never been peace. Is the obstacle to peace Sharon or Arafat?

BLAMING ISRAEL FOR SEPTEMBER 11

A whole contingent of professors blames America's trouble with militant Islam on our support of Israel. Ignoring that Israel is the only true democracy in the Middle East, they say that Arab rage over "Israeli aggression" caused September 11. Of course, it's false. Middle Eastern regimes would hate America even if Israel were destroyed. But truth is no obstacle to professorial bias.

"The American public is now waking up to the cost of the relationship with Israel," stated Professor Yehuda Lukacs of George Mason University after September 11.[19] Wrong. September 11 woke Americans up to the cost of a relationship with Saudi Arabia and Egypt.

Just hours after September 11, Professor Jim Lea of the University of Southern Mississippi blamed American support of Israel for the attacks. "The US has become to be closely identified with the current regime in Israel, Sharon, and its settlements, and its presence in East Jerusalem, and its use of the military in political assassinations, and in its air attacks," he expounded.[20]

Professor James G. Blight of Brown University reasons along similar lines. He blames Israel for the attacks, saying that "the US has never seriously entertained the idea of an equitable settlement in the Middle East," which stirs Arab anger at the United States.[21]

At the University of Georgia, Professor Alan Godlas quoted Palestinian Islamic Jihad terrorist Ramadan Abdullah's lecture to UGA students in order to explain the causes of September 11. One of the four causes he cited was—you guessed it!—that the US supports depriving Palestinians of their right of self-determination.[22] Nothing like swallowing whole the garbage terrorists are selling.

Professor Maysam al Faruqi of Georgetown University takes the cake. She says that the September 11 terrorists were frustrated at "the dispossession and killings of Palestinians who have been kept in refugee camps, more like concentration camps, for fifty years where they are born, live, and die without any hope of a normal life or the possibility to return to their homes and their lands."

When asked specifically if she was referring to US support of Israel as the cause of September 11, al Faruqi answered, "Primarily, yes. . . . The United States keeps vetoing any resolution from the United Nations addressing the matter . . . In this way, and in providing financial and military support to Israel, it becomes responsible in the eyes of the Muslims for what Israel is doing. Israel perpetrated and still perpetrates acts of terror, and those who help it are seen to be as guilty as Israel itself is."[23] Better keep an eye on this woman. It sounds as if she's not averse to ramming planes into buildings herself.

Osama bin Laden would approve of these professors. After all, they promulgate his agenda.

THE "JEWISH CONSPIRACY"

The Protocols of the Elders of Zion, the most notorious anti-Semitic document in modern history, has been debunked many times over. That work argued that Jews controlled the world. There is no global Jewish conspiracy. But many professors still believe in a Jewish-American political conspiracy to hijack the government, influencing government officials toward pro-Israel policies.

"Our President continues to issue toothless and ambiguous statements, while the Congress remains largely an 'occupied territory,'" accuses Professor Joe B. Nielands of UC Berkeley.[24]

The *Palestine Chronicle*, a heavily anti-Semitic publication, states that its purpose is to "expose the influence of the strong Jewish American lobby upon our government, media, and institutions." The board of the magazine includes Professors Noam Chomsky of MIT and Robert Jensen of the University of Texas, who serve alongside the likes of radical Palestinian terror-supporter Hanan Ashrawi.[25]

"Every US political figure of note, whether it's a campaigner in a small district in northern New York State or a presidential contender, has had to declare himself or herself an unconditional supporter of Israel, because of the power of the Israeli lobby," said the late Edward Said.[26] "The US administration is effectively controlled by the Christian right and the Israel lobby," Said stated.[27] The Jews controlling the government. Where have we heard this before? How about pre-WWII Germany? And Tsarist Russia? And Stalin's USSR?

An assigned reading for a UCLA political science class comes up with the same conclusion: "The truth about America's Israel lobby is this: it is not all-powerful, but it is still far too powerful for the good of the US and its alliances in the middle east and elsewhere." The reading slurs the Jewish-American community as having been "morally coarsen[ed]," and equates Palestinian terrorism against civilians with Israeli military retaliation against terrorists.[28]

When the teacher's assistant asked our class what we thought about the article, I responded that I found it extremely biased and morally abhorrent. "No," the TA said, "It was a very nice piece."[29] It wasn't a very nice piece. It was a pack of lies. But the "Jews run the government" notion seems to be popular among academics.

HAMAS, ISLAMIC JIHAD, AND OTHER CAMPUS GROUPS

"Does anybody here think that Israel shouldn't exist—that the extremist position represents the right and morally valid position?" Professor Donald

Moon of Princeton University asked students at a teach-in.[30] If students did think this, they'd probably be working on the faculty at a top-ranked university right now.

Harvard University faculty chose a special graduation speaker for their 2002 academic year. His name was Zayed Yasin, and his commencement speech was entitled "My American Jihad." Yasin insisted that the "jihad" mentioned in his speech referred to spiritual struggle against ungodliness and that he discussed jihad in order to "reclaim the word 'jihad' from the way it's been misused and abused."

Professor Richard Thomas, the chair of the committee that selected Yasin, defended his choice: "It appealed because it began with a personal perspective of a Muslim American, questioning whether he fit as an American, and as a Muslim. And then expanded that out to include all of us in terms of the struggle it promotes and it urges on all of us."[31]

Let's look a bit deeper at Mr. Yasin to see just how anti-jihad he really is.

In November 2000, Harvard's Muslim and Arab students held a fund-raising dinner on the Harvard campus to benefit charities in the Palestinian Authority. The "charities" were the Holy Land Foundation (HLF) and the Palestinian Red Crescent, both of which support terrorist groups like Hamas. The fund-raiser was coordinated by the Harvard Islamic Society and the Society of Arab Students. The president of the Harvard Islamic Society was none other than Zayed Yasin.

"I saw the HLF in action, and they were very professional. I've never heard anything bad about them," said Yasin. "The benefit of [these] foundations is that they are fairly transparent, that where their money goes is clear." So clear that the Anti-Defamation League and State Department officials already had them pegged as terror-supporting charities almost a year before the September 11 attacks. Yasin was clearly notified of the allegations against the "charities," and authorized the final go-ahead to the monetary transfer.[32] And as Yasin concedes, he feels that suicide bombings against Israeli military personnel are "a very difficult moral question. . . . I can see arguments on both sides."[33]

Yasin isn't the only Hamas supporter on campus. Mustafa Abu Sway taught about Islam at Florida Atlantic University. He has a PhD from Boston College, is an associate professor at Al-Quds University in Jerusalem, and has penned two books. He has also won an award from the Center for Theology and the Natural Sciences in Berkeley. He is a Fulbright scholar. He is also an active member of Hamas. When FAU was confronted with this information, they did nothing. Middle East experts Daniel Pipes and Asaf Romirowsky draw the obvious conclusion: "connections to Islamist terrorism [have become] acceptable and almost routine in Middle Eastern studies."[34]

Then there's Professor Sami Al-Arian. The tenured lecturer at the University of South Florida headed two front-organizations for terrorist groups. In one organization, Al-Arian employed a man who went on to become the head of Islamic Jihad, the terrorist group responsible for scores of suicide attacks in Israel. In the other, he employed a man who provided an interview with Osama bin Laden to ABC News.

That was only the beginning. Al-Arian used university rooms to host conferences with such notorious terrorists as Sheikh Rahman, the man incarcerated for planning to blow up tourist sites in New York. At a rally in Cleveland, Al-Arian spoke to the crowd under the title "head of Islamic Jihad," and led the crowd in chants of "Jihad is our path. Victory to Islam. Death to Israel. Revolution. Revolution until victory. Rolling, rolling to Jerusalem." A few weeks later, Al-Arian sent out a letter asking for donations to Islamic Jihad. At the time, then-President Bill Clinton had already frozen the US funds of Islamic Jihad, so this was clearly illegal.[35] Al-Arian was banished from campus only after Fox News' Bill O'Reilly interviewed him on the air and exposed him as a supporter of terror. By that point, he had taught at the university for sixteen years.[36]

Naturally, Al-Arian's colleagues supported him. The University of South Florida Faculty Senate refused a measure by University President Judy Genshaft that would fire Al-Arian. As the *St. Petersburg Times* reported, a large majority of the senators voted with Al-Arian. The moral minority was justifiably outraged. "If we condone this, what happens next?" questioned an angry and bewildered Joseph Kools, who teaches Army ROTC.[37]

Al-Arian's brother-in-law and former University of South Florida faculty comrade, Professor Mazen Al-Najjar, had worse luck than Al-Arian. Al-Najjar was detained by the INS for overstaying his student visa by twenty years and later accused by the Justice Department of having connections to terrorist groups, Islamic Jihad in particular.[38] Despite the skills of his defense council, Professor David Cole of Georgetown University, Al-Najjar couldn't get off the hook. The INS did its job and Al-Najjar was deported from the United States to an unidentified country in August 2002.[39]

At Northeastern University, Professor M. Shahid Alam shocked the country with his fervent defense of Palestinian terror. In an op-ed piece for the Egyptian English-language publication Al-Ahram, Alam wrote: "resistance is a Palestinian right, as it was a right of all colonised [sic] peoples who faced dispossession. Of necessity, dispossession is implemented by force, and it follows that resistance to the coloniser must also be violent. The question, therefore, is not why do the Palestinians resist, nor why do they resist by violent means. There is a different question before the world's conscience: why have we for fifty years abandoned the Palestinians to fight their battles alone, beleaguered by a coloniser whom they cannot fight alone?"[40]

Fellow Northeastern faculty members either offered wishy-washy condemnations of the piece or attempted to distance themselves from it. Professor Stephan Kane weakly objected to the piece, saying: "I'm angry, but by the same token I understand his frustration. But I think his arguments, his rationale and vitriolic behavior are unacceptable." The president of the university did not condemn the piece, but merely dismissed it as Alam's personal view on the matter.[41]

"GET OUT OF HERE, ZIONIST"

Zionists are unwelcome on campus. It's okay to be "culturally Jewish," and you're grudgingly tolerated if you're religious, but as soon as you say you believe Israel has a right to defend herself, there's hell to pay.

A student at UCLA sent me the following e-mail: "There is a general hostility towards anything related to Israel or Jews on campus, coming from all types of people at the university. I was advised to forward you this e-mail, sent by one of my teacher's assistants (who happened to be a Persian Muslim) to the entire class. This individual constantly utilized class time to impose her views of Israel on us relentlessly, and slammed any attempt for student feedback which contradicted her narrow views. Other students, even ones totally unaffiliated, felt she was extremely overpowering in terms of her views on Israel and authority over our grades. Though everyone was afraid to say anything, or bring it to the professor's attention, many were very troubled by her conduct."

The forwarded e-mail included by the student was stunning. The TA, Mona, encouraged her students to attend an upcoming rally entitled "NO OCCUPATION! NO TERROR! NO WAR!" and suggested that students read works by vitriolic anti-Israel authors like Howard Zinn, Noam Chomsky, Angela Davis, David Barsamian, and Lyndon LaRouche. Mona also suggested that students vote for LaRouche in his bid for the presidency.[42]

Perhaps the best example of the anti-Zionist attitude on campus can be found by contrasting UC Berkeley's treatment of former Israeli Prime Minister Benjamin Netanyahu with Colorado College's treatment of radical Palestinian spokeswoman Hanan Ashrawi.

On November 28, 2000, Netanyahu was scheduled to appear at the University of California in Berkeley. Two thousand people bought tickets to hear the former prime minister talk about the Israeli-Arab conflict. But soon, three to five hundred rowdy students and professors blocked off the entrance to the venue, waving signs reading "Zionism = Nazism," chanting "Support the Palestinians," and threatening violence. Netanyahu's security detail canceled his appearance due to the threat of violence. Meanwhile, Berkeley's police department did nothing to clear the protesters from the area, instead allowing them to disturb the peace without threat of arrest.[43]

The problems didn't end at Berkeley for Netanyahu. A similar protest shut down his speech at Concordia College in Canada, where anti-Israel protesters physically assaulted pro-Israel demonstrators.[44] Rabble-rousers planned to do the same at the University of Pittsburgh. "To call him a 'champion of peace,' as they did in the lecture series brochure, is unacceptable," explains Professor Ken Boas of the University of Pittsburgh,[45] a card-carrying member of Professors for Peace and Justice, a leftist pacifist group against all international conflict.[46]

Palestinian spokeswoman Hanan Ashrawi received a far different welcome at Colorado College than Netanyahu did at Berkeley. Despite the fact that Ashrawi is as anti-America and anti-Israel as Osama bin Laden, she spoke without hindrance before an auditorium crammed with students. Over the objections of thousands of Americans, including Colorado

Governor Bill Owens and former New York Mayor Rudy Giuliani, the speech went ahead as planned.[47]

In her speech, paid for with public dollars,[48] Ashrawi labeled Israeli policies "ethnic cleansing," and stated, in a clear reference to the Holocaust: "there's no justification for doing unto others what was done to you." She also called September 11 "an opportunity for a historic redemption of the Palestinian cause."[49]

It is almost unbelievable. As columnist Daniel Pipes notes, "Ashrawi is smack on the side of America's enemies in the War on Terrorism. For example, while the US government formally designates Hamas a terrorist group, Ashrawi states she doesn't 'think of Hamas as a terrorist group.' Also, she considers Israeli civilians living on the West Bank to be 'legitimate . . . targets of Palestinian resistance'—that is, legitimate targets for deadly violence."[50]

A legitimately elected leader of a liberal democracy is prevented from speaking on campus, while a supporter of Palestinian terrorism speaks her mind freely and openly. Is that free speech at work?

THE DIVESTMENT CAMPAIGN

Of late, there has been a campaign underway for American colleges to divest from the State of Israel. By divestment, proponents mean that colleges should take their money out of companies that invest in the Israeli economy. The movement is picking up steam as more and more professorial extremists climb aboard.

The movement began at Illinois State University, where Professor Francis A. Boyle called for divestment from Israel until Israel pulls out of the West Bank and Gaza, accepts the non-existent Palestinian right to return, and ceases defending itself.[51] Harvard University and MIT immediately jumped on board; fifty-seven faculty members from MIT signed the petition, and seventy-five Harvard faculty members affixed their names to the revolting document.[52]

Princeton University followed suit, with forty-three professors signing the divestment petition, blaming Israel for the Intifada and condemning it for "[violating] Palestinian human rights."[53] So did Columbia/Barnard, where 107 faculty members had signed the petition as of January 2004.[54] The University of Massachusetts also hopped onto the Jew-hating bandwagon; forty-five faculty members had signed the petition as of January 2004.[55] By October 2002, divestment petitions had spread to forty universities.[56]

The heart of the divestment movement is the University of California system. A whopping 223 UC faculty members had signed the UC divestment petition as of October 2003, including: ninety-six from UC Berkeley, fifteen from UC Davis, fourteen from UC Irvine, thirteen from UCLA, seven from UC Riverside, thirty-two from UC San Diego, five from UC San Francisco, sixteen from UC Santa Barbara, and twenty-three from UC Santa Cruz.[57]

The rhetoric of the professors is just as anti-Semitic as their support for divestment.

"Divestment can speak out loudly against Israel's invasions, illegal settlements, and systematic destruction of Palestinian civil society," declares Professor Karen Brodkin of UCLA. "[O]ppression breeds terrorism and that is exactly what the Israeli government has done and continues to do," babbles Professor Isgoushi Kaloshian of UC Riverside on the Faculty Statements page of the UC divestment campaign Web site.[58]

"Israel has made itself into a white colonial settler state, mimicking South Africa before the end of apartheid," spews Professor Lisa Rofel of UC Santa Cruz. "The Israeli occupation of Palestine and destruction of human rights and democracy is at least as severe as that of the South Africans," agrees Professor Daniel Boyarin of UC Berkeley.

"American financial and military support provides Israel with $10 million a day, blood money used to maintain its illegal and immoral occupation of Palestine. I oppose Israel's racist apartheid regime," writes Professor Leslie A. Mullin of UC San Francisco.

"For half a century, Israel has had military dominance in the Middle East but has not had peace. Military occupation, colonization, seizures of lands, destruction of houses and orchards, assassinations, expulsions have not brought security, but terror from both sides that will escalate to disaster," spouts Professor Susan M. Ervin-Tripp of UC Berkeley. "It is time for us to unequivocally side with peace and Palestinian independence in every possible way."

In October 2003, anti-Semites from across the country united at Rutgers University for the Third National Student Conference on the Palestine Solidarity Movement. Their goal: escalating their attacks on Israel and Zionism. Then they went back to their universities, and taught their students more of the same.

SELF-HATING JEWS

The obvious question in all of this: Where are the Jewish support centers, fighting back against the anti-Israel and anti-Semitic sentiment on campus? The answer: Many of them are fighting alongside enemies of the Jews.

At UCLA, the supposed Jewish leader is an apologist for Palestinian terror. Chaim Seidler-Feller is the head of UCLA Hillel, the UCLA wing of the largest national Jewish campus organization in the United States. He is also a professor of sociology and a rabid Peace Now activist who consistently sides with the Palestinians against Israel. Columnist Avi Davis described Seidler-Feller as "the cynosure for Los Angeles liberal-left causes, an organizer of conferences involving groups who spew the most venomous anti-Semitic and anti-Zionist rhetoric and an adamantine critic of all right wing governments—whether Israeli or American."[59]

Davis hit the mark with his description. At a memorial for victims of the Holocaust, Seidler-Feller spoke to the crowd of students, comparing Israeli treatment of Palestinians to Nazi treatment of Jews. Just because Jews were victimized in the Holocaust, he said, does not mean that Jews are "immunized from victimizing others."[60]

On May 29, 2002, syndicated columnist and talk show host Dennis Prager spoke about Israel to a crowd of about two hundred members of the UCLA community. In his speech, he explained why Israel has a right to defend itself against Palestinian terror and discussed the history of the State of Israel. Seidler-Feller, a vocal critic of Prager, introduced him to the crowd. After Prager's speech, Seidler-Feller strode to a microphone and challenged Prager's honesty and his arguments, stating to Prager that he was "exaggerating the case" for Israel.[61]

But Seidler-Feller wasn't done yet. He wrote a letter to the editor in the *Daily Bruin*, explaining his position. "[T]he Palestinians are still struggling to gain full freedom and currently live under the dual oppression of foreign dominance (the Israelis) and the corrupt and undemocratic rule of Arafat. Those of us in the Jewish/Israeli peace movement have said for years that it is essential to recognize that Palestine is home to the Palestinians."[62] This man is supposed to be a guide for Jewish students at UCLA. What a crock.

Another professor at UCLA, Gabriel Piterberg, also hates Israel, calling on Israel to capitulate to every Palestinian demand, even if the Palestinians continue terror attacks against Israeli civilians. He calls Israel's control over the West Bank "apartheid," and suggests a "bi-national state" as the solution to the conflict.[63] On his office door is a poster reading "End the Occupation." "It's mind-boggling," he says of Israeli treatment of Palestinians. Piterberg says he is "ashamed to be an Israeli citizen."[64] Is it surprising that UCLA hired Piterberg directly from Israel to come brainwash their students?

The Tikkun Community is a Jewish group led by Michael Lerner, a far-left anti-Israel propagandist. As the "About Us" section of the Tikkun Web site brags, "Tikkun has become particularly controversial for its support of the rights of Palestinians."[65] The board of the "Community" included (as of October 2003) Professor Susannah Heschel of Dartmouth College, Professor Cornel West of Princeton University (a noted "black supremacist"), Professor Doug Allen of the University of Maine, Professor Chet Bowers of the University of Oregon, Professor Tony Campolo of Eastern College, Professor Harvey Cox of Harvard University, Professor Gordon Fellman of Brandeis University, Professor Peter Gabel of the New College of California, Professor Robert Gottlieb of Worcester Polytechnic Institute, Professor Richard Lowery of Phillips Theological Seminary, Professor Ian Lustick of the University of Pennsylvania, Professor Shaul Magid of the Jewish Theological Seminary of America, Professor Svi Shapiro of the University of North Carolina in Greensboro, Professor Lawrence Simon of Brandeis University, Professor Paul Wapner of American University, and Professor Robin West of Georgetown University.[66]

Several of the aforementioned professors are considered Jewish leaders on campus—as members of the Tikkun Community, they are closer to Palestinian sympathizers. As are most other Jewish leaders on campus.

MOBILIZING AGAINST ISRAEL

The anti-Israel sentiment on campus grows stronger year by year with virtually no opposition. "Zionism" has become a dirty word on campus. Polls show that while the American public tends to heavily sympathize with the Israelis over the Palestinians (48 percent to 15 percent in a CBS News poll in April 2002[67]), college students favor Israel by only 35 percent to 22 percent, with 6 percent sympathizing with both sides.[68]

In private colleges and Northeastern colleges, students actually back the Palestinians. At private colleges, 34 percent back the Palestinians while 26 percent back the Israelis; in the Northeast, 36 percent back the Palestinians while 23 percent back the Israelis.[69]

On May 14, 2002, long-time anti-Israel, anti-American columnist Robert Fisk wrote a piece entitled "Why does John Malkovich want to kill me?" In the piece, Fisk quoted Professor Judea Pearl of UCLA, who wrote that Fisk was a "hate peddler." Naturally, this piqued my interest—a UCLA professor supporting Israel? What a rarity!

So I e-mailed Professor Pearl, asking if I could possibly interview him in one of my columns. He was hesitant to give an interview, because he was "having a problem now trying to avoid the general media," he said, but he wanted to sleep on the proposal. "But before I start my sleep," he wrote, "let me commend you on your courage to present the Israeli point of view on campus. I almost gave up hope of finding courageous students in UCLA, especially in the political science department."

I had no idea then, but Professor Pearl was the father of Daniel Pearl, the *Wall Street Journal* reporter brutally murdered by Islamic fanatics in Pakistan. After proclaiming his Jewish identity and his family connection to Israel, Daniel Pearl's throat was slit by the terrorists.

How sad that Jewish identity and sympathy for Israel evoke hatred and intimidation not merely in Pakistan, but on US college campuses as well.

11

THE BRUIN, THE BAD, AND THE UGLY

On May 23, 2002, after over a year writing opinion columns for the *UCLA Daily Bruin*, I was fired. Technically, I was suspended from the student newspaper for two quarters at the least, and possibly more if I didn't "feel remorse,"[1] according to my editor. My crime? Speaking out publicly against the pro-Muslim bias of the *Daily Bruin* editorial staff.

I first applied for an unpaid position as a *Daily Bruin* opinion columnist in December 2000, as a freshman. To my surprise, I was accepted. As the "token conservative," I immediately became the most controversial opinion columnist in the paper.

Everything was sailing along smoothly. I was free to write about any topic I wanted, except for the sacred cow of Political Correctness—the extremism of the Muslim Student Association (MSA) and *Al-Talib*, the Muslim student newspaper.

During my tenure at the *Bruin*, I had three different viewpoint editors. Two of them refused to let me write anything quoting MSA and *Al-Talib* documents. "We'll have to confirm your quotes with the MSA and *Al-Talib*," they said, as though I had fabricated direct quotations. Strangely, they never even checked with those organizations.

Twice I actually wrote articles about the MSA and *Al-Talib*, which were rejected. In all, I submitted thirty-two articles for publication while working for the Bruin; thirty were printed. The only two the *Bruin* wouldn't publish discussed the extremist Muslim sect on campus.

In May 2002, the second rejection threw me into direct conflict with the *Daily Bruin*. The *Bruin* had rejected a similar article earlier. They had rejected the idea of attacking the MSA and *Al-Talib* numerous times. But this time the viewpoint editor, Sarah,[2] agreed to print the column because it was timely—the week of my submission was the official MSA "Anti-Zionism Week" (which they renamed "Islamic Awareness Week" that year). She even agreed to have my article approved by the MSA and *Al-Talib*. "Have a backup column ready to go," she wrote, "in case we don't get confirmation of positions from the groups by Monday."

Time passed. I revised, restructured, and reorganized the column, but the basic message of the column remained the same—the Muslim student groups on campus were supporting terrorism. The viewpoint editor approved the article for printing. Then it happened. On May 14, at 1:55 P.M., I received an e-mail from an assistant viewpoint editor, John.[3] "Ben," he stated, "Ted[4] [the editor in chief] saw your column in a budget meeting and deciding [sic] not to run it. He thinks that it doesn't add anything to the debate and that we need fresh opinions on this debate. I'm sorry, but I can't do anything about it."

I wrote back to John, telling him that I could take a "different, less hostile tack." "It isn't so much that your article was too hostile per se," he answered, "but mainly that the opinion has been expressed before in a very similar way. . . . we do NOT need another column about who is right and who is wrong and who hates whom."[5]

That did it. My column didn't "add anything to the debate," they said. The *Bruin* did "NOT need another column about who is right and who is wrong and who hates whom." In my time at UCLA, I had seen columns comparing Ariel Sharon to Adolf Eichmann; columns justifying suicide bombings; editorials ripping Israel; *news* articles openly issuing calls to "Free Palestine." But the *Bruin* could not bear to print a column merely quoting the Muslim student media on UCLA campus.

So I called up KABC talk show host Larry Elder. At Larry's request, I had appeared on his show in November 2001 to discuss an article I wrote in the *Daily Bruin*, so we knew each other. He generously offered to interview me on the air on Monday, May 20, 2002.

On air, I said that there seemed to be a pattern of UCLA's catering to its Muslim population. I connected the *Daily Bruin*'s policy with UCLA's overall pro-Muslim stance. I discussed the use of mandatory student fees for student media; part of tuition at UCLA includes a required payment to the student media. For example, my tuition money pays for *Nommo*, the black magazine on campus, despite the fact that I disagree with their viewpoint. Callers were outraged at both the *Daily Bruin*'s censorship and UCLA's overtly pro-Muslim policies.

As soon as I entered the *Bruin* office on Tuesday afternoon, I knew there would be a heavy price to pay for the interview. One of the advisors for the *Bruin* approached me and asked if I had spoken to the editor-in-chief yet. "No," I answered. "He's not happy with you," the advisor responded.

On Wednesday, I received a message on my cell-phone from Sarah, the viewpoint editor, saying that she wanted to meet with me. I called her back at the office and told her I would meet her on Thursday.

Thursday, May 23, 2002: The showdown. I walked into the office, where the viewpoint editor immediately took me aside. She then proceeded to read me the riot act, despite the fact that she had been willing to run the article originally.

"I think what you did was distasteful," she snapped. "You should have come to us first if you had a problem."

"I don't have a problem with *you*," I explained. "You were willing to print my article. My problem is with the Ted [the editor-in-chief], and with Katy[6] [the former editor-in-chief]. It was the editor-in-chief who nixed my article, not you. And I did come to the *Bruin* first—I've asked you guys about an article on this topic at least four or five times."

"Well," she said, "I still find what you did extremely distasteful."

Sarah told me that I had broken several opinion columnist policies. First, I had taken an "outside interview" with Larry without the *Daily Bruin*'s consent. Second, she stated, I had not clearly identified myself as a "viewpoint columnist," an allegation that was untrue, since Larry repeatedly identified me as a columnist, and columnists by definition are not reporters. Third, I had failed to "seek editorial advice" from my editor before "interacting with the public about a sensitive or otherwise controversial issue."[7]

The *Daily Bruin* had set these policies in place in January 2002, four months before. Viewpoint columnists were not required to sign the policy, and were not legally bound by it.

"You are hereby suspended from the *Bruin*," she continued, "for a period of at least two quarters. You can reapply in Winter 2003."

After I left the office, I called Les Siegel, Larry's producer, to tell him about the firing. He again agreed to give me time on his show to discuss the firing: 5:00 P.M. the next day. And Les also got Sarah to join us. Ted, the editor-in-chief, could not be bothered with appearing on LA's longest-running afternoon talk show to discuss *his* decision—instead, he sent the viewpoint editor as a proxy.

As soon as the interview began, it became clear that the *Daily Bruin* had not fired me for breaking columnist policy, but for revealing their censorship.

"Sarah, this has nothing to do with what Mr. Shapiro said? In other words, if he had come on the show and said 'I think the *Daily Bruin* is a great newspaper,' he still would have been suspended?" Larry inquired of the viewpoint editor.

"Yes, he would have been," Sarah answered. "It had nothing to do with his content."

"If he had said 'I am here; I am not representing the school although I am a columnist. I am not representing the newspaper although I am a columnist.' would he have been home free?" Larry pressed.

"Yes," she stated.

Later in the interview, Larry found the hole in Sarah's argument: I had clearly identified myself as a *Daily Bruin* columnist in the previous interview.

"Sarah," Larry said to her, "by definition, a *columnist* does not represent the views of the newspaper. I've had a lot of people on my show, from the *LA Times*, for example, and they've not said, 'Oh, by the way, I'm not representing the newspaper.' I know you're not, you're a columnist!"

"Right," she admitted. "But Larry, you'd be totally surprised by how many people don't understand that distinction."

"Well, that's their problem, not yours, not Ben's!"

She floundered about for an answer, first suggesting that it was "an issue of credibility." "But," I interjected, "the *Bruin* isn't legally liable for anything I say."

"Sarah," Larry added, "with respect, I write for *Jewish World Review*, I write for WorldNetDaily.com. . . . [and I can tell you that] by definition, a columnist is giving his or her opinion."

So I wasn't fired because I misrepresented myself as a *Daily Bruin* representative. Why was I fired? For speaking out. Larry hit the nail directly on the head during the interview.

"Sarah," Larry asked, "[Ben has] been suspended for 'at least two quarters.' Why 'at least,' as opposed to two quarters, one quarter, three quarters?"

"That was a decision made by the editor-in-chief," she replied.

"Meaning what? When is he out of penance? What does he have to do in order to get back?"

"He can reapply in January. And he'll just need to reassure us that we'll be notified before he speaks with outside media."

"So the punishment will be determined based on his degree of remorse?"

"Um, you can phrase it that way if you like."[8]

One week later, I began writing a nationally syndicated column with Creators Syndicate. Creators graciously offered the *Daily Bruin* the opportunity to print my columns for free—the *Bruin* refused. They still refuse to print my columns. That's how free speech works at college newspapers.

THE DAILY BRUIN MORAL CODE

I wasn't exactly surprised when the *Daily Bruin* editorial staff and I ended up on opposites sides of a fight. After all, this was an editorial board somewhere to the left of Karl Marx. Pravda can't hold a candle to the *Bruin*.

The *Daily Bruin* was the first student newspaper in the country to endorse divestment from Israel. After comparing Israel to South Africa and Burma, the editorial board wrote: "in the case of Israel, there should be no ambiguity about the UC's responsibility; it needs to divest immediately."[9]

The editors also defended UC Berkeley's atrocious English class, "The Poetics of Palestinian Resistance." After UC President Richard Atkinson spoke out against the course, the *Bruin* editorial board ripped into him. "Neither the regents nor the president have any business involving themselves in determining individual course descriptions," they stated. "The foundation of a university is to promote new insight, even if it's on sensitive subjects. Unless students and professors are allowed to challenge popular beliefs and introduce new knowledge, the concept of academics itself is lost."[10]

The *Bruin* is absolutely opposed to the War on Terror. "President Bush is talking about marching us straight into a war with Iraq, and possibly the entire Middle East, but our generation remains silent," write the editors. Puffed up with self-importance, they continue: "Is a military campaign with ambiguous goals and uncertain motives worth sacrificing our peers and loved ones? Unless generation Y can answer with a resounding yes, the war on terror should go no further."[11]

They love to play the race card as well. When 2002-2003 UCLA Under-graduate Student Association Council President David Dahle nominated four students for the board, the *Bruin* immediately targeted their skin color. "The Undergraduate Students Association Council refused to appoint four white students nominated by President David Dahle to the judicial board on the grounds of a lack of diversity. They were right to do so. Dahle was wrong in not considering people of different ethnicities or backgrounds."[12]

The editorial staff tells students to proselytize for affirmative action. "[S]tudents can also educate communities about the ways affirmative action can benefit them—regardless of their race, gender or ethnicity. Through outreach and direct action, students can transform the consciousness of their communities and educate others of the need for affirmative action."[13]

And what of the *Bruin*'s opinion of UC Regent Ward Connerly's Racial Privacy Initiative, which would prevent applicants from having to state their race? "[RPI] will only erase any record of society's racially-motivated inequality. Minorities will keep bumping their heads on the glass ceiling, continue to make up 60 percent of inmates on death row, and, more directly affecting the UC, continue to have small representation on competitive campuses."[14] Should death row inmates be selected on the basis of diversity? The *Bruin* thinks so.

APPLYING FOR CAMPUS SLUT

Midway through 2001, the *Daily Bruin* editors needed something to spice up the paper. As in the Spice Channel. They added a "sex column." This wasn't out of the realm of normality for the editors who compared a Westwood sex shop with a Christian book store.[15] Here are some of the lowlights from the UCLA "sexpert" column:

- From an article entitled "Mastering art of sexspeak heightens passion in bed": "make sure it's your partner's name you're saying as you near climax. . . . tell us how much you love different parts of our bodies or how good we look naked. . . . Positive reinforcement will not only boost our self-confidence but also result in mutual, take-charge sex."[16]

- Column headlined "Do it the risky way: out in the open": "Sex was around long before societies came into existence or houses were built or the word 'conservative' had any legitimate meaning. . . . For some, exhibitionism is simply having sex in front of the window with the curtains pulled aside—living across the street from some of the fraternities, as I have, will give you a good idea of how to do this. For the really devilish ones, there is always the public bathroom at a bar."[17]

- From "Spice up your life by attending strip clubs": "Now the female body is definitely beautiful to all and therefore pleasing to watch. Many of you men out there may already know what I'm talking about. After all, you dominate the female strip club scene. Now ladies, isn't it high time you, too, realized what strip clubs have to offer? . . . How many of you ladies have ever felt something more than friendship for another female? . . . Of course, the thought left as quickly as it came because you were told that such a way of life isn't normal or accepted."[18]

- From a column entitled "Casual sex: it's not just for 'sinners' anymore": "College: the place where virginity gets lost in oblivion and where sex is usually only one party away. For most, it is not until college that we truly begin to understand the prevalence and nonchalance of sex—especially with the introduction of co-ed dorm halls. . . . Indeed, casual sex is a reoccurring theme of college life. . . ."[19]

Some of the raunchy sex trash isn't even relegated to the sex column. On May 9, 2002, the *Daily Bruin* ran an article on the front page titled "Recipes for Hot Sex." The graphic showed lingerie panties, handcuffs, and a sex toy. The piece described a lecture by Dr. Joan Irvine to a group of retirees, middle-aged couples, and younger women. "We were always taught the way to a man's heart is through his stomach—forget that, it's about six inches lower," she said. Irvine went on to describe myriad ways to spice up sex life, including the use of sex toys like whips. The *Bruin* gleefully reported this as news. "Sexual salvation may be only a pack of batteries away," the reporter panted.[20]

It's not just the *Daily Bruin.* The Yale University and University of Kansas newspapers also carry sex columns containing similarly graphic material. Tufts University's sex column is called "Between the Sheets"; California State University at Long Beach's is "Sex at the Beach." UC Santa Barbara has "The Wednesday Hump" column, and Cornell has "Come Again." Advice and discussion from these and other such columns include commentary on:

- canned phrases to use during sex[21]

- body-cavity searches to retrieve lost condoms[22]

- the porn industry's biggest sin being forgoing the use of condoms ("a bad example for the viewers")[23]

- various techniques for anal sex[24]

- how lesbians can have sex like heterosexuals[25]

And here's a gem from Ohio State University:

No, sex is not like a porno—like most guys think from their experiences. And sex is not something beautiful between two people—like most girls are taught to believe. Sex might possibly be the most absurd thing that can happen between two people. . . . Two people—faces contorted in a combination of pure joy and an Indian burn—fart as their two bodies writhe against each other.[26]

How charming. College papers make sex as romantic and spiritual as flatulence.

THE VAST LEFT-WING CONSPIRACY

A quick sampling of student newspapers around the country reveals that the incredibly leftist viewpoint on the editorial boards isn't relegated to the *Daily Bruin*. Pick a random date and a random college newspaper, and you're sure to find consistently liberal opinions from the editors. In this case, I used October 1-2, 2002. Let's see what the editors have to say:

The *Columbia Spectator* ran editorials on both days opposing an American attack on Iraq. The October 1 editorial stated: "The Bush administration's proposed war with Iraq is ill-conceived. It is grounded in tenuous assumptions, shallow rhetoric, and a reckless desire for glory. . . . President Bush's plan is a mistake. The United States should not go to war with Iraq." The following day, the editorial staff followed up by calling on Congress not to even *debate* an attack on Iraq: "The sudden debate over war with Iraq is robbing Americans of the government's attention at a time when it is critically needed. . . . Bush's personal ties to oil should not send America to war."[27]

The *Harvard Crimson* editorial staff lauded Senator Tom Daschle for his tantrum over a President Bush remark supposedly calling Democrats uninterested in national security: "Rightly infuriated, Daschle accused Bush and other Republicans of exploiting the war on terrorism for political gain and countered Bush's ridiculous claim . . . Daschle's speech is a welcome sign that the Democrats may actually begin acting like an opposition party, and Daschle like an opposition leader. It is their responsibility to offer much-needed criticism of Bush's budding doctrine of preemptive strikes."[28]

The *Yale University Daily News* editors called on the students to reject the US military recruiters' "occupation" of campus because of the military's "don't ask, don't tell" policy banning open homosexuals: "when military recruiters come to campus this month, the *News* urges law students and faculty to sign up for interviews, flood their Holiday Inn suite, and do as Harvard students did last month: Don't ask them about career options. Tell them about equal rights."[29]

Boston College's student newspaper ran the following editorial asking the administration to be more tolerant of homosexuals: "The BC administration's official stance on sexual orientation plays perhaps the biggest role in perpetuating BC's perceived intolerance. . . . We are the people who live in a community where people are not protected against discrimination based on sexual orientation, the people who live in a community where the administration chooses not to allow support for its gay, lesbian, bisexual, and transgender students, the people who endure the reputation of being bigoted against those who are different."[30]

You might think I'm only quoting universities where leftism is a part of the state heritage. But check out this random sample of quotes from editorial boards in heavily right-wing states from October 1-2, 2002:

At the University of Kansas, the *Daily Kansan* editorial board decried the university's supposed lack of minority students, despite a 12 percent increase from 2001 to 2002: "while we can congratulate KU recruitment for their baby steps in solving this diversity problem, that's really all they are: baby steps."[31] (Sixty-one percent of Kansans voted for George W. Bush in the 2000 election.)

An editorial from the *University of Montana Kaimin* bashed big business: "little by little, piece by piece, our environment and our allegiance are being sold to the highest bidder. . . . Our campus is a community, not a battleground for corporate dollars. We are students, staff and faculty, not consumers waiting for our next buying impulse to hit. Our space and our allegiance shouldn't be sold to the highest bidder."[32] (Bush won 64 percent of the vote in Montana.)

Editors of the *Idaho State University Bengal* insulted President Bush for his support of an attack on Iraq: "As Congress passes a resolution that gives bloodthirsty President Bush power to take military action against Iraq, the possibility of a conflict is more real now than ever before."[33] (Idaho went for Bush at a clip of 71 percent.)

The *University of Utah Chronicle* editorial staff begged the administration to shell out bucks for an inefficient recycling program: "You thought losing to Air Force was bad. Now we've been beaten by Brigham Young University. The U's conservative counterpart to the south has out-liberalled, out-environmentalled and out-social conscienced our venerated school in a battle of commitment to progressive ideals. . . . They're making the world a better place by recycling their waste, and we're not . . . Administrators can change the situation by giving greater funding to recycling and looking at programs already working on other campuses."[34] (Seventy-two percent of Utah voters pulled the lever for Bush.)

PEER PRESSURE

It isn't only the professors who shape the views of college students. The opinions of already-brainwashed peers also influence their views. And student newspapers have quite a reach. The *Daily Bruin* reaches approximately sixteen thousand people per day, on and off campus. Altogether, student newspapers are read by hundreds of thousands of students.

Student newspapers are interesting sources for another reason as well: They constitute a window into the mind of the indoctrinated student body. Students express their thoughts and feelings, their experiences and their views. Almost all of it is slanted to the left.

Rival student newspapers that print conservative material are often subject to student crime. On October 24, 2001, students stole one thousand copies of the *UC Berkeley Daily Californian* after the Ayn Rand Institute placed an ad entitled "End States Who Sponsor Terrorism." "What Germany was to Nazism in the 1940s, Iran is to terrorism today. Whatever else it does, therefore, the US can put an end to the Jihad-mongers only by taking out Iran," read the ad.

Student Zorros left flyers to mark their robberies. "We must take a stand against the continuation of a systematic policy of eliciting and reinforcing hatred and racism from our student newspaper," the flier stated. "Until the *Daily Cal* shifts policy we will not allow business to continue as usual. As a result, we have taken copies of today's issue of the newspaper." The flyer also called the Rand ad "irrational and inflammatory." Of course, instead of arguing about how "irrational" the ads were, the students stole the papers. The Keystone Cops of UC Berkeley vowed to hunt down the perpetrators. Despite *eight* previous newspaper robberies at Berkeley, the UC police has failed to arrest anyone.[35]

So students are left with only one side of the story—the smutty side.

From censoring conservative students in the name of political correctness to printing pornographic garbage on the front pages of the paper, student newspapers are examples of the kind of thought that dominates the universities. And with each student who enters the university system, indoctrination grows.

12

COLLEGE CLIQUES

Student groups are the lobbyists on campus. They print pamphlets. They hold protests. They whine. They shout. They fight. Groups like the African Student Association, Gay and Lesbian Association, Movimiento Estudiantil Chicano de Aztlán (MEChA), the Muslim Student Association, and their media outlets, like *Nommo, TenPercent, LA gente de Aztlán,* and *Al-Talib* all receive tuition money to spout their radical agendas.

At UCLA, the funding isn't split proportionally among groups, either. In the corrupt system, money is funneled into whichever group happens to control the student government. For example, in 2001-2002, the USAC budget review director was Mohammed Mertaban, a man who justifies suicide bombings. "We're in no position to condemn a suicide bombing because none of us has experienced what they've been though under fifty-three years of oppression," Mertaban states.[1] Not surprisingly, the Muslim Student Association received a total of $12,322.72 for programs; the Jewish Student Union received $0.00.[2]

What is more surprising is the base budget allocation to both groups. Up until the 2003-2004 school year, this money was supposed to be allocated based solely on the number of constituents in each student group. While there are at least as many JSU members as MSA members, the MSA received a whopping $5,203 while the JSU received only $1,243.[3]

In all, the JSU was the group that lost out the most in the money count, due to the fact that of all the student groups, they are the most conservative. The African Student Union received $7,803; the Gay and Lesbian

Association received $2,608; and MEChA received $7,636.75. The allocations were in no way proportionally representative of the different groups on campus.[4]

The trend continued in 2003-2004. While the standard for base budget funding changed from membership to a points system based on member retention and outreach, JSU continued to get the short end of the stick. In the end, JSU was forced to file a case with the Undergraduate Students Association Council judicial board.[5]

The cash keeps on flowing to the most radical student groups, and those who pay tuition can't do anything to stop it. And what these groups stand for is frightening.

"AFRICAN" STUDENT GROUPS AND NOMMO

The African Student Union is a national union with offices at most major colleges. These offices run independently of one another in general, but what they have in common is a goal to separate black Americans from other Americans.

The University of Georgia ASU constitution identifies all black Americans as Africans only, and lists as one of its goals "enabl[ing] African students and other Africans to share the cultural wealth of the African continent,"[6] despite the fact that many blacks have been living in America for generations and have never even visited Africa. The purpose of the University of Texas ASU is to "create critical student awareness of African issues, its pride, unity and development," according to its Web site.[7] The goal of ASU at the University of Syracuse is to "provide African student [sic] with a forum to express their culture."[8]

The ASU isn't the only "African" organization on campus. Another important black organization is the African Student Association. The purpose of the ASA perfectly reflects the purpose of the ASU: splintering the student body. The assumption that all black students are "Africans" is implicit in the name of the African Student Association. ASA members are "a dynamic group of students, *mostly Africans*, who undertake various activities including talks and cultural events with the goal of promoting awareness of the rich African culture and people," according to the University of

Massachusetts ASA.[9] But how many members of the ASA are actually African citizens? My guess is few.

Nommo is the black magazine at UCLA. Here are a few choice samples from *Nommo*:

- Here's a gem from the issue following September 11: "About 4,000 people lost their lives that morning. That is also when the slow torture of the meaning of justice began. Immediately after the attacks, just like the aftermath of the Oklahoma City bombing, Osama bin Laden, Muslims, and people of Middle Eastern descent were suspected. . . . Attorney General 'Ass'croft issued a national order to detain 5,000 men of Middle Eastern descent to be 'interviewed' by law enforcement. . . . The US government does a lot of dirt in the name of the American people and wonder [sic] why the United States and its interest are targeted by so-called terrorist groups. As f—ed [sic] we maybe [sic] over the events of 9-11, we can not allow ourselves to be blinded and fed bullsh— by our government. . . . President Dubya and Attorney General 'Ass'croft got their little kicks in by detaining hundreds for no reason. . . . Black folks, of all people, should not be silent on this issue. As black folks, we know what it is to be suspect in hiring and housing. And we know what it is like to always fit the description when pulled over. Our voices must be heard in support of Sikh, Middle Eastern, and South Asian brothers. Otherwise, our silence can potentially lend us to a similar fate as the 12 million people who died in Nazi death camps."[10]

- Askari Abdul Muntaqim weighs in with his take on American civilization: "I'm not suggesting that Amerikkka is civilized . . ."[11]

- Noluthando Williams asks if America is a terrorist state: "the US is a covertly dictatorial regime which stops at nothing to protect the interests of its elites. . . . So, before we rush to post up an American flag, sign up for the US armed forces, or spit slurs at Middle Easterners, because we truly want to do the right thing, we should ask ourselves what the right thing is. Who are the real culprits of global terrorism?"[12]

- On Zimbabwe: "Why are they kickin' white folks off the land in Zimbabwe? Of course, one reason is obvious. The land was violently stolen in 1890. . . . The white farmers, now the descendants of the original terrorists, have held the position that since they personally did not steal the land, they should be compensated for their land before leaving. . . . Now, before we start high-fivin' each other, we better examine the bigger picture, because if this is to become the trend in Africa, it should be a trend that improves the quality of life for those who suffer today as a result of colonialism and neo-colonialism."[13]

Besides bashing "Amerikkka," black student groups specialize in finding opposing political viewpoints "offensive." After the Indiana University *Daily Student* ran an anti-affirmative action cartoon by Dan Carino of San Jose State University, the Black Student Union went ballistic. The story made national headlines. A one-hundred-person town hall meeting was organized to discuss the "insensitive" cartoon. "We're basically here because we feel the [*Daily Student*] has a blatant disregard for the student body and constantly disrespects us," whined BSU President Gerald Mitchell. BSU political action chair Carolyn Randolph claimed that the *Daily Student* was "very exclusive and elitist." This despite the fact that 41 percent of IDS front pages during the time period in question contained at least one story about black issues.[14]

Cartoons are apparently a touchy subject. In 1999, the Rutgers University *Daily Targum* ran a cartoon strip entitled "Flaming Cyclops," by Gary Gretsky. The strip depicted a bunch of white people from "Hicksville"—these "white folks" insult anything unlike them. Speaking about black people, a white girl states that blacks are "always complaining" and that she's sick of them getting a "free ride." Another white character in the strip replies, "On a slave ship!" Obviously the point of the cartoon was to blast perceived white racism. As Professor Steve Adubato of Rutgers wrote, "Any responsible person—black or white—would understand that Gretsky was making an 'anti-racism' statement. Any idiot would know that the 'On a slave ship!' comment was intended to mock anyone, particularly a white person, who would never want to trade places with a black

American."[15] But the Black Student Union at Rutgers responded to the cartoon like a wounded tiger. "It could very well be true that [Gretsky] attempted to dispel racist notions. That, however, neither denies nor justifies the use of a comic strip to discuss a sensitive issue that affects a large part of the Rutgers population," sniveled Nadir Joshua, secretary of the Black Student Union. People who attended a rally to protest the anti-racism comic strip demanded that the *Daily Targum* "actively seek more representation from the minority community to prevent similar occurrences," give the staff sensitivity training, allow minority groups to run free ads in the newspaper, fire the editors that allowed the comic strip to run, and run a formal full-page apology in the *Targum*.[16]

Black student group hypersensitivity stretches to ridiculous lengths. A classic case-in-point: at Cal State Long Beach, the graphic design class posted a flier for their first art show; the flier was entitled "Our first hang." The flier contained a picture of a noose. The ASU went ballistic, demanding an apology to the entire African-American campus community for the ad, since nooses dredge up bad memories of lynchings. "We don't see just a noose. It is very offensive," complained ASU president Leilana Ford. The teacher of the graphics design class and the woman who approved the flier, Tanya Cummings, refused to apologize for the image. "We regret the way the poster was perceived, but I don't apologize for the image," Cummings stated. By the way—Tanya Cummings is black.[17]

HOMOSEXUAL GROUPS AND TENPERCENT

The Gay and Lesbian Association is another national organization with local bases across the country. At UCLA, GALA identifies itself as the "Queer Alliance."[18]

The Auburn University Gay and Lesbian Association constitution states that its purpose is "to provide support for gay, lesbian, bisexual, transgender people, their friends, and supporters . . . to educate the campus and community about gay, lesbian, bisexual, and transgender issues . . . to establish a campus and community environment free of prejudice based on sexual orientation."[19]

This sounds harmless enough in theory. In practice, GALA and groups like it are far more dangerous. They seek not just tolerance, but acceptance. If you don't accept homosexuality, you're labeled a "homophobe." One item on the gay group agenda is kicking ROTC off campus because of the military's "don't ask, don't tell" policy regarding homosexuality. Harvard University bans ROTC because of "don't ask, don't tell"; Kevin Jennings, a member of Harvard's Gay and Lesbian Caucus, says allowing ROTC to return to campus would be "a huge mistake."[20] ROTC is banned for similar reasons at Yale, Brown, Stanford, and Columbia.[21]

GALA's most prominent event is "National Coming Out Week," where they ask students and faculty to show their "gay pride." They sponsor ads in student newspapers listing gay people on campus. They plaster the campus with homosexual propaganda. At UCLA, they hang a banner over Westwood Boulevard in honor of the occasion.

And the campus gay clique rhetoric, as expressed by university-approved newsmagazines like *TenPercent*, is outrageous. It's insulting to homosexuals who are not promiscuous and do not wish to make their sexuality the focus of their identity. Check out the aggressive brand of homosexuality they promote:

- From a music review: "Straight, gay, bi—regardless of your orientation, this album will make you want to get it on. And I'm not talking anything clean or missionary; I mean dirty, rough. . . ."[22]

- "Every gay guy has a secret fantasy of being Queen Bitch."[23]

- Blasphemously comparing the creation of the world to the creation of homosexuality: "In the beginning, before Charles Gilber Chaddock coined the term 'homosexuality,' sexuality was a formless void and a darkness covered the face of gender, while a wind from God swept over the face of desire. Then God said, 'Let there be lesbians;' and there were lesbians. . . ." [24]

- Recommending anonymous gay sex: "When the room is dark, your boyfriend can be anyone."[25]

- "At TenPercent we are committed to putting the 'sex' back into 'homosexual.'" From there the magazine then went on to recommend various sex toys.[26]

- On the growing acceptance of homosexuality: "My heart fills with warmth as I watch two fathers stroll along the sidewalk with their daughter. I smile at an old lesbian couple sitting across from me on the bus. Love conquers all, I reason. It's just a matter of time before it'll all be OK. Gay people will have equal rights. . . . We'll settle for second-class citizenship because, someday, things will get better. Well, I am for once sick of waiting."[27]

At the University of North Carolina at Wilmington, one gay student group posted stacks of their magazine, *Queer Notes*, in the Student Union. The magazine contained a pornographic picture of one naked man standing behind another naked man, fondling his genitals. As Mike Adams, professor at UNCW and columnist, reported, "It appeared from the expression on his face, that he was also sodomizing the man standing in front of him." *Queer Notes*, like *TenPercent*, is sponsored by tuition money and is part of UNCW's stated "diversity mission."[28] But even if it weren't, does anyone think students leaving an Evangelical Christian gospel tract in the Student Union wouldn't face some sort of official sanction?

At Michigan State University, *Q*News* is the homosexual student newspaper. Here's a sample from a column by Jennifer Dunn, entitled "Rethinking Romantic Love":

I long for everything I know would destroy me, [sic] it's this death wish that is the most penetrating weapon of the male-supremacy. I'm dependent on him because a romantic relationship (or interaction) is the closest I can get to feeling as if I never existed. Men create the pain in me with their violence and rape and then I'm driven to them to wash it away.

Then, summing up the feelings of the student gay community, Dunn writes, "I'm calling on everybody to not copy or give in to heterosexual traditions."[29]

For the militant queer student body, scorning "heterosexual tradition" seems to be the key.

MECHA AND *LA GENTE DE AZTLÁN*

MEChA, the national Chicano campus organization, has a broader goal than merely uniting Chicanos under one banner. They seek to return the states of California, New Mexico, Arizona, Nevada, and Utah, which they call Aztlán, to Mexican rule. No, really. I couldn't make up stuff this ridiculous.

Don't believe me? Check out *El Plan Espiritual de Aztlán*, their basic philosophical document: "Aztlán belongs to those who plant the seeds, water the fields, and gather the crops and not to the foreign Europeans. We do not recognize capricious frontiers on the bronze continent. . . . With our heart in our hands and our hands in the soil, we declare the independence of our mestizo nation. We are a bronze people with a bronze culture. Before the world, before all of North America, before all our brothers in the bronze continent, we are a nation, we are a union of free pueblos, we are *Aztlán*."[30]

But wait, there's more! They not only want to "liberate" California, they want to do so by violent means. "Lands rightfully ours will be fought for and defended. Land and realty ownership will be acquired by the community for the people's welfare. Economic ties of responsibility must be secured by nationalism and the Chicano defense units." They call for the use of children in "resistance": "Those institutions which are fattened by our brothers to provide employment and political pork barrels for the gringo will do so only as acts of liberation and for La Causa. For the very young there will no longer be acts of juvenile delinquency, but revolutionary acts."[31]

The rhetoric doesn't stop there. As syndicated columnist Michelle Malkin reported, MEChA members from the UC system editorialized that federal immigration officials are "pigs" who "should be killed, every single one."[32] According to the Media Research Center, a 1998 statewide conference for MEChA at Cal Poly "welcomed more than one thousand students with a program that said 'Welcome to Cal Poly State Jewniversity" and a reference to 'Jew York.'"[33]

MEChA has plenty of resources to back their rhetoric. Malkin writes, "[MEChA] operates an identity politics indoctrination machine on publicly subsidized college and high school campuses nationwide that would make David Duke and the KKK turn green with envy."[34]

The MEChA militants reiterate their anti-Westernism and anti-Americanism in UCLA's *LA gente de Aztlán*:

- "It is not one, but all Nations under God, and in terms of Civilization, here, on this our homeland as Indigenous Peoples— the West is a Guest."[35]

- "The United States government has made the killing of innocent people standard practice to achieve political and economic goals. We must be able to understand that our blind support for US military actions in other countries is in essence supporting the deaths of countless innocent people around the world. We must understand that the mainstream media is consciously ignoring the deeper reasons for waging this war; money and oil."[36]

- "Our comunidad has always been under attack by the US government, particularly in times of war . . . our brothers and sisters were drafted and placed in the frontlines of battle, only to return to us in body bags."[37]

- "During the Spring of 1993, the University of Chicana/os in Lost Aztlán was reclaimed by the direct descendents of its territory. No, not the squirrels. Once again for a moment in time, the university with a historical array of grassroots political activism by people of color, became the site for Chicana/o Latina/o occupation. . . . Ten thousand people reclaimed their public university; a scene which has not been seen at UCLA since then nor before."[38]

MUSLIM STUDENT ASSOCIATION AND *AL-TALIB*

Perhaps the most extreme student group is the Muslim Student Association (MSA). They have been funding terrorist groups for years. As the Associated Press reported on December 22, 2001, "Muslim student organizations on college campuses have openly raised money for groups whose assets have been frozen by the US government because of alleged ties to terrorists. . . .

Altaf Husain, national president of the MSA, said his organization has no plans to stop raising money for various groups unless federal authorities crack down. He called suspicions about terrorist links post-attack 'hype,' and said it is up to the government to trace the money."[39]

Of course, the MSA immediately covered its tracks, condemning the Associated Press for printing the story. Using the age-old statement "you took me out of context," Husain complained: "This article is another example of irresponsible journalism that contributes to an atmosphere of animosity towards Islam and American Muslims." Husain then had the unending gall to call the *article* anti-American: "The US leadership, at its highest levels, called on Americans not to link their American Muslim counterparts with terrorism. Unfortunately, some journalists did not heed the call."[40]

This is a group that also attacks Jews with the old blood-libel lies. In anti-Semitic areas, Jews throughout history have been accused of using blood of Gentile children for Passover matzah or other ritual purposes. Nowadays, the MSA places blood libel posters around the San Francisco State University campus—the posters depict a soup can label with a Palestinian baby on it, and the words "Made in Israel" printed across the top.[41]

They publish pamphlets calling terrorist groups charitable organizations. They describe the terrorist group Hizbullah like a Middle Eastern Salvation Army: "Although their primary goal has always been resistance to 'Israeli' expansion into southern Lebanon, Hizbullah operates a wide array of social welfare programs. They construct hospitals, institutions for higher learning, research institutes, orphanages and centers for the physically disabled. They give financial assistance to young couples. . . . Their humanitarian assistance is available to the entire local population, regardless of religious denomination, or even religion."[42]

A quick trip to the MSA national Web site reveals just how fanatical the group is. On the one-year anniversary of September 11, the MSA released a statement. Under the guise of sympathy, the MSA took the opportunity to rip American foreign policy in Israel, Afghanistan, and Iraq. "Muslim-American students unequivocally condemn the senseless killing of civilians here in America, in Afghanistan, in occupied Palestine, in Indian-occupied Kashmir, in Chechnya, in Iraq, and in other parts of the world," read the press release.

The statement went on to condemn "the erosion of civil rights perpetuated by the Bush administration, namely the John Ashcroft-led Department of Justice since the 911 [sic] attacks," and the upcoming "unilateral and unjustified war on Iraq proposed by the Bush administration." And to deflect attention from global Muslim terrorism, the MSA also suggested that citizens "stand in support of shifting the Bush administration's attention to domestic issues such as the eroding surplus, education and welfare reform and the war on poverty and homelessness."[43]

Here's the scariest part: there are over five hundred Muslim student organizations on campus in the United States and Canada, with a constituency of over one hundred thousand.

Al-Talib, UCLA's Muslim newsmagazine, is far less devious than the national MSA. It openly supports terror and hates America. Mostafa Mahboob, the head of the newsmagazine, refused to stop printing ads for terror-funding organizations. "If the listed organizations were still able to advertise, the magazine would consider reprinting the ads as long as the groups were not proven guilty," he said, a full month after the listed organizations were declared illegal.[44] This is clearly in breach of federal anti-terrorism law, punishable by deportation. So far, the US government has not touched the students.

Lest you think Mahboob is a lone extremist, here are some excerpts from *Al-Talib*:

- "We must examine the West's motives in order to have a clearer understanding as to why it wants to control the underdeveloped world's population."[45]

- "Race and racism are deeply rooted in the very foundations of American society and the collective American psyche. . . . The current state of unequal distribution of educational resources, jobs and contracts based on race is based on a long history of institutionalized racism in the country. . . . people of color have never received special or privileged treatment in America—as a matter of fact they have received some of the worst treatment in human history at the hands of America."[46]

- In a piece entitled "UCLA Under Occupation": "How can such injustices go unnoticed? How can 300 UN Resolutions against Israel go unheeded? How can reports of human rights abuses by State Department, Middle East Watch and other agencies be ignored? It's called the Israel lobby. And its arms have a chokehold on UCLA . . . we too are living in an Israeli occupied territory."[47]

- The magazine shows two pictures and asks: "Which one of these two prominent Muslim activists will be next year's editor of Al-Talib?" One picture is of Mostafa Mahboob—the other is of Osama bin Laden.[48]

- "Get out of this defeatist mode of thinking, because it doesn't correspond to how things are. Whether we behold the truth of this or not, Allah is King of moments. It doesn't matter if Israel is well-financed, Serbia militarily superior, or US imperialism too powerful. Allah can change the state of affairs in a moment."[49]

- "I'm assuming that traditional Holocaust history is true, though of course there are libraries of compelling evidence to indicate that the numbers, accounts, and narratives are either exaggerated, or in some cases, wholly imaginary. Suffice it to say that proponents of a less gory account of Holocaust history are no longer fringe racists spouting nonsense, but now include a number of once-prominent historians who have been ostracized from university and intellectual circles that once held them in high esteem."[50]

- "America has rarely experienced death and destruction on its own soil. While the world mourns the daily robbery of its countless innocent lives, whether they are the struggling Palestinians or the starving Iraqis or the exploited Colombians, the United States has built a wall tear-proof and heartache-free, each cold brick symbolizing another foreign policy objective. . . . With the coming of death into this country, the US has entered Afghanistan so as to once again rob the world of its innocent lives."[51]

- "Yet few have asked the question, 'Why is Islam charged with the crime of Muslims in the first place?' Did anyone think to prosecute

Christianity when a ship called 'Jesus Christ' sailed the ocean blue filled with Muslim slaves from West Africa? Why isn't Judaism called to answer for the state terrorism of 'Israel?'"[52]

- "'Israel' and the United States were perceived as 'partners in crime,' as millions of indigenous Palestinians were forced to flee under pains of death. And the thousands of those who remained behind were massacred en masse by war criminals the likes of current Prime Minister Ariel Sharon, who continues to decorate his resume with the bloody ink of Palestinian children. . . . Is it any wonder, then, why there would be anti-American sentiment in the [Middle East] region?"[53]

- "While the world rushed to judgment blaming everyone from the rejoicing Palestinians to Saddam Hussein to Osama bin Laden, the Muslims rushed to the prospect that possibly Israel's Mossad or the CIA or even the state of India were responsible for the attacks that occurred on September 11th against the World Trade Centers and the Pentagon. Conspiracy or not, as the situation itself is hazy and unclear . . ."[54]

- "With the aftermath of Sept. 11, the spotlight has landed squarely on the Muslim community in America. We have become like the 'communists' during the McCarthy era, the clear victims of an unceasing witch-hunt."[55]

- "State sponsored terrorism has been the systematic policy of 'Israel' in subjugating millions of Palestinians in the Occupied Territories . . ."[56]

- "The truth is, our Western world is not quite the paradigm of freedom and equality of which we're taught to sing in our national anthem."[57]

SEPARATE BUT EQUAL

All of these groups rail against "segregation" and "unequal treatment." Then they go and hold their own graduation ceremonies.

At San Francisco State University, Chicanos and blacks have been holding separate graduations for years. The Chicano graduation is organized by MEChA.[58] The University of Texas holds graduations for American Indians, blacks, and Latino students. UC Santa Cruz has a commencement for gay, lesbian, bisexual, and transgender students.[59]

Michigan State University holds separate graduation ceremonies for black students. The University of Michigan has ceremonies for black, Latino, American Indian, and Jewish students, with each ceremony focusing on the "customs" of that group. "[I]f the Polish students came to us and said they want to do something to celebrate their culture, or the Hungarian students came to us, we would do the same thing for them," said John Matlock, a University of Michigan vice provost. "This is a reflection of our multicultural campus, and I think it's very healthy."[60]

UCLA is the center for separate graduation ceremonies. The university holds a graduation for homosexual students, which they call the Lavender Graduation. At that commencement, students wear rainbow tassels. There is also a graduation for Latinos, a graduation for blacks, a graduation for Filipinos, a graduation for Asian Pacific Islanders, a graduation for Iranians, and a graduation for American Indians.[61] About the only ones who don't have their own graduation are straight white males. But they will before long—if only by process of elimination.

SO MUCH FOR THE MELTING POT

It shouldn't be this way. Student groups should be places where people of similar backgrounds can go to share similar perspectives on current issues. The groups should exist for the support of the students, and to forward their opinions without becoming militant. Then the students should go back to the campus as young Americans, not anti-American ethnic minorities.

But in reality, student groups are radical factions fighting with each other for dollars and for the moderate students on campus. They use radical rhetoric, fight for radical goals, and in the end, tear the campus apart by polarizing the students. It becomes taboo for members of the ASU to talk to members of the JSU. There is no dialogue between active members of MEChA and anyone else, unless they're working together to form a more broad-based radical coalition.

Is college a place of open minds and open discussion? Not after the student groups are done with them.

13

SOLUTIONS

The brainwashing of students by the university system is one of the most severe problems plaguing America's youth. Under higher education's facade of objectivity lies a grave and overpowering bias, a bias that deeply affects the student body. To find viable solutions to this crisis, we must now answer three crucial underlying questions. Why are the universities so biased? Why do the students take their professors at face value? And what can we do to stop it?

WHY THE BIAS?

The bias of the universities has deep historical roots. As early as the 1930s, conservatives were warning of the increasing radicalism of the college professors.

"There are few colleges or universities where parents may send their sons and daughters without their being contaminated with some phase of the vilest of Communistic and allied teaching," cautioned Roscoe Dorsey of the *National Republic* magazine.[1]

Irving Kristol, now a conservative, remembers his socialist days at City College of New York: "If there were any Republicans at City—and there must have been some—I never met them, or even heard of their existence." At the time, CCNY had approximately twenty thousand students.[2]

The roots go even deeper. From its very inception, the goal of higher education has been to challenge the authority structure under the banner of open-minded inquiry.

Socrates was perhaps the first professor—a roving teacher enlightening the masses. His entire life was dedicated to challenging conventional thought, an exercise that eventually led to his demise when he was charged with "corruption of the young." The development of the university system broke from its generally rebellious nature during the Middle Ages, when colleges were required to receive licenses to teach from the pope, emperor, or king. Later, colleges became religious institutions, where students were taught their studies within the boundaries of godly morality. This vision of a religiously based educational system carried over to the time of America's founding. But with the increased separation of church and state came an end to religious control of the schools, and with that, a return to the Socratic philosophy of challenging authority.

Sometimes, when the authority structure has promoted vice, immorality, or totalitarianism, the professors have been invaluable in their refusal to accept, as in the former Soviet Union. At other times, when the authority structure is democratic, non-totalitarian, and classically liberal, as in the United States, professors have challenged this structure by preaching radical leftist doctrine.

It is this latter case which has arisen in the modern-day universities. Where the society preaches morality, the universities rebel against morality. Where the society embraces capitalism, the universities challenge capitalism. Where the society supports America, the universities disparage it.

Professors themselves readily admit their own rebellious (and hence leftist) tendencies. "[P]oll numbers show that Republicans are a small minority of the professoriate," declares Professor Lawrence Evans of Duke University. "True, and rightly so. In seeking faculty, universities look for people who can analyze and discuss matters of some complexity, who are unafraid to challenge the wisdom of simple solutions. . . . People like that usually vote for the Democrats. So what?"[3]

UCLA Professor Robert Watson agrees. "American universities have thrived, like the society as a whole, because we have a system for resisting the natural tendency of the authorities to want to dictate beliefs," he states.[4] Professors are "people who will question the self-worship and money-worship of American culture."[5]

WHY THE ACCEPTANCE?

Professors consistently champion the liberal line, but why do students buy it? Why don't they resist the indoctrination efforts of the university faculty?

The obvious answer is youthful naïveté. The innocence of college students blinds them to the motives of their professors. Students take everything at face value, instead of examining the professorial bias. Students also lack the tools, skills, and knowledge to challenge their professors. Acceptance is the easiest road, and the road most often taken. If the professor says that the sky is green, the sky must be green.

The infallibility of professors in the eyes of students is heightened by societal respect for the university system. The media seek out professors to comment on current events; parents spend their hard-earned dollars sending their children to liberal colleges. Therefore, students assume, there must be some inherent merit in the views of the professors who teach there.

Professors capitalize on the profound respect students feel for them. By telling students "think for yourselves" and "don't buy what your parents tell you," the professors set themselves up as the final authority on morality, politics, and society by discarding parents as moral arbiters. And students buy into it because they are always rebelling against their parents—and in college, this is a sanctioned and blessed activity.

WHAT CAN BE DONE?

The problem has many parts, so any solution must also be multi-pronged. Here are a few partial long-term solutions; a synthesis of these solutions should provide a long-term plan to combat indoctrination in the universities.

Pulling funds. An oft-proposed tactic is for conservatives to pull their money from major universities and demand even-handed teaching before reinstating their funds. This seems like a decent idea on the surface, but by itself, pulling funding does little to change university policy. Why? Because leftist and foreign funders will simply pick up the slack, entrenching liberalism more deeply into the university atmosphere.

For example, Saudi Arabia buys up American universities like they're going out of style. At the University of California, the Saudi government has created the King Abdulaziz Chair for Islamic Studies. At Harvard University College of Law, they funded the King Fahd Islamic Shariah Studies.[6] The King Faisal Foundation also gives major scholarships to up-and-coming Muslims students for "outstanding international researchers in science, medicine, Arabic literature, Islamic studies, and service to Islam."[7]

Theoretically, if conservatives were to pull money from universities, Saudi Arabia could become a main source of funding for universities, thereby dictating policy. As part of a comprehensive plan, however, pulling funds is a useful step, as I will explain shortly.

Start-up universities. Nothing is shocking the news world into moderation like the success of Fox News Channel. When CNN dominated the cable news airwaves, only one side of the story was being heard. Then, when Fox News opened its doors, its ratings shot through the roof. Where there's a market, there's a way.

Conservatives should begin a mass movement to start politically moderate universities. This means hiring from both sides of the political aisle. Using Fox News as a model, right-wing founded universities should strive to tell both sides of the story. Only one perspective should be banned: extreme anti-Americanism of the kind that blames America for September 11.

These universities should also shun tax money, following the lead of Hillsdale College. If these conservative-founded universities take tax money, they immediately become accountable to foolish restrictions leveled by the federal government.

This is where pulling funding from mainstream universities comes in. If funding is pulled as an end unto itself, it does little to change the situation. But if that money is simply shifted from mainstream liberal universities into the new, balanced universities, mainstreamers get the message. Just as cable channels like MSNBC moved slightly to the right once they realized that Fox News was taking their audience, mainstream universities will realize that they must move to the center or fall behind.

College rankings and job hiring. But funding in and of itself will not sustain the start-up universities. All universities need students, and the startups are no exception. The real problem becomes how to attract students from well-respected mainstream universities to the new, experimental universities.

There is only one reason that students go to a mainstream university, aside from the usual pap about "broadening the mind": to get a diploma in order to boost job prospects.

The system of "diploma ergo high-paying job" involves a serious problem for conservative start-up colleges. Hiring businesses recognize a university as legitimate and feel that graduates of that university will be good employees based on conventional rankings put out by publications like *US News and World Report*. If *US News* says that Harvard is a better school than UC Berkeley, for example, businesses will likewise seek graduates from Harvard over equal-ranking graduates from Berkeley. Students will follow the prospective jobs, and will desire admission to Harvard over admission to Berkeley.

This involves a major problem for start-up conservative universities: Many college ranking systems are slanted toward the left. UC Berkeley will always rank above Hillsdale College in the *US News and World Report* college rankings, no matter whom Hillsdale hires to teach.

The reason for that slant is very simple: the *US News* methodology will automatically yield higher results for liberal universities. The methodology takes into account "peer review," where biased college administrators rank other colleges. It takes into account financial resources, assuming that more money spent per student means a better education—by that token, public high schools should be mini-Oxfords. The methodology is self-perpetuating, since it takes into account retention of students by universities and quality of incoming classes—if the university ranks high, high-quality students would seek entrance, and no one would leave.[8]

Therefore, the only solution is for well-respected conservative publications to begin issuing college rankings. If the *Wall Street Journal* issued a report honestly ranking conservative schools alongside liberal schools, businesses would sit up and take notice. One criterion, noticeably absent from the *US News* methodology, should be average financial status after ten years for graduates or graduates' job satisfaction after a decade. The *US News* methodology of ranking according to what professors think, how much money is expended, and how many alumni give cash is pure nonsense.

Of course, no ranking system would gain legitimacy overnight. This is where conservative business owners must put their money where their mouth is. If they truly feel that indoctrination is not education, they must consider and hire excellent students from conservative schools for the same jobs where they now place excellent students from UCLA, Harvard, or any other liberal institution. Once conservative-owned businesses begin to legitimize right-wing rankings by hiring conservative graduates with the same frequency as Columbia graduates, students will begin flocking to the start-up conservative universities.

THE PLAN

In sum, I suggest a three-step course of action.

First, conservatives should redirect their funds from liberal colleges to conservative start-up colleges with equal distribution of professors across the ideological spectrum.

Second, new ranking systems should be installed and published by conservative news outlets in order to counter the anti-conservative bias of other ranking systems and provide a better resource for hiring businesses.

Third, conservative businesses must use the new rankings as a guide, in order to legitimize the systems and provide incentive for top-notch students to enter the start-up universities.

The policy I recommend is a long-term policy. Conservative-funded colleges with no tax money will not be easy to establish. Ranking systems will not flourish overnight. So, the short-term solution must be parenting. Bottom line: if parents do a good job teaching their children right from wrong, as I learned from my parents, when those children reach college age, they will be prepared to fight the liberal onslaught of the professors.

AND TO MY FELLOW COLLEGE STUDENTS . . .

Please, think for yourselves. When I say this, I really mean it. I do not mean that you must become a staunch conservative (although I believe reason tends toward it). All I ask is this: Question the motives of your professors. Pay attention to how they twist the facts, or editorialize during lecture. Ask them questions. Make them defend themselves. Make other students think before they buy into the professorial mindset.

The real mark of education is learning how to think. Swallowing whole what your professors say doesn't teach you to think—it teaches you to think what they want you to think. And that is indoctrination, pure and simple.

NOTES

INTRODUCTION

1. Robert M. Behrdahl, "Letter to the Editor: Berkeley: 'A Failure of Oversight' On Palestinian Poetics Course," *Wall Street Journal,* 17 May 2002.
2. Robert Stacy McCain, "Poll Confirms Ivy League Liberal Tilt," *Washington Times,* 15 January 2002.
3. Eleanor Yang, "Some see widespread liberal bias at colleges," *San Diego Union-Tribune,* 21 January 2003.
4. "The American Freshman: National Norms for Fall 2001," Higher Education Research Institute, January 2002.
5. Barbara Ortutay and Bimal Rajkomar, "UCLA students favor Al Gore," *UCLA Daily Bruin,* 8 November 2000.
6. David H. Gellis, "Harvard Law School Professors Kick Off Liberal Legal Group," *Harvard Crimson,* 3 August 2001.
7. UCLA administrator, e-mail message to author, 3 April 2001.

CHAPTER 1

1. UCLA Professor Joshua Muldavin, Geography 5, Lecture, 16 January 2001.
2. *NewsHour with Jim Lehrer,* 30 September 1998. Emphasis added.
3. Stanley Fish, "Condemnation Without Absolutes," *New York Times,* 15 October 2001.
4. "NAS/Zogby Poll Reveals American Colleges Are Teaching Dubious Ethical Lessons," NAS Press Release, 2 July 2002, http://www.nas.org/print/pressreleases/hqnas/releas_02jul02.htm.
5. John Leo, "At Postmodern U., professors who see no evil," *Jewish World Review,* 16 July 2002.
6. Sylvia Nasar, "Princeton's New Philosopher Draws a Stir," *New York Times,* 10 April 1999.
7. Paul Ehrlich, *Human Natures: Genes, Cultures, and the Human Prospect* (New York: Penguin USA, 2002), 2.

8. Dr. Paul R. Ehrlich, *The Population Bomb* (New York: Sierra Club-Ballantine, 1968), Prologue

9. As quoted by Michelle Malkin in her article, "Cop Haters Dearly Loved in Hollywood," *Capitalism Magazine*, 8 January 2001.

10. "Popular Music Under Siege," ACLU Briefer, http://www.aclu.org/library/pbr3.html.

11. Professor Lynn Vavreck, Political Science 40, Lecture, 24 January 2002.

12. Steve Lopez, "One Problem in Abu-Jamal's Crusade: He's Guilty," *Los Angeles Times*, 24 December 2001.

13. Benjamin Shapiro, "Effects of campus liberalism far-reaching," *UCLA Daily Bruin*, 20 November 2001.

14. "Judge may reject Olson guilty plea," *Los Angeles Times*, 2 November 2001.

15. According to the Sara Olson Defense Fund Committee.

16. Sharon Cohen, "Anti-war radical tells his story," Associated Press, 26 September 2001.

17. Don Babwin, "Northwestern Alumni Withhold Money," Associated Press, 1 November 2001.

CHAPTER 2

1. Robert Stacy McCain, "Poll Confirms Ivy League Liberal Tilt," *Washington Times*, 15 January 2002.

2. Phyllis Schafly, "Diversity Dishonesty on College Campuses," *The Phyllis Schafly Report*, April 2002.

3. Bruce Bartlett, "Conservative students versus their faculty," Townhall.com, 11 September 2003.

4. Jon Dougherty, "Campus commencements lean to left," WorldNetDaily.com, 3 September 2003.

5. Paul Kengor, "Reagan Among the Professors," *Policy Review Magazine*, December 1999.

6. Larry Elder, "Leftist bias in college—the denial continues," WorldNetDaily.com, 30 January 2003.

7. Robert Maranto, "For true diversity, include conservatives," *Baltimore Sun*, 31 July 2003.

8. Barbara Ortutay and Bimal Rajkomar, "UCLA students favor Al Gore," *UCLA Daily Bruin*, 8 November 2000.

9. Veronica Aguilar, "Poll: students liberal, campus politics dull," *Tufts Daily*, Spring 2002.

10. Knight Stivender, "Student poll reveals disparity in party support," *Daily Beacon*, 5 November 1996.

11. "Inauguration spells doom for democratic principles," Professor Robert N. Watson, *UCLA Daily Bruin*, 8 January 2001.

12. Payam Mahram, "Inauguration ceremonies go unseen," *UCLA Daily Bruin*, 22 January 2001.

13. UCLA Professor Matthew Baum, Political Science 20, Lecture, 11 January 2001.

14. Thomas E. Cronin and Michael Genovese, "Presidential politics in 2000," *Portland Oregonian*, 31 January 2000.

15. "A look back at Bush vs. Gore, one year later," *Daily Princetonian*, 7 November 2001.

16. "A look back at Bush vs. Gore, one year later."

17. Nicholas Zamiska, "Bush's Tax Cuts: A Shot in the Arm or the Foot?" *Yale Herald*, 30 March 2001.

18. Kelly Rayburn, "Address focuses on terrorism," *UCLA Daily Bruin*, 30 January 2002.

19. UCLA Professor Lynn Vavreck, Political Science 40, Lecture, 12 February 2002.

20. "The Ronald Reagan Home Page: Incomes," http://reagan.webteamone.com/incomes.cfm.

21. "The Ronald Reagan Home Page: Unemployment 1980-89," http://www.presidentreagan.info/unemployment.cfm.

22. "Bush's tax cuts: who benefits?" Institute for Public Accuracy, February 9, 2001. My emphasis.

23. "Bush's tax cuts: who benefits?"

24. "Bush's tax cuts: who benefits?"

25. "Election 2000—Still 'The Economy, Stupid'? MIT Economists weigh in . . .", MIT Sloan School Press Release, 31 August 2000.

26. Robert Watson, "Illogical, rude letters condemn too quickly," *UCLA Daily Bruin*, 25 February 2002.

27. Robert Watson, "Conservative outlook on economy not so great," *UCLA Daily Bruin*, 7 March 2002.

28. Geoffrey Nunberg, "On the bias," *Fresh Air*, 19 March 2002.

29. Thomas Hargrove and Guido H. Stempel III, "Many voters see bias in newspaper stories," Scripps Howard News Service, 11 November 2000.

30. ABCNews.com, 22 July 2002.

31. UCLA Professor Steven Spiegel, Honors Collegium 97, Course Syllabus.

32. UCLA Professor Lynn Vavreck, Political Science 20, Lecture, 28 February 2002.

33. Professor Scott Bowman, Political Science 167A, Lecture, 28 May 2002.

34. Samuel Kernell and Gary C. Jacobsen, *The Logic of American Politics* (Congressional Quarterly, 2000), 68.

35. "Welfare: Where do we go from here?: Opening Statements," *Atlantic Monthly* Roundtable, 12 March 1997.

36. "The Fallout of Welfare Reform," *Columbia University Record*, 20 September 1996.

37. "Welfare: Where do we go from here?: Opening Statements," *Atlantic Monthly* Roundtable, 12 March 1997.

38. Robert Rector, "The Good News About Welfare Reform," Heritage Foundation, 20 September 2001.

39. "UF Law Professor Warns Social Security Privatization Could Endanger Retirement Prospects For Millions," *University of Florida Law School News-Online*, 10 July 2001. Emphasis added.

40. *NewsHour with Jim Lehrer*, 24 July 2001.

41. Adrea Korthase, "Wayne St. discusses Bush's Social Security plans," *South End*, 11 February 2002.

42. "Raising minimum wage seems inevitable," CNN.com, 6 May 1996.

43. Eric Roston, "How much is a living wage?," Time.com, 31 March 2002.

44. "Commentary: The Case for a Minimum-Wage Hike," *Business Week*, 2 February 1998.

45. "Commentary: The Case for a Minimum-Wage Hike."

46. Larry Elder, *The Ten Things You Can't Say In America* (New York: St. Martin's Press, 2000), 113.

47. Sarah Beirute, "Brooker and Gillen face off on nationalized health care," *Oracle*, 15 April 2002.

48. Mary Lee Grant, "Texas poll: government should provide health care says 56 percent," Scripps Howard Texas Poll, 20 March 2000.

49. Kathleen Maclay, "Researchers help define what makes a political conservative," UC Berkeley News, 22 July 2003.

50. UCLA TA Darren Schreiber, Political Science 6, Section, 5 March 2002.

51. Mikhael Romain, "Panel discussion examines effects of Sept. 11 on minorities," *University of Oregon Daily Emerald*, 22 May 2002.

52. Professor Robert Watson, "Johnson fails to accept need for dissent in life," *UCLA Daily Bruin*, 20 November 2001.

53. Danielle Gillespie, "Liberals, radicals, or just activists?" *University of Oregon Daily Emerald*, 5 March 2002.

54. UCLA Professor Barbara Sinclair, Political Science 140A, Lecture, 15 January 2004.

55. UCLA Professor Kenneth Schultz, Political Science 121, Lecture, 30 May 2002.

56. UCLA Professor Lynn Vavreck, February 26, 2002.

57. Kernell and Jacobsen, *The Logic of American Politics*, 102.

58. Jim Powell, *FDR's Folly* (New York: Crown Forum, 2003).

59. Robert Stacy McCain, "Poll Confirms Ivy League Liberal Tilt," *Washington Times*, 15 January 2002.

60. Dexter Gauntlett, "Carnesale addresses US national security," *UCLA Daily Bruin*, 1 March 2002.

61. "News Conference—Union of Concerned Scientists," Federal News Service, 2 May 2001.

62. Robert Stacy McCain, "Poll Confirms Ivy League Liberal Tilt," *Washington Times*, 15 January 2002.

63. Debra Viadero, "Researchers at Center of Storm Over Vouchers," *Education Week*, 5 August 1998.

64. Viadero, "Researchers at Center of Storm Over Vouchers."

65. Kernell and Jacobsen, *The Logic of American Politics*, 489. Emphasis added.

66. Kernell and Jacobsen, *The Logic of American Politics*, 344. Emphasis added.

67. David Kaplan, "Professors sign statement opposing impeachment," *Rice News*, 12 November 1998.

68. "History professor testifies for Clinton," *New York Times*, 9 December 1998.

69. Christopher Chow, "Conservatives equal racists at MLA," Accuracy in Academia, 17 January 2002.

70. Jon Dougherty, "Campus commencements lean to left," WorldNetDaily.com, 3 September 2003.

71. Robert Salonga, "Students protest UCLA's invitation of Laura Bush to speak at commencement," *UCLA Daily Bruin*, 20 February 2002.

72. Howard Kurtz, "Al Franken: Throwing Punches and Punch Lines," *Washington Post*, 28 August 2003.

73. Michelle Malkin, "What's so funny about abstinence, Al Franken?," Townhall.com, 22 August 2003.

CHAPTER 3

1. "Comedy & Tragedy, 2003-2004," Young America's Foundation, 2003.

2. "Comedy & Tragedy, 2003-2004."

3. UCLA Professor Richard Sklar, Political Science 167A, Lecture, 7 May 2002.

4. Sklar, 23 April 2002.

5. "Struik straddled words of mathematics, Marxist politics," *MIT Tech Talk*, 14 September 1994.

6. Professor Cornel West, http://www.afroamerica.net/west.html.

7. Brandon A. Evans, "Forum offers socialism a needed outlet," *Daily Illini*, 17 November 1998.

8. Deborah Schoeneman, "Pulitzer Prize winner Kushner critiques America, pushes socialism," *Cornell Chronicle*, 18 February 1999.

9. Schoeneman, "Pulitzer Prize winner Kushner critiques America, pushes socialism."

10. Schoeneman, "Pulitzer Prize winner Kushner critiques America, pushes socialism."

11. UCLA Professor Richard Sklar, Political Science 167A, Lecture, 16 April 2002.

12. K. Watkins, "Free Trade and Farm Fallacies," *The Ecologist* v. 25, Nov/Dec 1996.

13. UCLA Professor Jurgen Essletzbichler, Geography 4 Syllabus, Fall 2000. Emphasis added.

14. Sarah H. Wright, "Merits of teaming capitalism and democracy discussed at colloquium," *MIT Tech Talk*, 18 October 2000. Emphasis added.

15. Wright, "Merits of teaming capitalism and democracy discussed at colloquium."

16. Maureen McDonald, "Urban crisis is historian's theme," *Detroit News*, 14 February 2001.

17. As quoted by Betsy Hart, "It's gettin' better all the time," *Jewish World Review*, 2 January 2001.

18. Elizabeth Goodman, "Ayn Rand's resurgence," *Penn State Digital Collegian*, 10 September 1999.

19. Teri Sforza, "Ayn Rand groups shrugs off old HQ," *Orange County Register*, 6 June 2002.

20. Hugh Aynesworth, "Texas town sees Red as Marxist professor rides tenure track," *Washington Times*, 27 March 2002.

21. Jennifer Hagin, "Lawsuits bolster Fla. coffers," *Daily Tar Heel*, 10 April 2000.

22. John Creed, "USA: Oil Firms Fund 'Tobacco Terrorism'," *Anchorage Daily News*, 7 November 2001.

23. Joe Light, "A question of conflict: the university and tobacco," *Yale Daily News*, 7 December 2001.

24. Geraldine Sealey, "Whose fault is fat?" ABCNews.com, 22 January 2002.

25. Sealey, "Whose fault is fat?"

26. Sealey, "Whose fault is fat?"

27. Paul Ehrlich, *Human Natures: Genes, Cultures, and the Human Prospect* (New York: Penguin USA, 2002), 266.

28. Robert Watson, "Conservatives quick to excuse war crimes," *UCLA Daily Bruin*, 10 May 2001.

29. UCLA Professor Joshua Muldavin, Geography 5, Lecture, 23 January 2001.

30. Eric Mann, *LA's Lethal Air: New Strategies for Policy, Organizing, and Action* (Los Angeles: Labor/Community Watchdog, 1991), 9.

31. UCLA Professor Joshua Muldavin, Geography 5, Lecture, February 1, 2001. Emphasis added.

32. Robert Watson, "Johnson fails to accept need for dissent in life," *UCLA Daily Bruin*, 20 November 2001.

33. Robert Watson, "Johnson fails to accept need for dissent in life," *UCLA Daily Bruin*, 20 November 2001.

34. Dana Cloud, "Pledge for the workers," *Daily Texan*, 1 July 2002.

35. UCLA Professor Marilyn Raphael, Geography 124, Lecture, 4 April 2002.

36. Eric Mann, *LA's Lethal Air: New Strategies for Policy, Organizing, and Action*, 35.

37. Mann, *LA's Lethal Air*, 36.

38. Mann, *LA's Lethal Air*, 46. Emphasis added.

39. F. Lappe, J. Collins, and P. Rossett, *World Hunger: Twelve Myths* (New York: Grove Press, 1998), 175.

40. UCLA Professor Jurgen Essletzbichler, Geography 4, Lecture, Week 6, Fall 2000.

41. Essletzbichler, Week 8, Fall 2000.

42. Essletzbichler, Week 6, Fall 2000.

43. Sean Axmaker, Amazon.com essential video, Editorial Review of *Roger and Me*.

44. UCLA Professor Jurgen Essletzbichler, Geography 4, Lecture, Week 6, Fall 2000.

45. Steve Pearlstein, "In Blossoming Scandal, Culprits Are Countless," *Washington Post*, 28 June 2002.

46. Pearlstein, "In Blossoming Scandal, Culprits Are Countless." Emphasis added.

47. Pearlstein, "In Blossoming Scandal, Culprits Are Countless."

48. "NAS/Zogby Poll Reveals American Colleges Are Teaching Dubious Ethical Lessons," NAS Press Release, July 2, 2002, http://www.nas.org/print/pressreleases/hqnas/releas_02jul02.htm.

49. "NAS/Zogby Poll Reveals American Colleges Are Teaching Dubious Ethical Lessons."

50. *NBC News/Wall Street Journal* Poll, July 19-21, 2002.

51. Steven Greenhouse, "Labor leaders and intellectuals are forging new alliance," *New York Times*, 22 September 1996. Emphasis added.

52. Greenhouse, "Labor leaders and intellectuals are forging new alliance."

53. "What We Stand For: Mission and Goals of the AFL-CIO," http://www.aflcio.org/aboutaflcio/about/mission/index.cfm. Emphasis added.

54. Federal Elections Committee Report, 30 June 2002, <opensecrets.org>.

55. UCLA Professor Joshua Muldavin, Geography 5, Lecture, 20 February 2001.

56. "The Great Reform of China: An Alternative View," Interview with Joshua Muldavin, *Intercom, Newsletter of ISOP*, Vol. 18, No. 7, May 1996.

57. "The Great Reform of China: An Alternative View," Interview with Joshua Muldavin. Emphasis added.

58. "The Great Reform of China: An Alternative View," Interview with Joshua Muldavin.

59. UCLA Professor Joshua Muldavin, Geography 5, class discussion board, Winter 2001.

60. "Cuba's Isolation Fosters Challenges, Along with Charms for Medical Teams," *Stanford Medical Staff Update*, June 1999.

61. "Going Home Could Be Good for Elian's Health," *SLU Newslink*, 3 April 2000.

62. "The Living Streets of Havana," Ken Gewertz, *Harvard University Gazette*, May 9, 2002.

63. Karl Marx and Frederick Engels, *Communist Manifesto* (Boston: Bedford/St. Martin's, 1999), 78.

64. F. Lappe, J. Collins, and P. Rossett, *World Hunger: Twelve Myths*, 175.

65. Thomas Sowell, *The Quest for Cosmic Justice* (New York: Free Press, 1999), 167.

66. Barry Commoner, "How Poverty Breeds Overpopulation," *Ramparts Magazine*, Aug/Sept 1975.

67. Eric Mann, *LA's Lethal Air: New Strategies for Policy, Organizing, and Action*, 71.

68. Paul Ehrlich, *Human Natures: Genes, Cultures, and the Human Prospect*, 322.

69. "Our Structure," Democratic Socialists of America, http://www.dsausa.org/about/structure.html.

70. "Where We Stand," Democratic Socialists of America, http://www.dsausa.org/about/where.html.

CHAPTER 4

1. Bimal Rajkomar, "Minority admits at UC near pre-SP-1 levels," *UCLA Daily Bruin*, 4 April 2001.

2. Eli C. Minkoff and Pamela J. Baker, *Biology Today: An Issues Approach*, 196.

3. B.P. Giri, "CSAS Hosts Seminar and Panel Discussion on Afghanistan and Pakistan," *University of Virginia Center for South Asian Studies Newsletter*, Fall 2001.

4. Kelly Rayburn, "Students unite to remember the Holocaust," *UCLA Daily Bruin*, 10 April 2002.

5. Dinesh D'Souza, *Illiberal Education: The Politics of Race and Sex on Campus* (New York: Free Press, 1991), 5

6. "Comedy & Tragedy, 2003-2004," Young America's Foundation, 2003.

7. "History 330 Syllabus," Oberlin College Web site, http://www.oberlin.edu/faculty/dmaeda/hist330/.

8. J. Lawrence Scholer, "The Failure of Middle Eastern Studies," *Dartmouth Review*, 4 February 2002.

9. J. Lawrence Scholer, "The Failure of Middle Eastern Studies."

10. Anne D. Neal, *Exfemina*, Independent Women's Forum, April 2001.

11. Eric Mann, *LA's Lethal Air: New Strategies for Policy, Organizing, and Action* (Los Angeles: Labor/Community Watchdog, 1991), 28.

12. Eric Mann, *LA's Lethar Air: New Strategies for Policy Organizing and Action*, 28.

13. Samuel Kernell and Gary C. Jacobsen, *The Logic of American Politics*, (Congressional Quarterly, 2000), 92.

14. Kernell and Jacobsen, *The Logic of American Politics*, 344.

15. Kelly Rayburn and Christian Jenkins, "Conference covers views on race, ethnicity issues," *UCLA Daily Bruin*, 29 May 2002.

16. Noel Ignatiev, Talk given at the conference "The Making and Unmaking of Whiteness," University of California, Berkeley, 11-13 April 1997.

17. Sara Russo, "Harvard University Fellow Advocates 'Abolishing the White Race,'" Accuracy in Academia, 10 September 2002.

18. *Schooled in Hate: Anti-Semitism on Campus*, Anti-Defamation League, 1997.

19. Vernellia R. Randall, "Institutional Racism in the US Health Care System: Statement to the Committee on the Elimination of Racial Discrimination," 24 January 2001, http://www.udayton.edu/~health/07HumanRights/WCAR02.htm.

20. Karen Feldscher, "Minorities seek greater respect," *Northeastern Voice*, http://www.voice.neu.edu/961024/survey.html.

21. Andrew Edwards, "UCLA faculty remembers course of events of riot," *UCLA Daily Bruin*, 29 April 2002.

22. Professor Donald E. Wilkes, "Lawlessness in law enforcement," *Campus Times*, 30 May 1991.

23. Phat X. Chiem, "The Verdict and the Violence," USC The Law School News Release, 29 April 2002.

24. "Building a Multiracial and Multiethnic Community in Los Angeles," *Inside Dominguez Halls*, December 2000/January 2001.

25. "Building a Multiracial and Multiethnic Community in Los Angeles."

26. Linda Deutsch, "The Legacy of Rodney King," ABCNews.com, 3 March 2001.

27. UCLA Professor Daniel Buring, Linguistics 1, Course Reader, Spring 2001.

28. Lisa Estey, "Ebonics creator: language is a tool," *Times-Delphic Online*, 4 March 1997.

29. "Ebonics Insider," *Stanford Magazine*, March/April 1997.

30. Todd Hardy, "Panel emphasizes value of Ebonics as teaching aid," *Arizona Daily Wildcat*, 28 February 1997.

31. Tamina Agha, "Ebonics supported at discussion," *Northeastern News*, February 26, 1997.

32. Linda Prendez, "Debate over Ebonics masks racism," Daily Forty-Niner, 26 February 1997.

33. Eric M. Jukelevics, "UA professor defends bilingual education," *Arizona Daily Wildcat*, 3 February 1999.

34. UCLA Professor Pamela Munro, Linguistics 1, Lecture, 8 May 2001.

35. Robert Stacy McCain, "Poll Confirms Ivy League Liberal Tilt," *Washington Times*, 15 January 2002.

36. John Mack Faragher, Mari Jo Buhle, Daniel Czitrom, Susan H. Armitage, *Out of Many: A History of the American People, Volume I: To 1877* (New Jersey, Prentice Hall, 1999), 88.

37. Faragher, Buhle, Czitrom, Armitage, *Out of Many: A History of the American People*, 100-101. Emphasis added.

38. Marty Toohey, "Legal experts want slavery reparations," *University of Oregon Daily Emerald,* 24 October 2001.

39. Carla Blumenkranz, "In talk, RIC professor calls slavery 'part of the American pedigree'," *Brown Daily Herald,* 18 October 2001.

40. Robert Chrisman and Ernest Allen Jr., "Ten Reasons: A Response to David Horowitz," http://www.umass.edu/afroam/hor.html.

41. Chrisman and Allen Jr. "Ten Reasons: A Response to David Horowitz."

42. Jake Lilien, "David Horowitz to speak at Amherst College," *University of Massachusetts Daily Collegian,* 12 March 2002.

43. Michael Mitchell, "Controversy Comes to Campus: A Response to David Horowitz," *Legacy Magazine,* 2002.

44. Ehrlich, *Human Natures: Genes, Cultures, and the Human Prospect,* 2.

45. Bimal Rajkomar, "Atkinson proposes dropping SAT I in admissions," *UCLA Daily Bruin,* February 20, 2001.

46. Rajkomar, "Atkinson proposes dropping SAT I in admissions."

47. Robert Salonga, "College Board expands SAT I with writing section, more complex math," *UCLA Daily Bruin,* 1 July 2002.

48. This is an actual question on a sample SAT test.

49. June Kronholz, "No Pimples, Pools, or Pop," *Wall Street Journal,* 18 July 2002.

50. Crystal Betz, "Panelists address educational access issues," *UCLA Daily Bruin,* 1 February 2002.

51. Daniel Golden, "To Get Into UCLA, It Helps to Face 'Life Challenges'," *Wall Street Journal,* 12 July 2002.

52. "Press Release: The Civil Rights Project Hails Decision in University of Michigan Affirmative Action Case," The Civil Rights Project: Harvard University, 14 May 2002.

53. Timothy Kudo, "Connerly proposes to bar ethnic questions," *UCLA Daily Bruin,* 15 February 2001.

54. Shauna Mecartea, "Petitions for privacy act underway," *UCLA Daily Bruin,* 27 April 2001.

55. Charles Proctor, "UCLA admissions probed," *UCLA Daily Bruin,* 22 October 2003.

56. Kim-Mai Culter and Janine Pliska, "Article Criticizes UC Berkeley Admissions," *UC Berkeley Daily Californian,* 7 October 2003.

57. David Limbaugh, "Targeting campus speech codes," Townhall.com, 16 August 2003.

58. Andrew Grossman, "College Lite: less filling, tastes great?" Townhall.com, 17 October 2003.

59. Andrew Grossman, "College Lite: less filling, tastes great?"

60. David Limbaugh, "Targeting campus speech codes," Townhall.com 16 August 2003.

61. http://speechcodes.org/schools.php?id=80.

62. http://speechcodes.org/schools.php?id=223.

63. http://speechcodes.org/schools.php?id=929.

64. http://speechcodes.org/schools.php?id=738.

65. http://speechcodes.org/schools.php?id=659.

66. http://speechcodes.org/schools.php?id=979.

CHAPTER 5

1. Robert Watson, "Scandal, dishonesty extend across party ideology," *UCLA Daily Bruin*, January 25, 2002.

2. Barbara Ortutay, "Campus Talk," *TenPercent*, Fall 2001, 12.

3. Rick Goldberg, "Shapiro incorrect about sexuality," *UCLA Daily Bruin*, October 12, 2001.

4. Jeff Thomas, "Visibility of gays a social necessity," *UCLA Daily Bruin*, October 12, 2001.

5. Kelly Finn, "Shapiro's wrong on coming out," *UCLA Daily Bruin*, October 15, 2001.

6. "And The Damned: Dartmouth's Worst," *Dartmouth Review*, 27 September 2002.

7. *UCLA General Catalog*, 1999-2001, 283.

8. "Members of the Center," Center for Sex Research, http://www.csun.edu/~sr2022/members.htm.

9. "University Course and Programs Committee: Undergraduate courses," May 7, 2003, http://www.uark.edu/depts/facsen/facsen2002to2003/TableA5703.pdf.

10. "Comedy & Tragedy, 2003-2004," Young America's Foundation, 2003, http://www.yaf.org/publications/c&t.asp.

11. "Comedy & Tragedy, 2003-2004," http://www.yaf.org/publications/c&t.asp.

12. "Comedy & Tragedy, 2003-2004," http://www.yaf.org/publications/c&t.asp.

13. "Comedy & Tragedy, 2003-2004," http://www.yaf.org/publications/c&t.asp.

14. "Truman State University Division of Language and Literature: Majors Offered," http://11truman.edu/majors.html/

15. "Department of English: Fall 1997 courses," http://www.uwm.edu/Dept/English/fall1997/f97lane2.shtml.

16. "Appendix: Courses Certified for 2000-2001 As Fulfilling The Undergraduate General Education Requirements," http://www.stanford.edu/dept/registrar/bulletin/bulletin00-01/pdf/Appendix.pdf.

17. "Comedy & Tragedy, 2003-2004," Young America's Foundation, 2003.

18. "Comedy & Tragedy, 2003-2004," Young America's Foundation, 2003.

19. "IWU Women's Studies Program—Course Offerings," http://titan.iwu.edu/~wstudies/courses.html.

20. "Comedy & Tragedy, 2003-2004," Young America's Foundation, 2003.

21. "Bryn Mawr: Feminist and Gender Studies: Courses," http://www.brynmawr.edu/femgen/courses02-03.shtml.

22. "English 331: Queer Literature/Queer Theory," http://www.brynmawr.edu/english/courses/331.html.

23. "Comedy & Tragedy, 2003-2004," Young America's Foundation, 2003.

24. Sarah R. Buchholz, "Complaints prompt professor to remove sex material on Web," *University of Massachusetts Chronicle*, 14 April 2000.

25. Claudette Riley, "Professor to spend year writing book," *Kansas State Collegian*, 6 February 1998.

26. "Gloria G. Brame, PhD, MPH," http://www.sexualhealth.com/experts/viewexpert.cfm?ID=85.

27. Daniel J. Wakin, "Keep the Sex R-Rated, NYU Tells Film Students," *New York Times*, 4 December 2003.

28. Editorial, "Give film profs voice in policy," *Washington Square News*, 3 December 2003.
29. Daniel J. Wakin, "Keep the Sex R-Rated, NYU Tells Film Students," *New York Times*, 4 December 2003.
30. Robin Clewley, "A Sprinkle of Porn, Art, Feminism," *Wired News*, 21 January 2002.
31. Matt Smith, "Public Enema No. 2," *SF Weekly*, 23 February 2000.
32. Kim Curtis, "Gross-Out Artist," Associated Press, Copyright 2000.
33. Curtis, "Gross-Out Artist."
34. UCLA Professor Lynn Vavreck, Political Science 40, Lecture, 7 March 2002.
35. Thomas Jefferson, Andrew A Lipscomb, ed., *The Writings of Thomas Jefferson: Volume I*, (Washington, D. C.: Thomas Jefferson Memorial Association, 1904) 226-227.
36. "UN group in 'showdown with religion'," WorldNetDaily.com, 8 August 2003.
37. Samuel Kernell and Gary C. Jacobsen, *The Logic of American Politics*, (Congressional Quarterly, 2000), 122.
38. Paul Ehrlich, *Human Natures: Genes, Cultures, and the Human Prospect* (New York: Penguin USA, 2002), 14.
39. "UNC task force recommends sexuality studies program," Associated Press, 29 July 2002.
40. Barbara Ortutay, "Transgender 101," *TenPercent*, Spring/Summer 2002.
41. "The ultra-fabulous and not-so glamorous homo class revue!" *TenPercent*, Winter 2002.
42. Randy Thomas, "Inching toward equality," *Ten Percent*, Spring/Summer 2002.
43. Leslie Hague, "Same-sex benefits a possibility," *Daily Illini*, 19 July 2002.
44. Bill Schackner, "Pitt Pressured Anew on Same-Sex Benefits," *Pittsburgh Post-Gazette*, 5 April 2000.
45. Bill Schackner, "CMU board OKs same-sex benefits," *Pittsburgh Post-Gazette*, 23 March 2000.
46. Susan Eckerman, "Class is Out," *TenPercent*, Fall 2001.
47. Eckerman, "Class is Out."
48. Eckerman, "Class is Out."
49. Robert Stacey McCain, "Promoting Pedophilia," *Washington Times*, 19 April 2002.
50. Lynn Franey, "Professor defends writing on pedophilia," *Kansas City Star*, 31 March 2002.
51. Robert Stacey McCain, "Promoting Pedophilia," *Washington Times*, 19 April 2002.
52. McCain, "Promoting Pedophilia."
53. McCain, "Promoting Pedophilia."
54. Lynn Franey, "Professor defends writing on pedophilia," *Kansas City Star*, 31 March 2002.
55. Garry Willis, "Priests and Boys," *New York Times Review of Books*, 13 June 2002.
56. Jessica Cantelon, "Coming-of-Age Film Sparks Conservative Criticism," CNSNews.com, 31 July 2002.
57. Peter Singer, "Heavy Petting," *Nerve Magazine*, March/April 2001.
58. Marjorie Garber, *Dog Love* (New York: Simon and Schuster, 1996), 149.
59. Marjorie Garber, *Dog Love* (New York: Simon and Schuster, 1996), 144.
60. John Leo, "It's grin-and-bare-it time at U.C. Berkeley," Townhall.com, 4 March 2002.

61. Sarah Gold, "Gypsy Rose Coed," Salon.com, 12 May 1999.

62. Eric Rich, "Wesleyan Brings Porn Into The Classroom," *Hartford Courant*, 8 May 1999.

63. Dave Ranney, "Senator plans to watch videos from KU sex class," *Lawrence Journal-World*, 2 May 2003.

64. "Text of letter from KU liberal arts faculty supporting Dailey," *Lawrence Journal-World*, 19 May 2003.

65. Associated Press, "Pornography classes proliferate on college campuses," *Portsmouth Herald*, 20 August 2001.

66. Ken Sato, "College can be time of sexual learning as result of new freedoms," *Orion Dimensions*, 8 November 2000.

67. Anna Stubblefield, "Dr. Ruth discusses keys to good sex," *Brown Daily Herald*, 5 December 2003.

68. Paul C. Reisser, "The Painful Hook in 'Hooking Up'," *Physician Magazine*, November/December 2001.

69. Laura Kipnis, "Off Limits," *MSN Slate Magazine*, 2 January 2004.

70. Dan Froomkin, "Professor fights for right to sex with coeds," *Orange County Register*, 26 June 1994.

71. Stuart Silverstein and Rebecca Trounson, "Student-faculty trysts banned," *Detroit News*, 15 December 2002.

72. Stuart Silverstein and Rebecca Trounson, "Student-faculty trysts banned."

73. Justin Scott, "UC May Ban Faculty-Student Romances, Sex," *Daily Nexus Online*, 15 May 2003.

74. Christopher Heredia, "S.F. State offers degree in sex," *San Francisco Chronicle*, 26 January 2002.

CHAPTER 6

1. "Judeo-Christian Tradition Best Basis for Environmentalism," *Religion and Liberty*, Volume 9, Number 2, March and April, 1999.

2. Shelley Smithson, "Big Plan on Campus," *Grist Magazine*, 31 July 2002.

3. UCLA Professor C. F. Brunk, Life Science 15, Lecture, 6 June 2002.

4. "Environmental Diplomacy," *Online Newshour Forum*, 12 December 1997.

5. Stephen Dinan, "GOP disputes global-warming cause," *Washington Times*, 30 July 2003.

6. UCLA Professor C. F. Brunk, Life Science 15, Lecture, 4 June 2002.

7. David Stauth, "Scientists warn about impacts of climate change," *Oregon State University News*, 24 July 1997.

8. Shelley Smithson, "Big Plan on Campus," *Grist Magazine*, 31 July 2002.

9. "Environmental Diplomacy," *Online Newshour Forum*, 12 December 1997.

10. "Researchers Rally for Kyoto Accord," *Harvard Focus*, 19 December 1997.

11. David Stauth, "Scientists warn about impacts of climate change," *Oregon State University News*, 24 July 1997.

12. UCLA Professor Kenneth Schultz, Political Science 121, Lecture, 4 June 2002.

13. Matt Boyd, "President's policy gets mixed reports," *Diamondback*, 2 May 2001.

14. *Newshour with Jim Lehrer*, 30 April 2001.

15. Huck Gutman, "Changes of historic magnitude," DAWN.com, 11 August 2001.

16. Sallie Baliunas, "The Kyoto Protocol and Global Warming," *Imprimis*, March 2002.

17. UCLA Professor Kenneth Schultz, Political Science 121, Lecture, 4 June 2002.

18. William R. Moomaw, "Who can stop the gas pains?," *Boston Globe*, 13 May 2001.

19. Kathleen Maclay, "Economists find no shortage of culprits behind high gas prices," *Berkeleyan*, 11 July 2001.

20. Sean Holstage and Bill Brand, "Davis to sign emissions legislation," *Oakland Tribune*, 20 July 2002.

21. Holstage and Brand, "Davis to sign emissions legislation."

22. David F. Salisbury, "Science, politics, speculation all key in assessing climate change," *Stanford Review*, 28 October 1998.

23. UCLA Professor C. F. Brunk, Life Science 15, Lecture, 30 May 2002.

24. Christopher Quinn, "GAS TAX: Roads outrun state's money Georgia's growth has left the ability to expand and maintain highways in the dust," *Atlanta Journal-Constitution*, 17 November 2001.

25. Jackie Calmes and Christopher Georges, "Economists say gasoline tax is too low," *Wall Street Journal*, 7 May 1996.

26. Calmes and Georges, "Economists say gasoline tax is too low."

27. "Professor discusses global warming," *MIT Tech Talk*, 2 May 2001.

28. Jennifer McNulty, "Environmentalists make a plea for 'patriotic' energy conservation," *UC Santa Cruz Currents*, 12 November 2001.

29. Bill McAllister, "Remote Arctic Refuge draws eco-tourists," Morris News Service, 26 July 2001.

30. Albert A. Bartlett, "Testimony: US House of Representatives: Committee on Science: Subcommittee on Energy," 3 May 2001.

31. John Gartner, "Budget Plan Fuels Energy Debate," *Wired News*, 5 February 2002.

32. Rory Hassler, "Gas prices on rise as summer nears," *Penn State Digital Collegian*, 12 April 2002.

33. George Will, "Dishonorable Slogan," *This Week with George Stephanopoulos*, 2 March 2003.

34. Marvin Olasky, "How to fight our addiction to Saudi oil," Townhall.com, 23 July 2002.

35. Brian Hansen, "Arctic Drilling Proposal Sparks Heated Debate," Environmental News Service, 1 November 2000.

36. Steven Dinero, "The real cost of drilling," *Christian Science Monitor*, 8 October 1999.

37. "Religious and Political Leaders Join to Oppose ANWR Drilling," Environmental News Service, 8 February 2002.

38. Terry McCarthy, "War Over Arctic Oil," *Time Magazine*, 19 February 2001.

39. "Prudhoe Bay Area Caribou Numbers Highest Ever," Petroleum News Alaska News Release, 22 December 2000.

40. Garrett Hardin, "Living on a Lifeboat," *BioScience*. v. 24, 1974, 561-568.

41. Paul Ehrlich, *The Population Bomb* (New York: Sierra Club-Ballantine, 1968), 66-67.

42. UCLA Professor C. F. Brunk, Life Science 15, Lecture, 18 April 2002.

43. Brunk, 14 May 2002.

44. Brunk, 16 May 2002.

45. Brunk, 23 May 2002.

46. Eli C. Minkoff and Pamela J. Baker, *Biology Today: An Issues Approach*, (London: Garland Publishing, 2000), 232.

47. UCLA Professor C. F. Brunk, Life Science 15, Lecture, 30 May 2002.

48. Allan Combs, "Conversations for a better world," http://rocky.unca.edu/~combs/conversations.html.

49. Julia Sommerfeld, "Will technology save us from overpopulation?," MSNBC.com, 12 October 1999.

50. Paul Ehrlich, *Human Natures: Genes, Cultures, and the Human Prospect*, 322.

51. Ronald Bailey, "Rebels Against the Future," *Reason Magazine Online*, 28 February 2001.

52. Neil Postman, "The Virtue and Intelligence of Moderation: An Address by Neil Postman," Regent University Journalism Conference, 28 February 1998.

53. Bonnie Dhall, "Media guru says computers isolate people," *Golden Gater Online*, 11 May 1995.

54. Media Relations, "UC Berkeley's 2001 Summer Reading List," Berkeley Press Release, 5 June 2001.

55. Editorial Staff, "The Life and Deaths of DDT," *Wall Street Journal*, 14 June 2002.

56. Editorial Staff, "The Life and Deaths of DDT."

57. UCLA Professor Joshua Muldavin, Geography 5, Section, 25 January 2001.

58. Richard A. Posner, "In over their heads," *Boston Globe*, 27 January 2002.

59. "The Preceptorials: 2000-2001," http://dolphin.upenn.edu/~precepts/spring02/eagles02.html.

60. UCLA TA Louis Lee, Life Science 15, Section, 24 April 2002.

61. Lee, Life Science 15, Section, 24 April 2002.

62. UCLA Professor C. F. Brunk, Life Science 15, Lecture, 30 May 2002.

63. UCLA Professor Joshua Muldavin, Geography 5, Lecture, 8 March 2001.

64. Ravi Batra, "Third World Agriculture: A Proutist Approach," *New Renaissance Magazine*, Volume 1, Issue 1, 1990.

65. Colin Morris, "Earth Institute's Jeffrey Sachs, Pedro Sanchez Address U.N. Goal of Eradicating Extreme Poverty By 2015 at Summit," *Columbia News*, 25 June 2003.

66. UCLA Professor C. F. Brunk, Life Science 15, Lecture, 4 June 2002.

67. "PBS: Harvest of Fear: Interviews: Jane Rissler," 2001, http://www.pbs.org/wgbh/harvest/interviews/rissler.html.

68. UCLA Professor C.F. Brunk, Life Science 15, Lecture, 4 June 2002.

69. Edward O. Wilson, "Building an Ethic," *Defenders Magazine*, Spring 1993.

70. Julian Simon, "Facts, not species, are periled," *New York Times*, 13 May 1993.

71. Philip S. Levine and Donald A. Levine, "The Real Biodiversity Crisis," *American Scientist Magazine*, January-February 2002.

72. Mark Shwartz, "Study suggests global extinction crisis more serious than previously thought," *Stanford University News Service*, 23 April 2002.

73. "State of the Planet: Episode 1: Is there a crisis?," BBC World, August 10-11, 2002.

74. Julian Simon, "Facts, not species, are periled," *New York Times*, 13 May 1993.

75. Edward O. Wilson, "Vanishing Point," *Grist Magazine*, 12 December 2001.

76. Wilson, "Vanishing Point."

77. Andrew Bernstein, "Environmentalism vs. Human Life," *Media Link: The Ayn Rand Institute*, 20 April 2001.

78. Glenn Woiceshyn, "Environmentalism, Eco-terrorism, and Endangered Species," *Capitalism Magazine*, 25 January1999.

CHAPTER 7

1. "Globalization and its Discontents," TIME Europe Web Exclusive, 30 January 2000.

2. David F. Salisbury, "Computer pioneer discusses atheism, artificial intelligence," *Stanford Report Online*, 17 March 1999.

3. "Interview: Steven Weinberg," PBS television program "Faith and Reason: Transcript."

4. Julie Emery, "Pulitzer Prize poet in Seattle," *Seattle Times*, 25 May 1972.

5. Arheun Kim, "Students, philosophers debate God's existence," *Diamondback*, 25 February 2000.

6. "Mind, Faith, and Spirit," *Princeton Daily Bulletin*, 26 April 1999.

7. Virginia I. Postrel, "Interview with the Vamp," *Reason Magazine Online*, Aug/Sep 1995 http://reason.com/9508/PAGLIA.aug.shtml.

8. William F. Buckley, *God and Man at Yale* (Chicago: Henry Regnery Company, 1951), 4.

9. Maggie Gallagher, "Ivy-covered bias," Townhall.com, 23 January 2002.

10. Dalia Sussman, "Who Goes to Church?," ABCNews.com, 1 March 2002.

11. Maggie Gallagher, "Ivy-covered bias," Townhall.com, 23 January 2002.

12. "Three Days of Hope," *Pennsylvania Gazette*, January/February 1999.

13. Christina Jenkins, "Students explore distinctions of spirituality vs. religion in society," *UCLA Daily Bruin*, 19 February 2002.

14. Joyce Howard Price, "Princeton bioethicist argues Christianity hurts animals," *Washington Times*, 4 July 2002.

15. Paul Ehrlich, *Human Natures: Genes, Cultures, and the Human Prospect* (New York: Penguin USA, 2002), 257.

16. UCLA Professor Joshua Muldavin, Geography 5, Lecture, 11 January 2001.

17. UCLA Professor C. F. Brunk, Life Science 15, Lecture, 22 April 2002.

18. William Lobdell, "4 Faces of Christianity's Future," *Los Angeles Times*, 15 February 2003.

19. Peter Smith, "Clergy, others call for tolerance of foreigners and Muslims," *Louisville Courier-Journal*, 13 September 2001.

20. Megan Over, "Religion panel explores diversity," *New Media Index*, 13 April 2000.

21. "Muslim Educator Dr. Nadira K. Charaniya is keynote speaker for Hebrew Union College—Jewish Institute of Religion's Rhea Hirsch School of Education Yom Iyun (Day of Study)," *HUC-JIR News*, 25 September 2001.

22. Brandon Johnson, "Panel offers answers," *Campus Carrier*, 20 September 2001.

23. Peter Smith, "Sermons strive for comfort, some answers," *Louisville Courier-Journal*, 17 September 2001.

24. Marvin Pittman, "Understanding More about Islam," *Harvard Graduate School of Education News*, 4 October 2001.

25. Koran 3:19, 9:30, 19:88, 4:56, 4:160, 41:26, 48:29, 5:36, 5:82, among others. N. J. Dawood, translator, *The Koran* (London: Penguin Classics, 1999).

26. "In the News," *BU Bridge*, 8 March 2002.

27. Jeff Burlew, "Forum sets the record straight on religions," *Tallahassee Democrat*, 14 December 2001.

28. Ken Gewertz, "Harvard's Muslims grieving, wary," *Harvard Gazette*, 20 September 2001.

29. Nancy Neff, "The politics of interpreting Islam," *On Campus*, 25 October 2001.

30. Jill Goetz, "New book introduces Westerners to Islamic principles of justice," *Cornell Chronicle*, 22 August 1996.

31. Koran 9:30, 5:51, and 5:36.

32. Jane Pek, "Misunderstood Muslims reach out to Yalies," *Yale Herald*, 22 February 2002.

33. Yvonne Chiu Hays, "Ahmed studies differences, seeks unity," *Princeton Weekly Bulletin*, 4 December 2000.

34. Crystal Kua, "Educators: Creation theory not scientific," *Honolulu Star-Bulletin*, 28 July 2001.

35. "Interview: Ron Number," PBS television program "Faith and Reason: Transcript."

36. "Americans more likely to believe creationism than evolution," *Catholic World News*, 19 August 1998.

37. Eli C. Minkoff and Pamela J. Baker, *Biology Today: An Issues Approach* (London: Garland Publishing, 2000),143.

38. Minkoff and Baker, 144.

39. Paul Ehrlich, *Human Natures: Genes, Cultures, and the Human Prospect*, 324.

40. Crystal Kua, "Educators: Creation theory not scientific."

41. Kua, "Educators: Creation theory not scientific."

42. Mia Taylor, "COBB COUNTY EVOLUTION DEBATE: Teachers on front lines of conflict," *Atlanta Journal-Constitution*, 24 August 2002.

43. Taylor, "COBB COUNTY EVOLUTION DEBATE: Teachers on front lines of conflict."

44. Rusty Pugh, "Christian college denied accreditation over creationist views," Agape Press, 10 May 2002.

45. Courtney Leatherman, "College Won't Renew Contract of Biology Professor Accused of Teaching Creation," *The Chronicle of Higher Education*, 31 March 2000.

46. "Husker Biographies: Ron Brown," Huskers.com (The Official Site of Nebraska Athletics), 14 July 2003.

47. Paul M. Weyrich, "Stanford: Christians Need Not Apply," *Free Congress Commentary*, 23 April 2002.

48. Weyrich, "Stanford: Christians Need Not Apply."

49. Anne Edison-Swift, "Lawmakers weigh medical conscience concerns," Capital News Service, 19 October 2001.

50. Andrea Garrett, "Intolerant Tolerance: Anti-Christian Bigotry on Campus," *Christian Broadcasting Network News*, 10 July 2002.

51. Tarleton Cowen, "Fling or forever?," *Daily Princetonian*, 8 October 2001.

52. Phyllis Schafly, "'Yale Five' Challenge Rule on Co-ed Dorms," *Education Reporter*, September 1998.

53. Anna Arkin-Gallagher, "'Yale Five' lose appeal in court," *Yale Daily News*, 12 January 2001.

54. Maggie Gallagher, "Ivy-covered bias," Townhall.com, 23 January 2002.

55. Eve Tushnet, "College students see the human face of abortion," *National Catholic Register*, 10-16 September 2000.

56. Michelle Gerise Godwin, "The Progressive Interview: Sarah Weddington," *The Progressive*, August 2000.

57. John Leo, "'Diversity' proponents should learn what the word means," *Jewish World Review*, 28 January 2002.

58. Megan Desario, "Abortion debate busts under eleventh-hour state pressure," *Daily Illini*, 21 January 1999.

59. Desario, "Abortion debate busts under eleventh-hour state pressure."

60. Geraldine Sealey, "Considering 'Partial-Birth' Ban," ABCNews.com, 24 April 2000.

61. Margaret A. Woodbury, "A doctor's right to choose," Salon.com, 24 July 2002.

62. "Abortion debate continues to rage over controversial laws," Medill News Service, 21 January 1998.

63. Ken Gewertz, "The Right to Die," *Harvard Gazette*, 6 June 1996.

64. "The Hemlock Board," The Hemlock Society of USA Web site, hemlock.org, 2003.

65. "Death with dignity national center: board and staff," Death with dignity Web site, deathwithdignity.org, 2003.

66. Marcella Bernard, "The Father of Health Law," *Harvard Public Health Review 75th Anniversary Issue*, 1997.

67. Joan Biskupic, "Unanimous Decision Points to Tradition of Valuing Life," *Washington Post*, 27 June 1997.

68. Jim Irwin, "Right-to-die movement working even without Kevorkian, backers say," Associated Press, 3 January 2000.

69. Gregg Krupa, "Few Kevorkian clients terminally ill," *Detroit News*, 7 December 2000.

70. Thomas Hargrove and Guido H. Stempel III, "75% say God answers prayers," *Detroit News*, 28 December 1999.

CHAPTER 8

1. John Leo, "Campus hand-wringing is not a pretty sight," Townhall.com, 1 October 2001.

2. Jennifer W. Sanchez, "UNM professor's resignation sought over Sept. 11 comment," *Albuquerque Tribune*, 26 September 2001.

3. UCLA Professor Dan O'Neill, Political Science 10, Lecture, 6 December 2001.

4. UCLA Professor Dan O'Neill.

5. Franklin Foer, "Disoriented," *New Republic Online*, 3 December 2001.

6. Walter Williams, "Elitist Contempt for American Values," *Capitalism Magazine*, 13 November 2001.

7. Peyton Knight, "'Progressive' America Haters," *Conservative Monitor*, October 2001.

8. Franklin Foer, "Disoriented," *New Republic Online*, 3 December 2001.

9. Walter Williams, "Elitist Contempt for American Values," *Capitalism Magazine*, 13 November 2001.

10. Williams, "Elitist Contempt for American Values."

11. John J. Miller and Ramesh Ponnuru, "Code Red Herring," *National Review Online*, 1 October 2001.

12. "American Morning with Paula Zahn: Interview with Noam Chomsky, Bill Bennett," CNN.com Transcripts, 30 May 2002.

13. "Final List: Seminars on September 11," UCLA College of Letters and Sciences Web site, Fall Quarter 2001.

14. Lisa De Pasquale, "'Blame America First' Teaches Youth to Embrace Islam," *Washington Times*, September 8, 2002.

15. Dana Cloud, "Pledge for the workers," *Daily Texan*, 1 July 2002.

16. Kate Morse, "The Academic Left's Contempt for America," *The American Enterprise Magazine*, 12 September 2002.

17. Audrey Crummey, "Experts on terrorism meet in small on-campus forum," *UCLA Daily Bruin*, 13 November 2001.

18. "Islam, bioterrorism hot college classes," CNN.com, 4 September 2002.

19. Jennifer McNulty, "Social scientists weigh in on terrorist attacks," *UC Santa Cruz Currents Online*, 25 September 2001.

20. Ben Shapiro, "Effects of campus liberalism far-reaching," *UCLA Daily Bruin*, 20 November 2002.

21. John Leo, "Campus hand-wringing is not a pretty sight," Townhall.com, 1 October 2001.

22. Ben Shapiro, "Effects of campus liberalism far-reaching," *UCLA Daily Bruin*, 20 November 2002.

23. Jennifer McNulty, "Social scientists weigh in on terrorist attacks," *UC Santa Cruz Currents Online*, 25 September 2001.

24. "SFSU Remembers September 11: Faculty," *San Francisco State University News*, 11 September 2002.

25. Marty Doorey, "Teach-in looks at factors that contributed to terrorism," *Inside BU*, 25 September 2001.

26. Karen Rosen, Melissa Mecija, and Brandon Evans, "Forums Examine Recent Attacks," *New University*, Fall 2001.

27. Jyni Ekins, "Sept. 11 led to many changes in US policy," *Iowa State Daily*, 12 September 2002.

28. "Final List: Seminars on September 11," UCLA College of Letters and Sciences website, Fall Quarter 2001.

29. Kate Morse, "The Academic Left's Contempt for America," *The American Enterprise Magazine*, 12 September 2002.

30. Joseph Craig, "Professor recalls tragic day," *State Hornet*, 11 September 2002.

31. John Leo, "Campus hand-wringing is not a pretty sight," Townhall.com, 1 October 2001.

32. Lisa De Pasquale, "'Blame America First' Teaches Youth to Embrace Islam," *Washington Times*, 8 September 2002.

33. "A Nation Takes Sides," *Northwestern Chronicle*, 4 October 2001.

34. "College students speak out," Americans for Victory Over Terrorism, 2-12 May 2002.

35. Marty Doorey, "Teach-in looks at factors that contributed to terrorism," *Inside BU*, 25 September 2001.

36. "Speaker: Terrorist Acts Inconsistent With Islam," *Advance on the Web*, 3 December 2001.

37. Dexter Gauntlett, "Panel gives insight into September 11," *UCLA Daily Bruin*, 4 October 2001.

38. "Speaker: Terrorist Acts Inconsistent With Islam," *Advance on the Web*, 3 December 2001.

39. "Professor Mark Berkson speaks to large First Friday crowd about Islam," *Hamline Weekly*, 4-11 January 2002.

40. Jennifer McNulty, "Hundreds turn out for Middle East teach-in," *UC Santa Cruz Currents Online*, 1 October 2001.

41. "Anti-Abortion Site on Trial," Reuters, 27 January 1999.

42. "Aftershock: Coming to Grips with Terrorism in America," University of Georgia Web site Forums, 17 September 2001.

43. "Moyers in Conversation," PBS.org, 19 September 2001.

44. Paul Powers, "What are the basic practices and beliefs of Islam, and what is 'Islamic fundamentalism'?," Lewis and Clark College Official Web site.

45. David F. Forte, "Religion is Not the Enemy," *National Review Online*, October 19, 2001.

46. "Transcript of President Bush's Address," CNN.com, 21 September 2001.

47. "A Statement of Conscience: Not In Our Name," http://www.nion.us/NION.HTM.

48. Jon Dougherty, "Professors blame US for terrorism," WorldNetDaily.com, 31 October 2001.

49. Angie Leventis, "Panel of University experts discuss attacks's aftermath," *Daily Illini*, 20 September 2001.

50. Taniquelle Thurner, "UW professors discuss the aftermath of Sept. 11," *Badger Herald*, 18 October 2001.

51. Debbie Gilbert, "Experts critical of war on terror," *Gainesville Times*, 11 September 2002.

52. Gilbert, "Experts critical of war on terror."

53. Jennifer McNulty, "Social scientists weigh in on terrorist attacks," *UC Santa Cruz Currents Online*, 25 September 2001.

54. McNulty, "Social scientists weigh in on terrorist attacks."

55. Kristina Wong, "Afghanistan still vulnerable, professor says," *UCLA Daily Bruin*, 26 February 2002.

56. Brad Knickerbocker, "As 'axis of evil' turns, Bush sees no blur of right, wrong," *Christian Science Monitor*, 6 February 2002.

57. Peijean Tsai, "'Evil' comment elicits Iranian reaction," *UCLA Daily Bruin*, 25 February 2002.

58. Jennifer McNulty, "Social scientists weigh in on terrorist attacks," *UC Santa Cruz Currents Online*, 25 September 2001.

59. Hemesh Patel, "Professors incorporate events into classes," *UCLA Daily Bruin*, 27 September 2001.

60. Kate Bramson, "Course about Vietnam War expands to encompass new campaign against terrorism," *George Street Journal*, 2 November 2001.

61. Marcelle Richards and Kiyoshi Tomono, "Bush takes anti-terrorism plan to American people," *UCLA Daily Bruin*, 21 September 2001.

62. Debbie Gilbert, "Experts critical of war on terror," *Gainesville Times*, 11 September 2002.

63. Gilbert, "Experts critical of war on terror."

64. Ann Coulter, "Liberalism and terrorism: stages of the same disease," Townhall.com, 6 July 2002.

65. Jennifer McNulty, "Hundreds turn out for Middle East teach-in," *UC Santa Cruz Currents Online*, 1 October 2001.

66. Marty Doorey, "Teach-in looks at factors that contributed to terrorism," *Inside BU*, 25 September 2001.

67. Ann Coulter, "My name is Adolph," Townhall.com, 12 September 2002.

68. "Keeping the Peace at Work," *Business Week Online*, 26 September 2001.

69. "Moyers in Conversation," PBS.org, 19 September 2001.

70. Megan Woolhouse, "Singled Out," *Courier-Journal*, 11 September 2002.

71. Scott Norvell, "Tongue Tied: A Report from the Front Line of the Culture Wars," FoxNews.com, 24 September 2001.

72. Steve Sexton, "School-sponsored 9-11 Remembrance Day to exclude patriotic symbols and religious references," *California Patriot Online*, 4 September 2002.

73. Christopher L. McCargar, "History Professor debates meaning of patriotism," *Zephyr*, 18 April 2002.

74. Sally Hicks, "Collection of Sept. 11 Essays Offers Dissenting Voices Amid 'Unreflective Patriotism,'" *Duke News and Communications*, 5 September 2002.

75. Vijay Prashad, "Shrouded by Flags," ZMag.org, 19 September 2001.

76. Todd A. Eisenstadt, "Coming of age as patriots: One professor's post-tragedy education," *Union Leader*, 21 September 2001.

77. Zoe Galland and Hope Glassberg, "Columbia U. Faculty Reflect on Surge of Patriotism," *Columbia Daily Spectator*, 2 October 2001.

78. L. Brent Bozell, "The Post Lauds a Lunatic," Media Research Center, 16 May 2002.

79. Andrea Peyser, "Once-proud campus a breeding ground for idiots," *New York Post*, 3 October 2001.

80. Walter Williams, "Elitist Contempt for American Values," *Capitalism Magazine*, 13 November 2001.

CHAPTER 9

1. Nicole Morgan, "Iraq war isn't right, say peace protesters," *Lexington Herald-Leader*, 21 October 2002.

2. Rachel Landman, "Students, faculty stage war protest," *Amherst Student*, 20 November 2002.

3. Mark Goldblatt, "Bitter Taste of Academia," *National Review Online*, 11 March 2003.

4. Gina Damron, "Faculty members join anti-war protest," *South End*, 27 February 2003.

5. Brian J. Foley, "Why Are We So Passive? Patriotic Protest for Professors," *CounterPunch*, 21 March 2003.

6. Professor Michael T. Klare, "Oiling the Wheels of War," *The Nation*, 7 October 2002.

7. Robert Jensen, "The US Drive to War: Smoking Guns and Big Guns," *CounterPunch*, 6 February 2003.

8. Sarah H. Wright, "MIT community members rally to protest Iraq war," *MIT TechTalk*, 2 April 2003.

9. Andrew Dys, "Anti-war voices ring out at rally," *Herald*, 14 February 2003.

10. Rebecca Walsh, "Karl Rove Returns to the U.," *Salt Lake Tribune*, 14 November 2002.

11. Yehia El Mogahzy, "Wake up America," *Auburn Plainsman*, 23 January 2003.

12. Michael Rooke-Ley, "A plea for peace: US, Iraqi scholars gather in Baghdad to oppose war," *The Register-Guard*, 26 January 2003.

13. Carlos Ramos-Mrosovsky, "Visions of the Impossible: Truth, Falkhood, and International Relations," *Daily Princetonian*, 4 December 2002.

14. Michael Hardt, "Global Elites Must Realise That US Imperialism Isn't In Their Interest," *Guardian*, 18 December 2002.

15. Ronnie D. Lipschutz, "Pathways to Empire," *UC Santa Cruz Currents Online*, 9 September 2002.

16. Daniel Pipes, "American Academics Who Hate America," *Capitalism Magazine*, 19 November 2002.

17. Daniel Pipes and Jonathan Calt Harris, "Does Columbia U hate America?," *Jewish World Review*, 1 April 2003.

18. Cindy Yee, "Students, faculty protest for Iraq peace," *Chronicle Online*, 10 October 2002.

19. Alon Ben-Meir, "Behind Mr. Bush's Fixation on Saddam," Universal Press International, 29 September 2002.

20. Walt Brasch, "Scoring the US/Iraq War," *CounterPunch*, 16 November 2002.

21. John McCaslin, "The Beltway Beat: Pass the Mayo," Townhall.com, 29 March 2002.

22. David Usborne, "Bush forced to play down talk of war," *Arab News*, 11 August 2002.

23. Alan Elsner, "Domestic, personal issues may sway Bush on Iraq," Reuters, 9 August 2002.

24. Chalmers Johnson, "The Real Casualty Rate from America's Iraq Wars," *Znet*, 3 May 2003.

25. Brian J. Foley, "War Cries: Weapons of Mass Distraction . . . Or Something Worse?," *CounterPunch*, 8 November 2002.

26. "Kerry's 'Regime Change' Comments Draw Fire," FoxNews.com, 3 April 2003.

27. "Kerry's 'Regime Change' Comments Draw Fire," FoxNews.com, 3 April 2003.

28. Kellia Ramares, "Preemptive impeachment," *Online Journal*, 4 January 2003.

29. "Members of MIT community rally to protest Iraq war," *MIT News*, 20 March 2003.

30. Ginny Meriam, "Protesters gather at UM to rally against war with Iraq," *Missoulian*, 21 November 2002.

31. Andrea Brunty, "Anti-war sentiments broadcast across Ferg Plaza with 'Forum Against War in Iraq,'" *Crimson White*, 14 February 2003.

32. Brianna Blake, "Protesters in D.M. decry plan for war," *Des Moines Register*, 31 January 2003.

33. "Anti-war statement by 65 Filipino educators," Bulatlat.com, 24-30 November 2002.

34. Bruce Ackerman, "Two Fronts," *American Prospect Online*, 27 January 2003.

35. Robert Jensen, "The US Drive to War: Smoking Guns and Big Guns," *CounterPunch*, 6 February 2003.

36. "Some Analysis of Powell's Speech," Institute for Public Accuracy, 6 February 2003.

37. Editorial, "The Case Against Iraq," *New York Times*, 6 February 2003.

38 "Experts can discuss impact of possible war," *Purdue News*, 5 February 2003.

39. "Members of MIT community rally to protest Iraq war," *MIT News*, 20 March 2003.

40. Majorie Cohn, "Invading Iraq Would Violate US and International Law," *JURIST: The Legal Education Network*, 2 September 2002.

41. Scott Cawelti, "Bush is taking United States to wrong place," *Waterloo-Ceder Falls Courier*, 2 February 2003.

42. Richard Falk and David Krieger, "War with Iraq is Not Bush's Decision," *CounterPunch*, 19 September 2002.

43. Emil Guillermo, "In Praise of the Protesters," *San Francisco Chronicle*, 25 March 2003.

44. Cindy Yee, "Students, faculty protest for Iraq peace," *Chronicle Online*, 10 October 2002.

45. John Buchel, "Peace groups act as human shields," *Badger Herald*, 11 February 2003.

46. Leslie Scrivener, "Peace Activist Implores Pope to be 'Ultimate Human Shield,'" *Toronto Star*, 6 March 2003.

47. Professor Bill Quigley, "America, Yes! War, No.," *JURIST: The Legal Education Network*, 12 November 2002.

48. Rajiv Chandrasekaran, "Activists Bring War Protests to Baghdad," *Washington Post*, 14 January 2003.

49. Michael Rooke-Ley, "A plea for peace: US, Iraqi scholars gather in Baghdad to oppose war," *Register-Guard*, 26 January 2003.

50. Rooke-Ley, "A plea for peace: US, Iraqi scholars gather in Baghdad to oppose war."

51. Kellia Ramares, "Preemptive impeachment," *Online Journal*, 4 January 2003.

52. Joe Krauss, "US, Iraq Tensions Fuel Campus Debate," *Hoya*, 25 October 2002.

53. Erwin Chemerinsky, "By Flouting War Laws, US Invites Tragedy," *Los Angeles Times*, 25 March 2003.

54. Hugh Hewitt, "Commentary and Consequences," *Weekly Standard*, 26 March 2003.

55. Robert Digitale, "'Kill the President' Prof Won't Be Fired," *Press Democrat*, 22 July 2003.

56. Jim Sparkman, "'Kill the President' Prof at SRJC Answers Back, I Think," Chronwatch.com, 24 August 2003.

57. Ron Howell, "Columbia Prof's Remarks Spark Furor," New York Newsday.com, 28 March 2003.

58. Peter Cannavo, "Is Asking Key Questions Anti-American?," CollegeNews.org, 12 February 2003.

59. Gloria LaBounty, "War over the war," *Sun Chronicle*, 6 April 2003.

60. Cris Barrish, "Dissenters pressured to keep quiet," *Delaware Online: The News Journal*, 5 April 2003.

61. Bill Marvel, "What is patriotism?," *Dallas Morning News*, 5 April 2003.

62. Walter Williams, "Elitist Contempt for American Values," *Capitalism Magazine*, 13 November 2001.

63. Janita Poe and Dan Chapman, "Dissent seen as healthy—or traitorous," *Atlanta Journal-Constitution*, 23 March 2003.

64. David Horowitz, "Moment of Truth: For the Anti-American Left," Townhall.com, 31 March 2003.

65. "Top 10 Activist Campuses," *Mother Jones*, October 2003.

66. Kate Zernike, "Professors Protest as Students Debate," *New York Times*, 5 April 2003.

CHAPTER 10

1. Lee Green, "CAMERA ALERT: Letter by Martin Luther King a Hoax," Committee for Accuracy in Middle East Reporting in America, 22 January 2002.

2. Lawrence Summers, "Address at morning prayers," 17 September 2002, http://president.harvard.edu/speeches/2002/morningprayers.html.

3. M. Shahid Alam, "Extending the boycott," *Al-Ahram Weekly Online*, 29 August– 4 September 2002.

4. Joan Peters, *From Time Immemorial*, (New York: J. KAP Publishing, 2000), 16.

5. Mitchell G. Bard, *Myths and Facts: A Guide to the Arab-Israeli Conflict*, (United States of America: American Israeli Cooperative Enterprise, 2001), 169-171.

6. Peters, *From Time Immemorial*, (New York: J. KAP Publishing, 2000), 13.

7. UCLA Professor Luke Bresky, English 80, Lecture, 16 October 2001.

8. "Major International Issues: Racism, Israel's occupation," Institute for Public Accuracy, 29 August 2001.

9. Fouad M. Moughrabi, "A Special Relationship at Risk," *Washington Report on Middle Eastern Affairs*, April 1989.

10. Mouyyad Hassouna, "Instructor's insight into controversy," *Spectator Online*, 15 March 2001.

11. Professor Nancy Kanwisher, "Opening Comments," 6 May 2002, http://www.harvardmitdivest.org/nancyspeech.html.

12. Roger Kimball, "The Intifada Curriculum," *Wall Street Journal*, 9 May 2002.

13. "Fact Sheet on English R1A: 'The Politics and Poetics of Palestinian Resistance'," *Berkeley News*, 24 July 2002.

14. *NewsHour with Jim Lehrer*, 23 July 2002.

15. Christopher Bollyn, "Ariel Sharon's Final Solution: 'Cleanse' Palestine," *Spotlight Online*, 10 April 2001.

16. Ashley Burrell, "Continuing conflict in Mideast sparks student, faculty reactions," *Penn State Digital Collegian*, 4 February 2002.

17. "Terrorist Attacks Against US to Subside in Coming Year," *University of Alabama News*, 14 December 2001.

18. Andrew Chang, "So Close, So Far Apart," ABCNews.com, 22 April 2001.

19. Peter Grier, "The US & Israel," *Christian Science Monitor*, 26 October 2001.

20. John Dudley, "Questions surround terrorist attack," *Student Printz*, 12 September 2001.

21. "James G. Blight: Professor of International Relations (Research)," Choices Educational Program, http://www.choices.edu/interviews/blight.cfm.

22. "Humanistic Values in a Time of Crisis," September 11: UGA Responds, 24 September 2001, http://www.uga.edu/news/september11/forums/values.html.

23. "A Theological Reflection on September 11," http://www.georgetown.edu/centers/woodstock/report/r-fea67.htm.

24. "Faculty Statements," http://www.ucdivest.org/statements.php.

25. "About Us," The Palestine Chronicle Web site, http://www.palestinechronicle.com/aboutus.php.

26. David Barsamian, "Intifada 2000: The Palestinian Uprising," Zmag.org, November 2000.

27. Edward Said, "Arafat is only interested in saving himself," Independent.co.uk, 20 June 2002.

28. Michael Lind, "The Israel Lobby," *Prospect Magazine*, April 2002.

29. UCLA TA Monica Arruda de Almeida, Political Science 121, Discussion section, 17 April 2002.

30. Jennifer Greenstein Altmann, "Forum encourages frank talk about difficult ethical issues," *Princeton Weekly Bulletin*, 29 April 2002.

31. Dave Marash, "War of Words," ABCNews.com, 5 June 2002.

32. Lauren R. Dorgan and David H. Gellis, "Dinner May Benefit Alleged Hamas Supporters," *Harvard Crimson*, 13 November 2000.

33. Marash, "War of Words," ABCNews.com, 5 June 2002.

34. Daniel Pipes and Asaf Romirowsky, "Fulbright's Terrorist Tie," *New York Post*, 20 October 2003.

35. *The O'Reilly Factor*, 22 August 2002.

36. Barry Klein and Babita Persaud, "Faculty leaders refuse to back Al-Arian firing," *St. Petersburg Times*, 10 January 2002.

37. Klein and Persaud, "Faculty leaders refuse to back Al-Arian firing."

38. Josh Gerstein, "US Cites Terror Ties," ABCNews.com, 24 November 2001.

39. Rachel La Corte, "US ousts Palestinian ex-prof suspected of links to terrorists," Associated Press, 23 August 2002.

40. M. Shahid Alam, "Extending the boycott," *Al-Ahram Weekly Online*, August 29-4 September 2002.

41. Ed Hayward, "Prof shocks Northeastern with defense of suicide bomber," *Boston Herald*, 5 September 2002.

42. Rachelle Davidoff, e-mail to author, 26 June 2002.

43. Joe Eskenazi, "Protesters force cancellation of Netanyahu talks here," *Jewish Bulletin News of Northern California*, 1 December 2000.

44. Daniel Pipes, "The Arab-Israel Conflict on Campus," *Capitalism Magazine*, 18 September 2002.

45. Mackenzie Carpenter, "Netanyahu visit to Pittsburgh has police on alert," *Pittsburgh Post-Gazette*, 21 September 2002.

46. Pittsburgh Professors for Peace and Justice Web site, http://www.pittppj.org/committees.html.

47. Carpenter, "Netanyahu visit to Pittsburgh has police on alert," *Pittsburgh Post-Gazette*, 21 September 2002.

48. Dave Curtin and Becca Blond, "Arab speech stirs Springs," *Denver Post*, 13 September 2002.

49. Valerie Richardson, "Palestinian speaker roils Colorado college," *Washington Times*, 13 September 2002.

50. Daniel Pipes, "The Arab-Israel Conflict on Campus," *Capitalism Magazine*, 18 September 2002.

51. Francis Boyle, "In Defense of a Disvestment Campaign Against Israel," *CounterPunch*, 20 May 2002

52. "Join Harvard-MIT Petition for Divestment from Israel," http://www.harvardmitdivest.org/petition.html.

53. "End the Israeli Occupation – DIVEST NOW!," http://www.princetondivest.org.

54. "CU Divestment Campaign Signature List," http://www.columbiadivest.org/sig_list.html.

55. "Signatories to the UMass Divest from Israel petition," http://www-unix.oit.umass.edu/~uri/Palestine/Signatures.htm.

56. Rachel Pomerance, "Divestment conference is a showdown," *Jewish News of Greater Phoenix*, 11 October 2002.

57. "University of California Petition for Divestment from Israel," http://www.ucdivest.org/petition.php#sigs.

58. "Faculty Statements," http://www.usdivest.org/statements.php. Quotes immediately following also from this site.

59. Avi Davis, "The Jewish People's Fifth Column," Standwithus.com, 22 April 2002.

60. Kelly Rayburn, "Students unite to remember the Holocaust," *UCLA Daily Bruin*, 10 April 2002.

61. Kelly Rayburn, "Prager claims Israel is legitimate," *UCLA Daily Bruin*, 30 May 2002.

62. Chaim Seidler-Feller, "Israel's solid case doesn't need exaggeration," *UCLA Daily Bruin*, 6 June 2002.

63. Christina Jenkins, "Academic panel discusses Mideast conflict," *UCLA Daily Bruin*, 1 May 2002.

64. Kelly Rayburn, "Jewish professor condemns actions of Israel," *UCLA Daily Bruin*, 24 April 2002.

65. "About Tikkun," http://www.tikkun.org/about_us/index.cfm.

66. "About Tikkun: Board Members," http://www.tikkun.org/about_us/index.cfm/action/board_members.html.

67. CBS News Poll, 15-18 April 2002.

68. "College students speak out," Americans for Victory over Terrorism, 2-12 May 2002.

69. "College students speak out."

CHAPTER 11

1. Larry Elder Show, 790 KABC, Los Angeles, 24 May 2002.

2. Name changed to protect personal privacy.

3. Name changed to protect personal privacy.

4. Name changed to protect personal privacy.

5. *UCLA Daily Bruin*, e-mail message to editor, 15 May 2002.

6. Name changed to protect personal privacy.

7. "*UCLA Daily Bruin* Viewpoint Columnist Policy."

8. Larry Elder Show, 790 KABC, Los Angeles, 24 May 2002.

9. Editorial Board, "UC must respect human rights, divest," *UCLA Daily Bruin*, 8 July 2002.

10. Editorial Board, "Only faculty should decide course policies," *UCLA Daily Bruin*, 1 October 2002.

11. Editorial Board, "Students must be wary of 'war on terrorism'," *UCLA Daily Bruin*, 22 September 2002.

12. Editorial Board, "USAC correct in refusing nominees," *UCLA Daily Bruin*, 27 September 2002.

13. Editorial Board, "There's still work to be done now that SP-1, 2 are gone," *UCLA Daily Bruin*, 22 May 2001.

14. Editorial Board, "Carnesale should take a stand on RPI," *UCLA Daily Bruin*, 26 August 2002.

15. Editorial Board, "Community has right to patronize sex shop," *UCLA Daily Bruin*, 31 January 2002.

16. Keely Hedges, "Mastering art of sexspeak heightens passion in bed," *UCLA Daily Bruin*, 12 August 2002.

17. Chez Shadman, "Do it the risky way: out in the open," *UCLA Daily Bruin*, 17 October 2001.

18. Chez Shadman, "Spice up your life by attending strip clubs," *UCLA Daily Bruin*, 3 October 2001.

19. Chez Shadman, "Casual sex: it's not just for 'sinners' anymore," *UCLA Daily Bruin*, 6 August 2001.

20. Marcelle Richards, "Recipes for Hot Sex," *UCLA Daily Bruin*, 9 May 2002.

21. Yvonne K. Fulbright, "Dirty words will whet her desire," *Washington Square News*, 2 October 2003.

22. Beth Van Dyke, "Race to the Bathroom," *Daily Nexus Online*, 14 May 2003.

23. Amber Madison, "Porn and Sexuality," *Tufts Daily*, 16 April 2003.

24. Kate McDowell, "Going Down the Dirt Road," *Cornell Daily Sun*, 13 March 2003.

25. Kathy Greaves, "It's hetero pride every other week," *Daily Barometer Online*, 14 May 2003.

26. Paul Shugar, "Smarter than the average woman (at least)," *Post Online*, 3 April 2003.

27. Spectator Managing Board, "Eye on America," *Columbia Spectator*, 2 October 2002.

28. The Crimson Staff, "Speak Out, Democrats," *Harvard Crimson*, 1 October 2002.

29. The News' View, "Don't welcome 'don't ask, don't tell,'" *Yale Daily News*, 2 October 2002.

30. Editorial Board, "We deserve an explanation," *The Heights*, 1 October 2002.

31. Editorial Board, "KU officials must continue to boost minority count," *University Daily Kansan*, 2 October 2002.

32. Jessie Childress, "Corporate contracts go deeper than what we're drinking," *University of Montana Kaimin Online*, 1 October 2002.

33. Editorial, "Our View: Bush's war not supported by international community, former commanders," *Idaho State University Bengal*, 25 September 2002 (Posted through October 8, 2002).

34. Editorial, "The Chronicle's View: Get with the recycling times," *University of Utah Chronicle*, 2 October 2002.

35. Cyrus Farivar, "*Daily Cals* Stolen, Replaced With Protester Flyers," *Daily Californian*, 25 October 2001.

CHAPTER 12

1. Peijean Tsai, "Students reflect on current situation in Israel," *UCLA Daily Bruin*, 9 May 2002.

2. "Undergraduate Students Association Programming Fund," UCLA, http://students.asucla.ucla.edu/Funding/board_programming_fund.html. Besides the figures listed here, the MSA also received an additional $2,408 for "Islamic Awareness Week" during Spring Quarter.

3. "2001-2002 Base Budget Allocations," UCLA, http://students.asucla.ucla.edu/Funding/budget_board_info.html.

4. "2001-2002 Base Budget Allocations," UCLA.

5. Melody Hanatani, " Friend 'Friend of the court' filed for JSU's case," *UCLA Daily Bruin*, 20 January 2004.

6. "The Constitution," University of Georgia ASU, http://www.uga.edu/asu/const.html.

7. "African Student Union," http://www.utdallas.edu/student/union/asu.html.

8. "About Us," ASU at University of Syracuse, http://students.syr.edu/afsu/about%20us.html.

9. "Welcome to the homepage of the African Students Association (ASA) at the University of Massachusetts, Amherst," ASA at University of Massachusetts, http://www.umass.edu/rso/african/mainpage.html. Emphasis added.

10. Terelle Jerricks, "Buckshot," *Nommo*, Fall 2002, Vol. XXXIII, Iss#1.

11. Askari Abdul Muntaqim, "Souls in Kaptivity," *Nommo*, Fall 2002.

12. Noluthando Williams, "A Voice of Critical Consciousness," *Nommo*, Fall 2002.

13. Noluthando Williams, "Time For Sum Axion (Buckshots)," *Nommo*, Spring 2002.

14. Christina Galoozis, "Town hall meeting addresses cartoon," *Indiana Daily Student*, 26 February 2003.

15. Steve Adubato, "Political Correctness is Out of Control," Caucus Educational Corporation, 4 November 1999.
16. Cathleen Lewis, "Hundreds protest offensive campus comic strip," *Tiger Online Edition*, 13 October 1999.
17. Joyce Kelly, "Noose poster incites reaction," *CSULB Online 49er*, 14 October 2002.
18. "About Us," UCLA GALA, http://qa.gaybruins.com/ .
19. "Constitution," Auburn Gay and Lesbian Association, http://www.auburn.edu/student_info/agla/constitution.html.
20. "Harvard alumni urge return of banned ROTC," CNN.com, 11 October 2001.
21. Ben Shapiro, "Banned on campus," Townhall.com, 20 June 2002.
22. Melissa Coats, "Music Review: Peaches: Teaches of Peaches," *TenPercent*, Fall 2001.
23. Bryan Chin, "You gotta have it: The 10 essential albums for every gay boy," *TenPercent*, Fall 2001.
24. Amanda Schapel, "The Genesis of LGBTQ2IA: The lesbian, gay, bisexual, transgender, queer, questioning, intersex, ally continuum," *TenPercent*, Fall 2001.
25. Ben Lee Handler, "Heart-a-choking?," *TenPercent*, Winter 2002.
26. "All I want for Christmas is . . . Toys! Toys! Toys!," *TenPercent*, Fall 2001.
27. Barbara Ortutay, "Letter from the editor," *TenPercent*, Winter 2002.
28. Mike Adams, "The thought police police," Townhall.com, 20 October 2003.
29. Jennifer Dunn, "Rethinking Romantic Love," *Q*News*, 24 June 2003.
30. "El Plan Espiritual de Aztlán," http://www.panam.edu/orgs/MEChA/Aztlán.html.
31. "El Plan Espiritual de Aztlán."
32. Michelle Malkin, "Bustamante, MEChA and the media," Townhall.com, 20 August 2003.
33. Tim Graham, "Cruising Past Cruz's Racial Controversies," *Media Reality Check*, 17 September 2003.
34. Michelle Malkin, "Bustamante, MEChA and the media," Townhall.com, 20 August 2003.
35 Tupac Enrique Acosta, "The West is a Guest," *LA gente de Aztlán*, Winter 2002.
36. M.E.Ch.A. de UCLA, "State of Aztlán," *LA gente de Aztlán*, Winter 2002.
37. M.E.Ch.A. de UCLA, "State of Aztlán."
38. Victor Cuevas, "Cindy Montanez," *LA gente de Aztlán*, Winter 2002.
39. Don Thompson, "Student groups probed for alleged terror ties," *Chicago Tribune*, 22 December 2001.
40. "AP irresponsibly links American Muslim Student Organizations to Terrorism," MSA National Press Release, 26 December 2001.
41. Adrienne Sanders, "Jews blast State hate," *San Francisco Examiner*, 17 May 2002.
42. MSA Pamphlet "Zionism: The Forgotten Apartheid."
43. "MSA National: A Time to Recover, Heal Our National Wounds," MSA National Press Release, 11 September 2002.
44. Rachel Makabi, "Reports link terrorist, student organizations," *UCLA Daily Bruin*, 8 January 2002.

45. Suhail Abdullah, "Cutting Off the Underdeveloped World: The Agenda Behind Population Control," *Al-Talib*, December 2000.
46. Li'i Furumoto, "Fighting for Diversity in Our Schools," *Al-Talib*, December 2000.
47. Editorial staff, "Best of *Al-Talib*," *Al-Talib*, May 2001.
48. Editorial staff, "Best of *Al-Talib*."
49. Mohamed Marei, "How Slaves become Kings," *Al-Talib*, May 2001.
50. Yusuf Abdulla, "Death for Sale: The Commercialization of the Holocaust," *Al-Talib*, May 2001.
51. Editorial staff, "Crossing Unforseen Borders: Reflections on the Aftermath of September 11," *Al-Talib*, November 2001.
52. Hisham Mahmoud, "Guilt by Association: Islam Under Oath," *Al-Talib*, November 2001.
53. Mahmoud, "Guilt by Association: Islam Under Oath."
54. Salar Rizvi and Reem Salahi, "Muslims in America: Living in the Memory of 9/11," *Al-Talib*, November 2001.
55. Editorial staff, "They Came for Us," *Al-Talib*, February 2002.
56. Dena Elbayoumy, "Carnage Covered Up," *Al-Talib*, May 2002.
57. Leen Salahi, "Culture and Religion: Blended to Confusion," *Al-Talib*, May 2002.
58. LaTasha Johnson, "Graduating Chicano students hold private commencement," *GoldenGater*, 16 May 1996.
59. Marc Levin, "Commencement 2002 Achieve New Degree of Political Correctness," Newsmax.com, 18 June 2002.
60. Erik Lords, "At MSU, plans for pomp create friction," *Detroit Free Press*, 5 April 2002.
61. John Leo, "Now there are even separate graduation ceremonies," *Jewish World Review*, 17 April 2001.

CHAPTER 13

1. Robert Cohen, "Activist Impulses: Campus Radicalism in the 1930s," http://newdeal.feri.org/students/essay01.htm.
2. Irving Kristol, "From *Memoirs of a Trotskyist* by Irving Kristol," PBS Online, http://www.pbs.org/arguing/nyintellectuals_krystol_2.html.
3. Lawrence Evans, "Voting IQs," Newsobserver.com, 23 September 2002.
4. Robert Watson, "Johnson fails to accept need for dissent in life," *UCLA Daily Bruin*, 20 November 2001.
5. Robert Watson, "Conservatives quick to excuse war crimes," *UCLA Daily Bruin*, 10 May 2001.
6. "Overview of kingdom's support for islamic studies worldwide," February 2002, http://www.saudiembassy.net/press_release/02-spa/02-15-Islam.htm.
7. "Postdoctoral Researcher Receives Royal Support," *Around the School: News and Notices of the Harvard School of Public Health*, 10 December 1999.
8. Robert J. Morse and Samuel L. Flanigan, "How we rank schools," *US News and World Report*, http://www.usnews.com/usnews/edu/college/rankings/about/04rank_brief.php, 2004.

ACKNOWLEDGMENTS

I have been extremely fortunate to be helped and guided by a multitude of kind and generous people. This book is the result of their wisdom, aid, and encouragement.

First and foremost, I must thank David Limbaugh, a scholar, a gentleman, and my mentor. Without him, this book never would have been written or published. David is a true prince of a human being, a truly righteous person.

Thanks to David Dunham and the wonderful people at Thomas Nelson/WND Books. Thanks especially to Joel Miller, my editor at WND Books, whose help in both getting this book published and honing it to a fine point has been invaluable. His advice during the publishing process has made it a pleasure.

Thanks to Rick Newcombe and the folks at Creators Syndicate for having the courage to syndicate my column and the faith to stick with it. Without their vision, I'd still be writing for the *UCLA Daily Bruin.*

Thanks to Katherine Searcy, my editor, who has sharpened my columns, checked my facts, and dealt with my at-deadline phone calls.

Thanks to the many friends and teachers I have had the pleasure of learning from: Andrew Breitbart, a brilliant analyst and a good friend; Ann Coulter, whose kindness, humor, and knowledge have been a touchstone; and John Fund, a craftsman with the pen and an endless source for information and aid. Thanks also to Michael Barone, Brad Miner, and Barry Farber for their encouragement and inspiration.

Thanks to Jon Garthwaite and Jennifer Biddison at *Townhall.com,* the first outlet to carry my column—their support from the start has heartened me and spurred me to ever-greater efforts.

Thanks to all of my friends in the radio talk show business. Their dedication makes the difference for millions of Americans, me included.

Thanks to Mrs. Caroline Brumm, my elementary school principal, who was there to lend me *The Hobbit* and push me to achieve. Thanks to Ms. Debbie Ginnetti, my fourth-grade English and history teacher, who told me not to let "Potential" be written on my tombstone. Thanks to Rabbi Nachum Sauer, whose guidance has kept me on the straight and narrow.

Thanks to my three younger sisters—having to listen to me drone on about my column and book is a thankless fate, but they handle it with grace and style.

Thanks to my loyal readers: without you, all of the words in the world mean nothing.

Finally, I want to thank God for giving me the ability and opportunity to make a difference.

INDEX